WALKING
WITH DINOSAURS
A NATURAL HISTORY

Tim Haines

This book accompanies the 1999 BBC television series, *Walking with Dinosaurs*.
Executive producer: John Lynch
Series producer: Tim Haines
Producers: Tim Haines and Jasper James

Commissioning editor: Sheila Ableman
Text editor: Caroline Taggart
Project editor: Martha Caute
Art director Linda Blakemore
Designer: Martin Hendry
Illustrations: Gary Hincks
Picture research: Deirdre O'Day

First published in 1999 by BBC Worldwide Ltd.,
80 Wood Lane, London W12 OTT

Text © Tim Haines 1999 The moral right of the author has been asserted.
Design © BBC Worldwide 1999
BBC commissioned photographs © BBC Worldwide 1999

DK

A Dorling Kindersley Book
www.dk.com

Publisher: Sean Moore
Text editor: Jennifer Quasha
Project editor: Barbara Minton
Art director: Dirk Kaufman
Designer: Gus Yoo
Production director: Lou Bilka

First American Edition, 2000
Published in the United States by Dorling Kindersley Publishing, Inc.
95 Madison Avenue
New York, New York 10016

Library of Congress Cataloging-in-Publication Data
Haines, Tim.
Walking with dinosaurs/by Tim Haines.–1st American ed.
p.cm.
ISBN 0-7894-5187-5 (alk. paper)
1. Dinosaurs literature. (1. Dinosaurs.) l. Title.
QE862.D5 H22 2000   99-37311
567.9–dc21   CIP

Set in Monotype New Baskerville and Stone Sans
Printed and bound in Great Britain by Butler & Tanner Ltd., Frome & London
Color reproductions by Radstock Reproductions Ltd.,Midsomer Norton
Jacket printed by Lawrence Allen Ltd., Weston-super-Mare

Previous pages: page 1 *Allosaurus;* **pages 2–3** *Tyrannosaurus*

Contents

New Blood

TRIASSIC
220 MILLION YEARS AGO

Time of the Titans

LATE JURASSIC
155 MILLION YEARS AGO

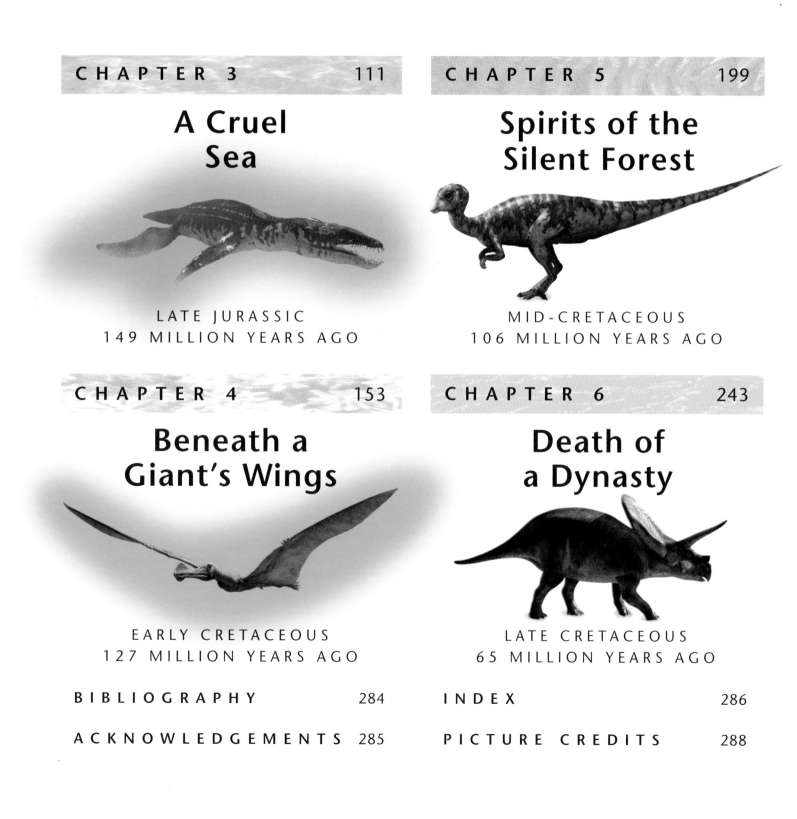

Introduction

No PERIOD ON Earth has gripped the human imagination more than the time of the dinosaurs. For over 150 years dinosaurs have fascinated scientists and lay people alike – perhaps because these creatures seem so completely alien to anything currently found on Earth, and yet they were frighteningly real. Their very size and power tempt us to try to picture them. But how can we imagine such a different world?

To begin with, visualize the changes in the landscape you would see in front of you if you were to go back in time; get rid of all the houses and roads, and then all the fields and fences. That's just the surface. Now replace grass and open ground with ferns and low, palm-like cycads. Convert any trees you can see into conifers – not the familiar plantation-pine types but older species like monkey puzzles – and spread them out over the landscape. Pull the birds out of the air, change the noise the insects make, and turn up the temperature. Finally, place a herd of enormous, loud reptiles in front of you and watch as groups of alarmingly fast predators stalk them. This book attempts a similar mental exercise, conjuring up the world of the dinosaurs. It is not intended to be an encyclopedia; it is an experience.

The trouble is that we are separated from these prehistoric scenes by a staggeringly vast time. Millions and millions of years have passed during which the remains of these magnificent creatures have been scattered, eroded, and buried. While mountains ranges have come and gone and oceans have risen up and drained away, a few of these remains became locked in the rocks and turned to stone.

All that we know about dinosaurs comes from these scraps of evidence that have survived the aeons as fossils. It is the paleontologists' job to interpret the clues, but for these scientists it is at once a fascinating and frustrating study. To

OPPOSITE A blast from the past: a dinosaur predator launches himself out from a group of ancient column pines. He is a carnivore with a basic body design that did not change for millions of years: its characteristics were two strong legs, a long tail, grasping arms, and sharp teeth.

THE TIME OF THEIR LIVES

LIFE ON EARTH probably began about 4500 million years ago, but for almost 4000 million of those years, life forms were largely single-celled creatures, such as bacteria and algae. Larger, more complex animals began to evolve during the Cambrian period, about 550 million years ago. During the so-called 'Cambrian explosion', a blizzard of new shapes and forms appeared. Many lasted only a short time, but some started mighty dynasties of creatures, such as the arthropods and molluscs that are still with us today. From a human viewpoint the most important development was the appearance of tiny animals with primitive backbones, the first vertebrates. This proved a good basic design for large size.

The period since the Cambrian is divided into three 'eras' – the ancient Paleozoic when life was dominated by water, the middle Mesozoic when giant reptiles ruled the world, and the modern Cenozoic when mammals and birds took over. The Paleozoic started with barren land and teeming seas. It took around 100 million years for the first complex organisms to conquer land. So while the first plants and insects struggled to establish themselves on the hostile ground,

the sea already had a rich variety of life, from giant carnivorous fish to extensive reefs. During the latter part of the Paleozoic, land was fully colonized. Small plants became trees and then forests, and insects became hugely successful. Millions of years after this the vertebrates crawled onto the land and, first as amphibians and then as reptiles, learned to exploit this harsh énvironment.

By the end of the Paleozoic, 245 million years ago, reptiles ruled on land and fish in the sea. But then they almost all died out at the end of the Permian. This ushered in the Mesozoic period, which started with a long period of recovery. Soon the old Paleozoic reptiles, called mammal-like reptiles because they were the ancestors of mammals, began to be replaced by the dinosaurs. For the rest of the Mesozoic – 170 million years – dinosaurs were the dominant animals on land. In the seas other giant reptiles took over all the large predator niches. Mammals evolved but remained restricted in numbers; birds appeared, and plants transformed completely by evolving flowers – but the dinosaurs strode on. Finally, at the end of the Mesozoic, 65 million years ago, another extraordinary mass extinction wiped out all the dinosaurs except the birds. The modern

A female *Tyrannosaurus*, the ultimate prehistoric predator, inspects her nest. No matter how large they were, dinosaurs always appear to have reproduced by laying eggs on the ground.

Cenozoic era opened with a great number of of smaller animals, such as mammals and birds. These diversified and some returned to the water, evolving into whales. Gradually, the rich variety of mammals with which we are familiar today appeared; finally, in the last blink of an eye on this vast time scale, humans evolved from the apes.

This time spiral charts the evolution of life from the Cambrian period, when the first complex creatures began to evolve, until the present day. Two of the biggest mass extinctions in life's history are marked at the beginning and the end of the Mesozoic era; the last brought to an end the age of dinosaurs.

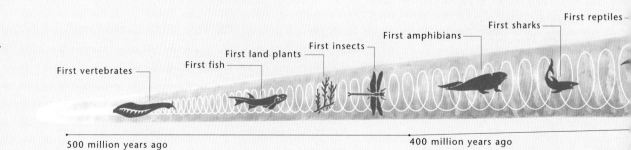

First reptiles

First sharks

First amphibians

First insects

First land plants

First fish

First vertebrates

500 million years ago

400 million years ago

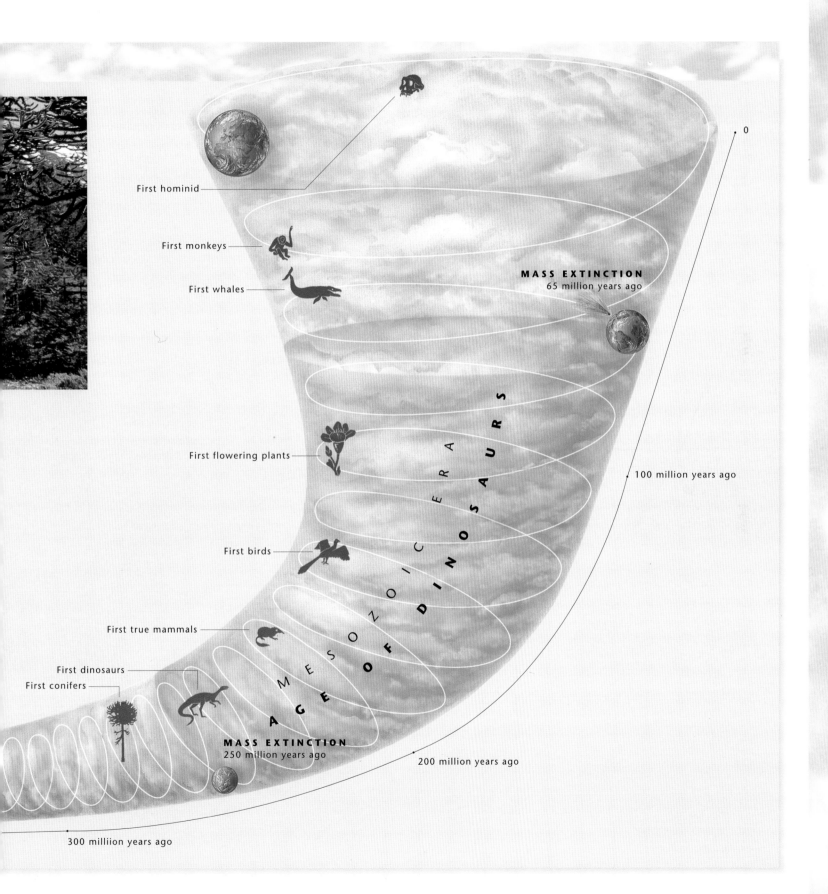

0

First hominid

First monkeys

MASS EXTINCTION
65 million years ago

First whales

First flowering plants

100 million years ago

First birds

M E S O Z O I C   E R A

A G E   O F   D I N O S A U R S

First true mammals

First dinosaurs

First conifers

MASS EXTINCTION
250 million years ago

200 million years ago

300 milliion years ago

9

expert eyes a fossil can hold a mass of information. It can reveal its age, the shape of the animal to which it belonged, and the other creatures to which it was related. But try to take this further - to discover how the animals lived - and the fossil record becomes teasingly elusive. Patterns of footprints, teeth marks, and the configurations of bones can be used as a starting point for many stories, but which one is right? The behavior that created these clues does not fossilize, and, therefore, the truth about them will never be known for sure.

Ultimately, speculating about most dinosaur behavior is unscientific because the theories cannot be tested. A zoologist might spend ten years in the field studying a living animal before he or she feels confident enough to

A WORLD IN MOTION

The first dinosaurs lived on a huge, crab-shaped continent that stretched from pole to pole in the middle of one vast ocean.

Even though the giant continent was breaking up, the great sauropod herds of the Jurassic could still walk from the northern tip of Africa to Australia.

TRIASSIC
220 MILLION YEARS AGO

PANGAEA

PANTHALASSA
OCEAN

LATE JURASSIC
155 MILLION YEARS AGO

TETHYS
OCEAN

PANGAEA

EARLY CRETACEOUS
127 MILLION YEARS AGO

ALTHOUGH THE GROUND beneath our feet may feel solid, it is in fact on the move, at about the same speed as our fingernails grow. During the unimaginably long time that life has existed on Earth, this has meant that the continents have danced across the globe in all sorts of configurations. In addition to altering the very face of the Earth, these movements have an enormous effect on the globe's climate because of the changes they make in ocean currents and wind patterns.

The moving continents also carry the hapless plants and animals that are living on them through different climate zones. So, for instance, during the Cambrian period Australia was in the northern hemisphere, then over millions of years it drifted through the tropics down to the South Pole and back up to where it is today. For life on Earth the ground rules are constantly changing.

The age of the dinosaurs started with one giant continent that slowly began to disintegrate. There were no ice-caps, and sea levels were sometimes much higher than those of today. Toward the end of the Mesozoic the landmasses began to look more as they do today, but they are, of course, still on the move and one day they might reform into another giant continent.

interpret its behavior. So how can we possibly claim to know the structure of a *Triceratops* herd? The answer, of course, is that we can't, but we do know that these animals existed and reproduced, so it seems well worth trying to find out more about how they might have lived.

This book aims to help the reader imagine this ancient and alien world more completely by drawing together all the elements of which science is certain and using reasoned speculation to fill the gaps. There are various ways I have tried to achieve this, both in the text and in the pictures.

To create the stories I spent two years talking to scientists and reading primary and secondary paleontological sources. With the help of a skilled team of researchers, we slowly focused in on those creatures of which enough was

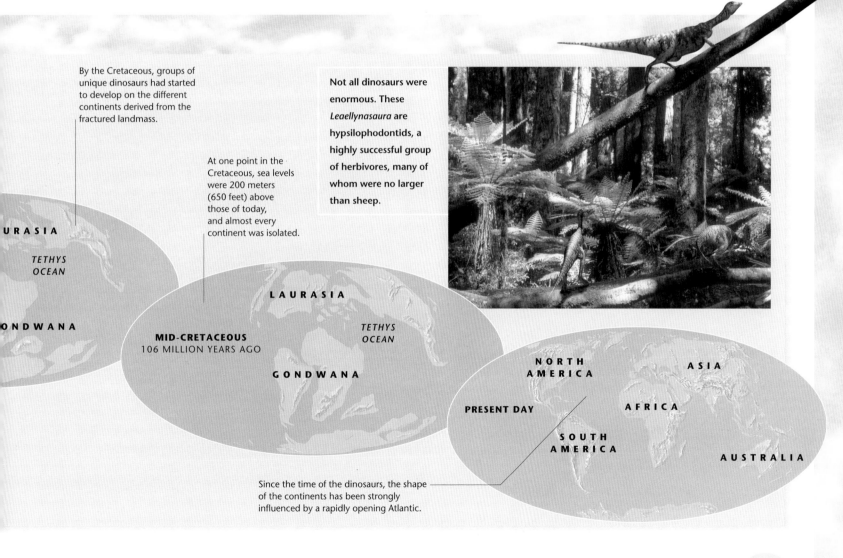

By the Cretaceous, groups of unique dinosaurs had started to develop on the different continents derived from the fractured landmass.

At one point in the Cretaceous, sea levels were 200 meters (650 feet) above those of today, and almost every continent was isolated.

Not all dinosaurs were enormous. These *Leaellynasaura* are hypsilophodontids, a highly successful group of herbivores, many of whom were no larger than sheep.

URASIA

TETHYS OCEAN

GONDWANA

LAURASIA

MID-CRETACEOUS
106 MILLION YEARS AGO

TETHYS OCEAN

GONDWANA

NORTH AMERICA

ASIA

PRESENT DAY

AFRICA

SOUTH AMERICA

AUSTRALIA

Since the time of the dinosaurs, the shape of the continents has been strongly influenced by a rapidly opening Atlantic.

THE MIGHTY DYNASTY OF DINOSAURS

THIS FAMILY TREE illustrates how a group of ancestral reptiles from the Paleozoic era managed to diversify and dominate the Mesozoic world. When reptiles first appeared they formed three main groups distinguished by different types of skulls. Today these forms live on in turtles, birds, and crocodiles, and mammals. Later the marine reptiles evolved as another distinct group, but they left no modern descendants.

At the beginning of the Triassic the turtle line became restricted to a few heavily armored forms and remains so to this day. The ancestors of birds and crocodiles – archosaurs – did well, but the age really belonged to the massive mammal-like reptiles. As the Triassic progressed, these huge creatures went into decline, but they produced new species that were much closer to what we would now call a mammal. By

the beginning of the Jurassic period small, hairy, warm-blooded mammals had evolved, but they were few in number and were to remain so for the next 130 million years.

Significantly, the Triassic saw the blossoming of the archosaurs. From small, swift animals they produced large carnivores, hefty herbivores and even the delicate flying pterosaurs. They also gave rise to the dinosaurs. The arrival of this group around

PALEOZOIC ERA　　　　　　　　　　**TRIASSIC**　　　　　　　　　　**JURASSIC**

250 million years ago

200 million years ago

• CHAPTER 1　　　　　　　　　　　　　　　　CHAPTER 2

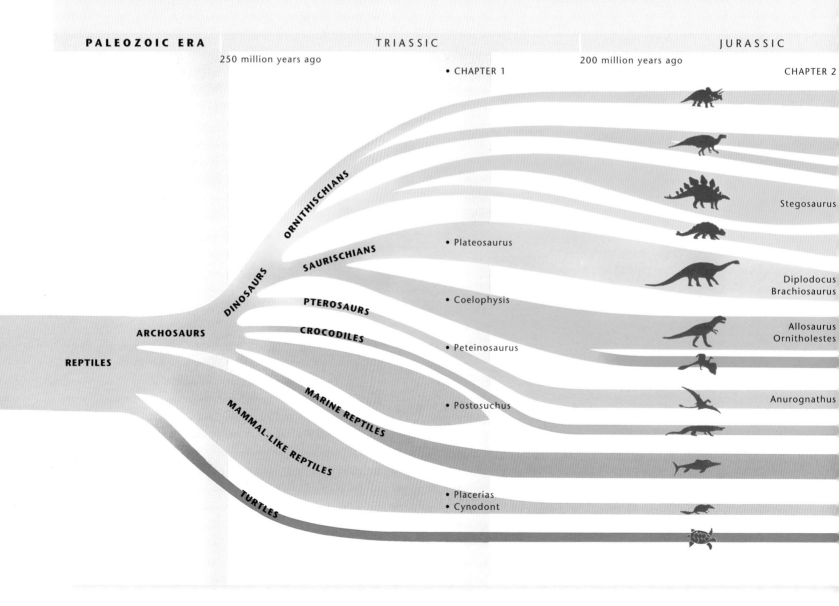

ORNITHISCHIANS

SAURISCHIANS

DINOSAURS

PTEROSAURS

ARCHOSAURS

CROCODILES

REPTILES

MARINE REPTILES

MAMMAL-LIKE REPTILES

TURTLES

• Plateosaurus

• Coelophysis

• Peteinosaurus

• Postosuchus

• Placerias
• Cynodont

Stegosaurus

Diplodocus
Brachiosaurus

Allosaurus
Ornitholestes

Anurognathus

the middle of the Triassic at first made little impression, but by the end of this era they dominated life on Earth. There were two major groups – the saurischians and the ornithischians – distinguished by the different structure of their hips. During the Jurassic the saurischians, made up of the carnivorous theropods, and giant herbivorous sauropods, were highly successful. Next, through the Cretaceous, the ornithiscians took off, and by

Last flourish: by the end of the time of the dinosaurs, the duck-billed hadrosaurs, like these *Anatotitan*, were the most common herbivores to roam the earth.

the end the duckbill and horned ornithisician dinosaurs were by far the most common herbivores. Then, 65 million years ago, all these creatures died out, leaving a few small feathered theropods and mammals.

CRETACEOUS

150 million years ago	100 million years ago	65 million years ago
• CHAPTER 3	• CHAPTER 4 • CHAPTER 5	CHAPTER 6 •

Torosaurus • **CERATOPSIANS**
Horned dinosaurs

PACHYCEPHALOSAURS
Domed-headed dinosaurs

Anatotitan • **HADROSAURS**
Edmontosaurus • Duck-billed dinosaurs

• Iguanodon

• Muttaburrasaurus

• Leaellynasaura **IGUANODONTIDS**

HYPSILOPHODONTIDS

• Polacanthus **STEGOSAURS**

Ankylosaurus • **ANKYLOSAURS**
Armored dinosaurs

SAUROPODS

• Eustreptospondylus • Utahraptor Tyrannosaurus • **THEROPODS**

• Iberomesornis **BIRDS**

• Rhamphorhynchus • Tapejara
• Ornithochieris Quetzalcoatlus • **PTEROSAURS**

CROCODILES

• Liopleurodon
• Ophthalmosaurus
• Cryptoclidus

Didelphodon • **MAMMALS**

TURTLES

known to help us form a complete picture. For instance, we chose *Coelophysis* to feature in Chapter 1, not because it is the earliest dinosaur ever found but because it is a typical early dinosaur, and we know a lot about it. Because we also wanted to describe dinosaurs' relationships with the plants and animals around them, we were naturally led to the world's richest fossil beds. Ghost Ranch in New Mexico produced hundreds of *Coelophysis* and, together with related beds, provided information that allowed us to add other creatures to its world – herbivores, a range of possible prey and a giant predator.

In large, well-preserved fossil beds scientists are also far more likely to

BUILT TO LAST

DINOSAURS WERE THE first land animals truly to be designed for speed and agility. Their bones were strong but light; they had an elegant upright posture, tails for dynamic balance, and highly energetic metabolisms. They made other animals such as mammals look clumsy.

Fast little reptiles existed before the dinosaurs and there is some controversy about how and when dinosaurs evolved. But the most popular current theory has dinosaurs first appearing as small, two-legged carnivores in the mid-Triassic, around 235 million years ago with a combination of features that marked them as different. These include an extra hole in the skull,

grasping hands and specialized ankle-bones, but it is dinosaurs' hips that are most distinctive. They had five fused sacral vertebrae that helped to create a very strong hip. Together with a specialized socket for the thigh bone, this gave dinosaurs their powerful upright posture. A long tail put their center of balance firmly over the pelvis, allowing them to run on two legs. This also freed their front limbs for catching food. All this was helped by a highly specialized skeleton. Many of their bones contained air sacs, like birds, and in the course of evolution they reduced many bones that were not absolutely necessary for structural strength. For their size, dinosaurs were probably surprisingly light.

The earliest-known dinosaur was found recently in Argentina in rocks about 228 million years old. It was called *Eoraptor*, or dawn hunter, by its discoverer, Paul Sereno. If dinosaurs did all come from animals like *Eoraptor*, they must have evolved very quickly. Within a few million years, another very different type of dinosaur had appeared – a heavy, four-legged herbivore called a prosauropod, the forerunner of the giants who came to dominate the Jurassic world.

Fused hip

Long balancing tail

Lightweight hollow bones

Grasping hands

Upright bipedalism

Hinged ankle bone

Structurally sound: the skeleton of *Coelophysis* shows many of the features of the earliest dinosaurs, which helped make them so successful on land.

discover clues to animal behavior, such as the incidence of cannibalism indicated by *Coelophysis*, or *Tyrannosaurus* teeth marks in a *Triceratops'* hip. Where scientific evidence of this sort was available, I incorporated it into the animal behavior described in the main text; there are boxes throughout the book which detail some of the best examples of this evidence, describe major discoveries, and explain some of the assumptions I have made. Most of the descriptions of movement, attack, defense and feeding are based on good fossil evidence.

In more speculative areas, such as sociability, parental care, and mating, however, I often had to resort to comparison with modern animals. It is worth remembering that dinosaurs were basically large, ground-nesting reptiles. Also we know that modern-day crocodiles are related to dinosaurs' ancestors and that birds are their descendants, so dinosaurs could be seen as the missing link between these two groups. If neither group shows a particular behavior – such as live birth – it is unlikely that the dinosaurs did.

Sometimes the stories are just reasoned guesses. For instance, I suggest that the little insectivorous pterosaur *Anurognathus* used the back of the giant herbivore *Diplodocus* as a feeding platform to hunt insects. There is no evidence for this, and it is hard to think of anything that could prove it. But given that a lot of insectivorous birds use large herbivores as feeding platforms nowadays, it is very possible that pterosaurs did the same in the age of the dinosaurs.

The structure of the book is intended to help readers imagine that they are observing dinosaurs from a hide such as those used by present-day naturalists and wild-life observers. Each chapter uses the evidence of one of the major fossil beds to help create a picture of a moment in time – usually no more than a year in the life of an individual creature – and is set in a specific place. Although covering brief periods, the stories are intended to reflect more widely the fate of different animal species, hence the decline of *Placerias* in Chapter 1 and the success of *Diplodocus* in Chapter 2.

The age of the dinosaurs covers a period from about 235 million years ago to about 65 million years ago, which is most of the geological era known as the Mesozoic (meaning 'middle life'). The era is divided into three periods – the Triassic, Jurassic, and Cretaceous. In selecting the stories on which to base a chapter, all of which are set in one of these periods, I have tried to cover significant moments in dinosaur history, as well as choosing a variety of geographic situations and climatic conditions. In the narrative I have used the geological names for extinct mountain ranges and oceans to emphasize how different the Earth then was from our own time.

In the photographs, as in the text, we tried to get as close as possible to reality. During the research period, we talked to paleobotanists about the flora of the Mesozoic and sought locations across the world where the vegetation is still similar to that era. We found a unique collection of little 'lost worlds,' where ancient botanical species persist, despite modern invaders such as the grasses. Our photographs included the monkey puzzle forests of Chile, the redwoods of California, the tree fern and podocarp forests of New Zealand, Australian cycads, and the bizarre araucaria of New Caledonia. These were used as background settings for our dinosaurs.

The dinosaur models were all based on the very latest scientific reconstructions, and again, it was useful that we chose well-known animals – the more information the model-builders had, the better the sculpture. These models were then digitized and reformed in the computer. Their skins were added, and then they were posed.

The skin patterns were largely speculation. Skin imprints have been found, but coloration will always be a mystery. The guesses in our pictures involved some assumptions. For instance, unlike most mammals, both crocodiles and birds see in color, so we assumed that color was important to the dinosaurs. If so, features such as camouflage, counter-coloration, and visual displays would have been common. On the very large creatures this does not

HOW NATURE'S GARDEN GREW

AT THE BEGINNING of the Mesozoic, many of the plant groups that had thrived during the previous era (the Paleozoic), such as the horsetails and club mosses, were still important, especially in wet areas. But change was in the air, and primitive, wind-pollinated conifers were becoming widespread. In the course of the Triassic period they became the dominant trees on the planet, producing many different types and eventually forming mighty forests of

which we can still see echoes in the redwood parks of northern California. Ferns continued to be a highly successful group, covering both open and understorey habitats. They appear to have been the closest the Mesozoic got to grass. Cycads (of which a few species still exist) and ginkgoes (whose sole surviving representative is the ginkgo tree) were also common, mostly as shrubs and trees. There were also several groups of plants that have left no modern descendants: these include the seed ferns,

the shrubby bennettites, and a number of conifer families.

The dinosaurs would have seen little of the colorful, chaotic growth of the flowering plants we are so used to today. This vast group, which now includes everything from oak and mahogany trees to cacti and grasses, made a very unassuming appearance in the middle of the Mesozoic. By the end, it had blossomed enormously, but ferns and conifers probably still dominated.

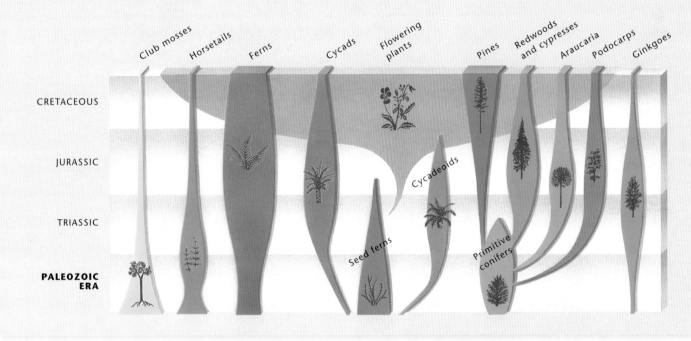

mean they were striped, but they could have had colorful flashes and crests.

The overall effect of *Walking with Dinosaurs* is to transport you back to the prehistoric world of the dinosaurs while at the same time showing you more about the fossil findings and scientific discoveries from which our knowledge comes. I hope readers of all ages will enjoy this natural history of some of the most extraordinary creatures that have ever lived on Earth.

220 MILLION YEARS AGO

New Blood

THE EARTH 220 MILLION YEARS AGO. The world in the Triassic period is a very different place from the one we know today. The vast Panthalassa Ocean covers two-thirds of its surface. A single continent, Pangaea, occupies the rest of the globe, stretching virtually uninterrupted from the North to the South Pole. There are no ice-caps. In fact, the ocean currents make the polar regions of Pangaea monsoonal. Most of the remaining continent is hot and dry.

This is a planet of extremes, and on its surface life is a struggle. The plants and animals of the Triassic are the survivors of a mass extinction that wiped out 95 percent of their population about 30 million years before.

At first, while the complex web of life slowly began to rebuild, it looked as if the familiar Permian fauna would reappear, with the mammal-like reptiles dominating. However, things began to change. Now reptiles have returned to the

The shape of things to come: young Coelophysis in the late evening light. Their lightweight, agile bodies are ideally suited to the demands of the seasonal Triassic landscape.

oceans and have become the top marine predators. Most successful among these are the sleek, fish-shaped ichthyosaurs. On land, reptiles have produced other new designs. There are crocodile-like creatures in the rivers, flying pterosaurs in the air, and small, hairy mammals on the ground. None of these, however, is destined to rule the Mesozoic.

Instead, out of the Triassic wilderness has come a group of animals ideally suited to this tough new world. Fast and adapted to drought, they are the dinosaurs. At first they were small, agile predators, standing erect on two legs, with grasping hands and sharp teeth. However, they are quickly evolving into larger forms and, with each passing millennium, they are increasing their domination of life on Earth.

The Triassic meadows and prairies would have been covered in ferns, low cycads, club mosses, and horsetails. There was no grass and the herbivores had to cope with a variety of plants.

A RACE FOR SUPREMACY

DURING THE TRIASSIC the single landmass of Pangaea (whose name means "all Earth") was at its most extensive, with China and part of South-East Asia separated as island continents. Only at the very end of this period did the first cracks in this huge land appear, when Africa and North America began to separate. The poles had no snow and were heavily monsoonal, probably lashed by severe storms. On the other hand, the equatorial regions would have been dominated by hot, dry deserts. The Triassic period was not "ruled" by any one group of animals. Instead, many completely different families of creatures came and went before the dinosaurs appeared.

At the beginning of the Triassic period, the great Permian extinction (see page 00) left an empty world with animal populations biased toward one or two successful survivors. It was millions of years before life on Earth really recovered. The first group to show more diversity was the invertebrates. Several ancient groups, such as spiders, scorpions, millipedes, and centipedes, weathered the extinction and started to thrive again at the beginning of the Triassic. Although many orders of insects were eliminated, when the recovery got under way, more modern species replaced the old, including grasshoppers, bugs, chewing stick insects, and primitive beetles. From then until the present day, insects have been one

Spiders are an ancient group of animals and, as this Cretaceous fossil shows, have changed little since the time of the dinosaurs.

continuous success story, increasing in variety and remaining unaffected by other global extinctions.

One of the insects' early advantages was that they had mastered flight, something no other group succeeded in doing for millions of years. Several reptiles experimented with methods of gliding and flying, probably in an

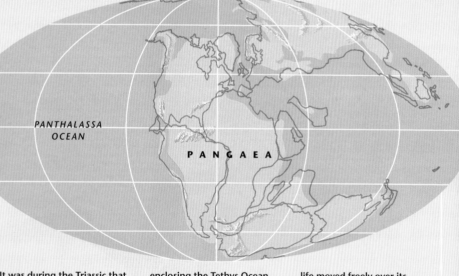

PANTHALASSA OCEAN

PANGAEA

It was during the Triassic that the supercontinent of Pangaea reached its maximum size. All the continental plates pushed together to form one landmass that ran from pole to pole. In the north and south two arms of land stretched eastward, half enclosing the Tethys Ocean. The rest of the globe was covered by the huge Panthalassa Ocean, twice the size of the modern-day Pacific. Although the sea occasionally isolated portions of Pangaea, the similarities between the flora and fauna across the world suggest that life moved freely over its surface, both on land and in the water. The northern and southern arms would have been seasonally lush because they caught the rain on the prevailing winds, but this robbed the center of the continent of water, creating extensive deserts.

attempt to harvest some of these insects, but it was not until the mid-Triassic that the flying pterosaurs appeared.

Among the second group, the plants, horsetails, and club mosses ceased to dominate the landscape, but continued to produce giant species. Ferns adapted to dry conditions and took over the open areas, and the conifers became the most common trees. At the beginning of the Triassic only primitive conifers existed, but they diversified into cypresses, redwoods, Araucaria (related to the modern monkey puzzle), podocarps, and pines. In the arid environment that prevailed in most of Pangaea, conifers had an enormous advantage. Most other plants needed water in order to reproduce, and conifers relied on the wind to spread their seed.

Seed ferns were common in the southern hemisphere. These look identical to ferns in the fossil record but had a different way of reproducing. They were extinct before the end of the Mesozoic era, but many people believe they were the ancestors of the flowering plants.

Marine creatures were harder hit by the Permian extinction than life on land. Some time during the early Triassic, reptiles helped repopulate the oceans by evolving into large marine predators.

There were nothosaurs, long-tailed fish eaters with four paddle-like limbs, and placodonts, squat reptiles that specialized in picking shelled mollusks off rocks. However, the most successful marine reptiles were the dolphin-like ichthyosaurs who evolved into fast-pursuit predators that would still be eating fish and squid 130 million years later.

Early Triassic land reptiles were similar to those of the Permian, dominated by the bulky mammal-like dicynodonts, which gave rise to the cynodonts and then to the mammals. However, instead of becoming more diverse,

Whip scorpions are some of the oldest members of the spider family. Creatures like these were probably among the first predators on land over 400 million years ago.

Dragonflies were very common before dinosaurs evolved. They survived into the Triassic, but for the first time experienced competition from rival aerial predators – the pterosaurs.

they faded away. By the Jurassic period all that was left of the entire group were small insectivorous mammals. In the middle of the Triassic a separate group of reptiles, the archosaurs, arose and produced a range of herbivores and predators. These creatures were better adapted to dry conditions and offered faster and more agile designs. Out of the archosaurs evolved crocodiles and dinosaurs, creatures that would reign for the next 150 million years. The dinosaurs divided into the carnivorous theropods and two groups of giant herbivores, sauropods, and ornithischians. For the first time herbivores were large enough to graze on trees, and they had vast fermenting guts for coping with tough vegetation.

However, dinosaurs did not "take over" because of some innate advantage. Another major extinction occurred and many groups of reptiles that had appeared to be thriving disappeared. This extinction was not like the one in the Permian. It was swift and might have been caused by the large meteor that landed in Quebec around this time. And, unlike the great extinction that was to kill off the dinosaurs 150 million years later, the large creatures seem to have been the survivors. By the time the Jurassic period started the world belonged to the dinosaurs.

These rare Araucaria trees in New Caledonia represent one of the earliest groups of conifers. Being drought-resistant and pollinated by wind made conifers highly successful during the Triassic.

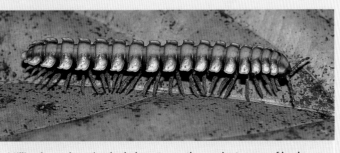

Millipedes and centipedes belong to another ancient group of land invertebrates from the pre-Triassic. Although the fossil record shows that they were rare in the Mesozoic, their success today makes this unlikely.

The Heat Returns

It is midday and the high fern scrubland has started to shimmer in the heat of the sun. The rains have left, but the ferns and club mosses still form a deep, lush mat over the rolling uplands. From beneath the green fronds comes the din of Triassic insects, lacewings, scorpion flies, and damselflies flitting from plant to plant. Centipedes and millipedes crawl among roots still damp from the morning's heavy dew. For the animals that live here it is a time of plenty. However, ahead lies the dry season, nine months of drought and hardship.

The scrubland lies on the western edge of central Pangaea, between forested lowland swamps to the north and the Mogollon Highlands to the

EXPERIMENTS IN LIFE

MOST OF THE ANIMALS in this chapter are loosely based on finds at Ghost Ranch in New Mexico (see page 46) and the Petrified Forest in Arizona. However, two have been drawn in from further away because during this time Pangaea was one continent and fossil finds show that there were remarkable similarities between habitats all over the world. The reason for choosing this moment in the varied history of the Triassic is that Ghost Ranch provides such detailed information about one particular early dinosaur, *Coelophysis*.

Coastal swamps

Fern uplands

MOGOLLON HIGHLANDS

A small area on the western coast of Pangaea. The uplands have the Mogollon Highlands to the south and a long inlet bounded by marshes to the north. To the east there is nothing but endless desert.

COELOPHYSIS

A highly adaptable little carnivorous dinosaur that was both an active hunter and a scavenger. Probably solitary most of the time, but during the dry season would occasionally concentrate in large groups around food and water resources.
EVIDENCE Hundreds of skeletons found at Ghost Ranch in New Mexico, including several whole skeletons and juveniles. Also found in the Petrified Forest in Arizona.
SIZE Maximum length of 10 feet (3 meters) and standing just under 3 feet (1 meter) at the hip. Weighed about 100 pounds (40 kilograms).
DIET An opportunistic carnivore and occasional cannibal.
TIME 222–215 million years ago.

POSTOSUCHUS

The biggest carnivore of its time, typical of a group of fast predators that evolved before the dinosaurs and developed their own unique upright posture.
EVIDENCE Several finds in the Petrified Forest in Arizona.
SIZE Maximum length of 20 feet (6 meters) with a powerful skull over 20 inches (50 centimeters) long. It could rear up to a height of about 6 feet 6 inches (2 meters).
DIET Active carnivore.
TIME 222–215 million years ago.

south. Scattered among the ferns are tall, pencil-like araucaria trees, but the thin shapes of these conifers provide little shade for the inhabitants of the scrubland. The largest animal here is Placerias, a bulky reptilian herbivore whose herds dot the open ground for as far as the eye can see. The adults grow to over 10 feet long and weigh up to a ton. Placerias are naturally a dull, mottled green, but these herds are stained red by the soil in which they habitually grub. The most striking thing about them is their head ornamentation: they have heavy skulls with two long horns that extend down on either side of their mouths. They use these horns to dig into the ground and to tear up whole plants, consuming them roots and all. The mouth itself ends in a beak that slices through the tougher vegetation. While Placerias feed, they plough up

PLACERIAS

The last of the large mammal-like reptiles that dominated the Permian era and the early Triassic period. They fed in large herds and defended themselves with two long tusks.

EVIDENCE The main Placerias find is just southeast of the Petrified Forest in St. Johns, Arizona, where 40 individuals were found in one place.

SIZE Maximum length of 10 feet (3 meters), but weighed well over a ton.

DIET Mainly low vegetation, but probably dug for roots as well.

TIME 226–220 million years ago.

PLATEOSAURUS

The best known of the prosauropods, the first of the giant dinosaur herbivores. Probably lived in herds and its size gave it a larger range of plants on which to feed. Also had strong clawed hands and a powerful beak.

EVIDENCE Several species have been identified from more than 100 fragmentary and complete skeletons found in Germany and France.

SIZE Perhaps grew as long as 30 feet (9 meters), making it able to graze at a height of 10–13 feet (3–4 meters). Weighed about 4 tons.

DIET A complete range of plants from trees to ferns.

TIME 216–210 million years ago.

CYNODONT

A group name for the ancestors of true mammals, more mammal than reptile. Some of them may have lived in pairs in burrows.

EVIDENCE The body shape described in this chapter is based on a cynodont called *Thrinaxodon*, found as a complete skeleton in South Africa. Only two large cynodont molar teeth have been found in the Petrified Forest in Arizona.

SIZE *Thrinaxodon* was no larger than a cat, but the Petrified Forest teeth indicate a bigger animal, at least 5 feet (1.5 meters) long.

DIET Most cynodonts were carnivorous, although their crushing molars could also have coped with seeds and roots.

TIME 222–215 million years ago

PETEINOSAURUS

One of the earliest known pterosaurs, it had short wings, a long stiff tail, and pin-like teeth for catching insects.

EVIDENCE Two skeletons found in the foothills of the Italian Alps near Cene.

SIZE Wingspan of 2 feet (60 centimeters) and a skull about 2 ½ inches (6 centimeters) long.

DIET Insects.

TIME 228–215 million years ago.

Triassic dawn: a small group of Placerias grazing in a meadow of tangled fern welcome the morning sun. Just after the wet season a thick carpet of ferns covers the high scrubland and thousands of Placerias are to be found grubbing in it.

bare patches of red earth, but the ferns have extensive root systems and will recover from this damage by next year.

During this time of year the adult Placerias are outnumbered by the juveniles. Each juvenile is only one foot long and barely visible above the ferns. At the beginning of the wet season the adults laid clutches of eggs in the loose, red soil and now, three months later, the herds are overrun with small, fat hatchlings. From the moment they hatched the young have had to cope with life alone. There is no bond between parent and offspring. In fact, the adults seem oblivious to the presence of the hatchlings. The youngsters have an innate ability to grub in the ground, and although they lack the adults' long facial horns, these small green reptiles quickly learn to find the club moss roots and fern shoots they need to grow. They also stick close to the herd, either for protection or to take advantage of the roots the adults leave behind .

Ground force: many of the scrubland plants have adapted to a long, dry season by producing large storage roots. Placerias' long cheek horns and powerful beak enable it to dig deep enough to feed on these roots.

By midday, most of the Placerias have stopped feeding and sit digesting their morning's work. With no grinding teeth, they rely on fermentation in their huge guts to extract nutrients from their diet. This process creates a lot of waste gas and their rumbling guts are clearly audible from some distance.

When the temperatures climb into the upper 80s, the herd begin to move. Led by the older adults, they head for the river valleys that cut across the scrubland to find shade and water. Placerias are low-slung animals and walk by swinging their legs out and around, their bodies twisting with each step, giving them a kind of swagger. Watching their slow progress through the heat haze is like a flashback to an ancient time millions of years earlier, when all land animals walked with this semi-erect posture. Placerias are the last of a dying race. Their kind no longer dominates the Triassic fauna. It seems that every time there is a long drought their numbers are badly hit, and afterward other species are quicker to recover. This means that over the past few millennia Placerias populations, once abundant across Pangaea, have become reduced and sparse. Now they are an endangered species, and here, near the Mogollon Highlands, is one of the few places where these magnificent beasts still survive in groups like their original numbers.

While the herd moves down from the high scrubland, they enter cycad groves and clumps of conifers. Tall column pines and maidenhair trees provide welcome shade. When the vegetation becomes dense, the Placerias follow game trails that have been trampled on by countless generations of herbivores. This forces them into single file, which is dangerous. In the open scrubland Placerias are capable of defending themselves against most predators. Besides

THE MOTHER OF ALL EXTINCTIONS

AROUND 30 MILLION years before the dinosaurs evolved, life on Earth very nearly died out. The facts about the great extinction at the end of the Permian period are staggering. In terms of pure destruction they dwarf the more famous cataclysm 185 million years later that wiped out the dinosaurs. Ninety-five percent of life perished. On land, flourishing ecosystems collapsed and whole animal dynasties, including giant amphibians and predatory reptiles, disappeared. Even the insects were decimated. In the sea it was worse. Ancient communities of sea lilies and corals were swept away, and the trilobites, which had thrived in the oceans for millions of years, were driven to extinction.

The problem for scientists trying to explain this event is identifying a killing agent lethal enough to have wiped out such huge numbers of both plants and animals on land and in the sea. There is no shortage of theories. Some have blamed volcanoes. The

There are many theories about the Permian extinction, but desertification on land and stagnation at sea is one of the most plausible.

volcanic rock formations known as the Siberian Traps were being formed at the time and over half a million cubic miles (2.5 million cubic kilometers) of lava spewed out over thousands of years could have poisoned the atmosphere. Others say a comet could have hit the Earth, which happened at the end of the dinosaur era, or that an intense ice age somehow made Earth uninhabitable. All these theories taken individually pose problems and many scientists favor the idea of a more gradual killer. After all, the period

of extinction lasted millions of years. It is now widely believed that at the end of the Permian nearly all the species on the planet died of suffocation. Lack of oxygen is a very effective killing agent on land and in the sea.

The extinction might have been triggered by the unification of all the continents into the giant landmass Pangaea. This eliminated thousands of miles of coastline and created vast inland deserts. Sea levels fell and the land heated up. Then the oceans started to warm and, as the variation in temperature between the poles and the Equator lessened, marine currents and circulation declined. The seas began to stagnate, triggering chemical changes that released carbon dioxide into the atmosphere. This created a super greenhouse effect. Life on Earth began to roast.

Fossil remains tell us that there were few survivors of this event. It was not until the mid-Triassic period, about 20 million years after the extinction, that the former rich diversity of life returned.

their general bulk, their face horns and powerful beaks are formidable weapons. However, in the closeness of this high scrub and forest, they are vulnerable to ambush. The herd begin to cough and grunt as the tension rises, and the hatchlings bunch close to the adults.

Their fears are well founded. No more than 10 yards from the path, shaded by some low tree ferns, lies a Postosuchus. Almost 20 feet long, she has a massive skull with a jaw full of slicing teeth. She is at the top of the food chain. Her back is covered in dark brown plates that form camouflaged armor and provide her body with a rigid strength that supports her on upright legs. Not only is she well protected, but she is fast.

Postosuchus are lone hunters and have perfected the art of ambush. Motionless, this female watches the herd cross in front of her. Slowly her head turns as she focuses on her intended victim. Normally she would study the herd for a while, seeking out signs of weakness before picking on the sick or injured, but with so many juveniles present, she has plenty of choices. She rises to her feet and pauses. Her body is superficially crocodilian in shape but her head is noticeably different. The snout is very deep, giving her a powerful bite. Also visible when she stands up are the long, strong legs tucked under her body that give her terrifying speed.

With a rustle of tree ferns, she darts forward. She picks on a hatchling that has stopped on the edge of the trail to feed. The small Placerias has just enough time to let out a piercing cry before the Postosuchus' jaws crush its ribcage. A ripple of alarm spreads through the herd. The large adults bellow and toss their heads in a threatening display of horns. However, the Postosuchus has already retired to the undergrowth with her prize, quickly dismembering the tiny animal and swallowing its parts whole. In the absence of any visible threat or alarm calls, the herd rapidly calms. Within minutes, it is like there had not been an attack. The Placerias continue down to the river. However, the Postosuchus has not finished with the herd. She will attack several times, taking four or five young, and none of the adults will attempt to pursue her.

This is the Placerias way. The herd is a loose group of individuals with no social structure to protect the young. Instead, they rely on quantity. Females become sexually mature after four years, and thereafter, if they survive, will produce eggs every year for more than 20 years. Each clutch may have as many as 30 eggs in it, meaning a female could easily produce 600 offspring in her lifetime. However, out of those she is lucky if two or three live to reproduce. Drought and predators take a huge toll.

By early afternoon the herd has reached the river. Its waters are swollen by the recent rains and they flow through dense stands of horsetails. The tall rod-like stems of these plants cluster along the bank, and some of the oldest plants rise several yards out of the mud. The trail the Placerias have been following ends at a bend in the river, where a long beach of red silt has built up and several stunted podocarp trees have replaced the horsetails. The herbivores line up along the water's edge to drink. Nearby a few slick green metoposaurs cluster around each other in the shallow water. These slab-headed amphibians and others like them used to dominate the ancient waterways, just as Placerias did the land, but now other reptilian predators are taking over. On the opposite bank a line of crocodile-like phytosaurs bask in the sun, their slender mouths wide open. With the arrival of the herd, some slip into the water to investigate. Phytosaurs are powerful predators living mostly on fish, such as the freshwater sharks, that are plentiful at this time of year. Although the Phytosaurs can grow 20 feet long, they would never tackle a fully grown Placerias, but a phytosaur could easily drag a Placeria hatchling to its death. Fortunately for the juveniles, the drinking herd presents the phytosaurs with a forest of tusks that protects the smaller animals splashing in the shallows.

LEFT Invincible carnivore: with his armored back and powerful jaws, Postosuchus is the top predator in these uplands. A fully grown adult can reach more than 15 feet long and only fears other Postosuchus.

Further downstream, the river falls over a series of shallow rapids, and broad, sluggish pools have developed along the edges. Here insect larvae feed off detritus, and in turn larger animals, such as crayfish, eat them. Within one of these pools a lungfish is killing a crayfish, his crushing jaws making short work of the crustacean's hard shell. However, the lungfish himself is being stalked. Right above him near the pool stands a thin, elegant reptile. He balances on his back legs, his head poised low over the water and his tail thrusted out behind, constantly making small adjustments to keep his body still. This is a small dinosaur called Coelophysis.

Dinosaurs are relative newcomers to the arid Triassic landscape and evolved from lightly built running reptiles. Already they have diversified into a number of different species, but Coelophysis remains true to the original design, a small, two-legged predator. Using his tail like a counter-balance, he is considerably lighter and more agile than his other reptilian contemporaries. He also has grasping hands, sharp recurved teeth, and excellent eyesight.

On this particular stifling afternoon, he is fishing. He watches a fat lungfish slide through the mud only a few centimeters beneath the surface. This Coelophysis is a mature adult just under 10 feet long from nose to tail and weighing around 80 pounds. The lungfish, which might be one quarter of the dinosaur's weight, is a mouthful. The Coelophysis will have to get his attack right first time or he could end up in the water. A blue damselfly lands on his motionless snout. He tilts his head to judge the true position of the lungfish beneath the surface and strikes. His curved teeth hook the prey and he catchs it with a powerful swing of his tail and flick of his head. Then he pins it down with his clawed feet and dismembers it.

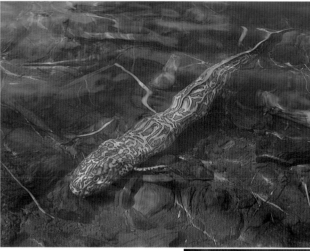

Fish out of water: a lungfish moves through the shallows, hunting small crustacea. Within the blink of an eye, he becomes a meal for a hungry Coelophysis. The dinosaur uses his recurved teeth to hook the fish and then, by articulating his lower jaw, easily slices the meat into smaller portions.

The Coelophysis' method of eating is simple. Except for some small nipping teeth at the front, all his teeth are the same, shaped like a double-edged knife with serrated edges, excellent for slicing through meat. His lower jaw is hinged in the middle, allowing him to move his upper and lower teeth against each other so that he can "saw" through difficult pieces. With such a formidable dental array, he makes quick work of his fish meal, dismembering large pieces and then throwing his head back to swallow each piece whole. Within five minutes, he has 22 pounds of fish being digested in his stomach and he moves off to find some shade.

Most of the Placerias herd have finished drinking and are sitting in the shallows keeping cool. Some of the young have wandered deep into a forest of old horsetail stems, grazing on the new growth pushing out of the silt. Behind the horsetails, at the end of the beach, is a high, sandy bank. An overhang is held in place by the corm-like roots of a nearby club moss, and hidden beneath this is the entrance hole to a cynodont burrow. Inside the chamber a pair of 3-foot-long cynodonts lie curled up asleep. Although they are distantly related to the huge Placerias outside, their heads, shoulders, and backs are covered in thick, black, hair-like scales, and their faces have long whiskers.

This is a mated pair and snuggled against the female's stomach are three cubs. The mother laid eggs toward the end of the last dry season and the cubs hatched in the middle of the monsoon. Since then the female has remained in the burrow, feeding her young from special milk glands on her belly. The cubs themselves are hardly recognizable as cynodonts. They are still half-blind and naked except for patches of pimples on their backs where their hair will grow. They are incapable of walking, and their stubby limbs wave helplessly if they lose contact with their mother in the burrow. In fact, they are completely dependent. Nowhere else in the Triassic is the bond between parent and young so strong. However, with so few young, cynodonts cannot afford to lose any. During the cubs' confinement, the parents will have to defend it aggressively.

'Already dinosaurs have diversified into a number of different species, but Coelophysis remains true to the original design, a small, two-legged predator.'

The afternoon progresses. The Placerias herd leaves the river and returns to the scrubland. While the sun drops toward the horizon, the sting is taken out of the heat. This is when the cynodonts awake. They are creatures of the night and a day's rest has left them hungry. The male stretches his long, thin body and crawls to the opening of the burrow. He sniffs the warm evening air and sets out for a night of hunting. The cynodont can see only in black and white, but he has very good night vision. This allows him to hunt without the unwanted attention of swift daylight predators such as dinosaurs. It also helps him to catch a few small, sluggish reptiles by surprise. Tonight it does not take long. He emerges from a tangle of ferns with a little gliding reptile clamped in his mouth. Once inside his burrow, he shares his prize with his partner. At this stage the cubs are oblivious to the catch since all their nutrition comes from their mother's milk. Within a month they will be needing raw meat and then both parents will have to work hard to feed them.

FURRY ANCESTORS

MAMMALS ARE AN ancient group of animals. We can trace our ancestors back to the late Carboniferous period 300 million years ago when a group of reptiles with a distinctively different-shaped skull evolved. These have been called mammal-like reptiles because their skeleton had certain mammalian characteristics, even though on the outside they would still have looked like reptiles. During the Permian era, they became the dominant group of animals on land. Fossils from South Africa show that these communities were rich and diverse, with a range of predators, large herbivores, and even burrowing animals. Although, like all animals, they were hit hard by the great extinction, they continued to be the most common reptiles into the early Triassic. However, gradually other types of reptiles took over and eventually dinosaurs replaced all other large animals on land.

Ironically, while the dinosaurs began their reign, the mammal-like reptiles were becoming more mammal than reptile. The cynodonts emerged and formed an almost perfect link between the two groups. Cynodonts had long bodies and ran on four crouched legs with a side-to-side movement like that of reptiles. However, they also had mammal-like features and specialized teeth, including molars, incisors, and canines. Their lower jaws were formed out of one bone, rather than the seven found in reptiles, and two of the redundant bones had migrated upward to form the delicate structure of the middle ear. Most significantly, fossil cynodont skulls reveal a pattern of small holes in the snout that suggest nerve roots supplying whiskers. Whiskers are specialized hairs, and

The perfectly preserved skull of the Triassic cynodont *Thrinaxodon*, found in the Karoo Basin in South Africa. Many mammalian features, such as differentiated teeth and the distinctive lower jaw, can be clearly seen.

suggest that cynodonts were covered in fur, needed for temperature control. This means that they were probably warm-blooded. Yet while mammals were clearly achieving an advanced state, their numbers were shrinking. For the next 150 million years our ancestors were confined to the undergrowth while dinosaurs ruled the Earth.

The Earth Cracks

It is now five months since there was any rain, and the river's level is falling. It used to flow past the bank where the cynodonts have burrowed, but now it is 60 feet from their entrance. Here and there dried clam beds bear witness to its increasingly rapid retreat. The old riverbed is a dry red mud and is beginning to crack in the savage Triassic sun. Occasionally, small holes betray the presence of buried lungfish. A month ago, when the river shallows began to stagnate, they burrowed down into the mud, wrapping themselves in a cocoon and waiting out the dry season in a dormant state. If need be, they can survive like this for several dry seasons, as long as they are not detected by a Coelophysis and dug out.

Despite the dryness, the river's edge still buzzes with insect life. Dragonflies patrol their hunting ranges above the horsetails, catching slower insects on the fly. Dragonflies have existed for more than 100 million years and although these brightly colored species are large, with 6-inch wingspans, they are nothing compared to their giant ancestors. Meganeura, a dragonfly that died out in the Permian era, had a wingspan of almost 2 feet.

On a log beside one of the more dense patches of horsetails sits a Peteinosaurus. He belongs to a group of animals called pterosaurs, or flying reptiles. Pterosaurs are not the first reptiles to take to the air since there are plenty gliding between column pines nearby, but they are the first to develop a flapping flight.

The Peteinosaurus sits flat on the log with his head and neck following the insect activity above him. A dense mat of short, fine hairs covers his head and shoulders and runs down his back. He holds onto the log with three short, clawed fingers on each hand. His last finger has grown into a long spar that supports the leading edge of his wing. While he sits, it is folded up across his back, just touching its partner on the other side. Attached to this is the thin skin of the wing, which runs from the tip of his wing finger down to his ankles.

Everything about this creature is delicate, from his almost transparent wings to his paper-thin bones. The Peteinosaurus has a wingspan of about 2 feet with a straight tail about 8 inches long, but he weighs little more than 3.5 ounces. In

OPPOSITE **Ready for take-off: a Peteinosaurus hangs under the shade of a podocarp tree, scanning the sky for the next careless insect that might flit within the range of his needle-sharp teeth.**

pursuit of flight, pterosaurs have shed everything that might weigh them down. In fact, they have to keep their wings folded, otherwise they would have trouble staying on the ground. Since they have to eat, pterosaurs still have relatively large mouths, about 2 inches long. He eats mainly insects, and a dragonfly is the perfect size.

Suddenly, the Peteinosaurus rocks on to his back legs and jumps. His wrists flick out his wings and he is airborne. His large eyes have already picked out his

TAKING TO THE AIR

FOR MILLIONS OF years insects were the only creatures that could fly, but at some point in the early Triassic, pterosaurs followed them into the air. No one can be sure where these unique creatures came from because there are no "missing links" to connect them to any other group of reptiles. The first pterosaur to appear in the fossil record is *Eudimorphodon*, already a highly evolved flier capable of plucking fish from the water. In the past it has been described as a sister group to dinosaurs, but many paleontologists believe that *Eudimorphodon*'s origins go back further, perhaps to the Permian. There is evidence that many reptiles evolved adaptations for gliding flight. One animal grew extensions at the end of its ribs that helped it parachute between trees, another had a large membrane between its hind legs, and there was one with long scales growing out of its back that it could use to help it glide. Among all these experiments, one group of creatures climbed into the trees and used a flap of skin that ran from the front legs to the back to help them glide.

However, the early pterosaurs took their approach to flight further. Their bones became lighter, and one of the fingers on

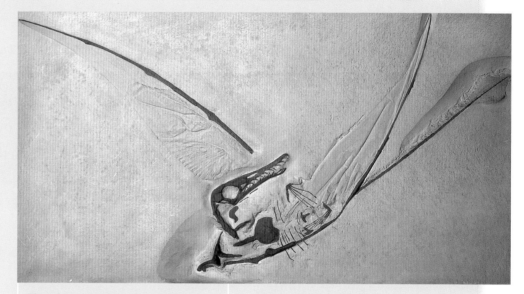

The origin of pterosaurs is a mystery. Without any apparent link to earlier reptiles, they suddenly appear in the fossil record as specialist fliers with paper-thin bones and long wing fingers.

their hands, probably the fourth, began to grow. Eventually they lost their fifth finger and evolved a long wingspan with three little claws in the middle. The skin stretched out from the legs and body to the finger, creating a wing. Their shoulders and breastbones strengthened to support enlarged muscles and they stopped gliding and started powered flapping flight. Besides bats and birds, pterosaurs are the only vertebrates to have done this and they were the first.

From then on the group stuck with the same basic body for 165 million years. Throughout, they occupied a specific niche, partly due to the way they conquered the air. Unlike birds, they required all four limbs for flying and therefore could not develop running or aquatic forms. However, it is clear that their design was ideal for active gliding, and during the Cretaceous they became giants of the air, traveling huge distances.

prey, and though his wings beat faster, he holds his head still, tracking the victim. Only four seconds after taking off, the pterosaur intercepts the dragon-fly, grasping its thorax and upper abdomen in his mouth with a crunch.

It is noon and the temperatures do not get much hotter in this part of Pangaea. All the moisture is being sucked out of the vegetation and the shade offers little relief for the inhabitants. The heat is even beginning to reach the cynodonts in their deep burrow, and parents and young sleep fitfully. The warm scent of mammal has attracted the attentions of two Coelophysis, who approach the entrance with care. The larger of the two cautiously puts his snout into the tunnel. About one foot inside it is met by the male cynodont coming out. The Coelophysis barks in alarm as he tumbles down the bank away from the angry parent. The cynodont remains half out of his burrow, snarling at the dinosaurs.

The two Coelophysis know the cynodont is too large and powerful to be an easy meal, so they trot down the bank and stop about 50 yards away, but continue to watch the hole. Eventually, the cynodont returns to his agitated family, leaving the two dinosaurs to watch.

The heat of the day passes slowly and by sunset a temperature difference between the high scrubland and the river valley sets up a breeze. The cynodonts wake and groom each other. The three cubs are now taking on many adult features, the dark, beady eyes, fine hair on their backs, and specialized teeth for chewing and biting. For some weeks now they have been making short excursions to the burrow entrance, playing under the watchful eye of one parent while the other goes out hunting. This evening the male climbs out of the nest to check for danger. The two dinosaurs have disappeared, but on the opposite side of the river several phytosaurs are tearing at a Placerias carcass in the water. The cynodont picks up the smell of meat in the air and scampers down the bank to get a clearer view.

Water cooler: under a vicious midday sun, and with a large expanse of wing membrane to absorb heat, small pterosaurs, such as Peteinosaurus, frequently splash themselves with water and use the evaporation to keep themselves cool.

The three cubs have started to clamber out of the burrow after their father. The first sits at the entrance, taking in the unfamiliar smells. A Coelophysis that has been standing motionless among the trees steps down and plucks the cub from the entrance. The pinch of the dinosaur's razor-like teeth is the first and last time the cub will feel pain and he squeals with alarm. The male cynodont launches himself up the bank, but it is too late. The Coelophysis accelerates down the riverbank. Even carrying food, he can reach speeds of almost 18 miles per hour and the low-slung cynodont has no hope of catching him. Soon the squeals stop.

Meanwhile, the burrow is under siege. Even though the rest of the cynodont family retreated inside after the attack, there were more Coelophysis among the trees and now they are determined to flush out the occupants. The male cynodont returns to scatter four or five large Coelophysis around his burrow. He then backs in, snapping at the dinosaurs around him. It is a lost cause. As soon as he disappears the Coelophysis approach the hole and start to scratch away its edges. Several times during the night the cynodonts try to chase the dinosaurs away, but they keep coming back. By morning the tunnel is only half as long as it was.

Inside, the cynodonts react to their change in fortune in the only way guaranteed to help them survive. The mother kills and eats her cubs. Though this may seem strange, it is done efficiently and without delay. At the point when escape with the young becomes impossible, it is only sensible that the cynodonts should benefit from all that nutrition. Under extreme circumstances like this, the drive to nurture is overtaken by the need to survive.

The cynodonts choose the early evening to leave the burrow. The flock of Coelophysis are surprised by their exit, and although a large female attempts to chase them, a raking blow from the male cynodont dissuades her. The other dinosaurs start to dig at the hole again. The attractive smell of mammal inside will hold the flock's attention for some time, until the burrow turns cold. Then they will lose interest.

OPPOSITE **Coming out fighting: once they have been discovered by the Coelophysis, the adult cynodonts know it will be impossible to rear young in the burrow, so they abandon it. The Coelophysis will continue digging at the hole for as long as the cynodonts' scent remains fresh.**

41

While the fleeing cynodonts push their way through the horsetails, they startle a resting Peteinosaurus. The little pterosaur flits low over the river, then rises up the other side of the valley. Below him stretches the fern scrubland. The scenery has changed radically since the end of the rainy season. Instead of the lush fern carpet, only a few dull green and grey patches survive. Large areas have been torn up by the Placerias and in the distance, a cloud of dust betrays the presence of a feeding herd. In the dry scrubland soil their method of rooting creates so much dust that they are almost hidden from view. Although there seems to be little nutritional value left on the scrubland, many of the ferns store water in their roots and this is what the Placerias want.

Nearby, in a cycad thicket, a male Postosuchus is lying uncomfortably in the shade of the broad cycad leaves. His mouth is thick with frothy saliva and his usually sleek brown scales are spattered with blood and dust. He shifts his back legs to reveal a long, deep tear over his giant thigh muscles. The only thing that could have produced such a wound is the tusk of a fully grown Placerias.

During the dry season, food gets scarce for all the animals, including Postosuchus. Not only can the herbivores' horns gore easily, but also their beaks are powerful enough to break bones. This male must have been driven by hunger to try a bold attack on a herd of Placerias. The wound is several days old and there are signs that it has become infected. Atleast with the gathering darkness, the Postosuchus can expect some relief from the heat, but in all other respects his situation is about to get worse.

Postosuchus are fiercely territorial. In the dry season, males and females must patrol an area of many square miles to ensure their food supply. Female territories tend to be smaller but more rigorously defended than those of males. Territorial battles can be violent, sometimes resulting in the death of one of the combatants. This protectionism extends even to unborn rivals. If an adult of either sex comes across a nest of Postosuchus eggs, he or she will devour most of them and destroy those they cannot eat. Juveniles tend to grow up in dense forests, where they can avoid direct contact with adults, but should they wander into more open areas, the adults will eat them too.

A female Postosuchus, who has been hunting in the river valley, has been drawn up on to the scrubland in the hope of finding stragglers in the Placerias herds. She is wary since she knows she is in another's territory. She stalks toward the herd and moves within 50 yards of the grove, where the wounded male is watching her intently. Suddenly, she picks up his scent in the evening

LEFT Evenly matched: two Placerias kill a Postosuchus. The Postosuchus is fast and powerful, but once he has lost the advantage of surprise, he would not be wise to attack the Placerias since these solidly built herbivores can inflict deep wounds with their cheek horns.

43

breeze. She arches her back and shows her teeth. When he sees this threat posture, he limps out of the cycads, bellowing and waving his armored tail. While he comes closer to the female, he starts throwing dust at her with his forelimbs, snapping aggressively.

However, she does not yield. She is younger than the wounded male and, as a female, slightly larger. Since he has failed to rear up on his back legs, and she can smell the wound on his leg, she feels bold. Postosuchus' back legs are much longer than the front ones and they frequently rear up in confrontations, revealing their distinctive yellow-striped underbelly and making them look more impressive. Sometimes two individuals will wrestle standing on their back legs, clawing at each other in a trial of strength.

The female rears up, issuing her own threats. The deep wound on the male's back leg makes him incapable of matching her challenge. He tries to arch his back to intimidate the intruder, but the confrontation is turning against him. He backs off and she advances. Then he turns and runs. He is limping badly and she pursues him, biting at his back legs. In the last light of the day he crashes into the denser undergrowth above the river valley. He has lost his territory and it is unlikely that he will be given the chance to recover from his wounds. His days are numbered.

A Thirsty Landscape

NOVEMBER—LATE DRY SEASON

It is now eight months into the dry season. The scrubland looks like a baking red desert with dead fern stumps littered across its surface. The dark green araucaria stand out against their barren surroundings because their long tap roots allow them to get water from deep in the earth. Despite outward appearances, there is still plenty of animal life up here. Insects that lived among the greenery earlier in the year have left eggs that will hatch with the arrival of the rains. Also, the dry red earth between the fern stumps is covered in small holes. Many burrowing invertebrates survive, no matter how high the temperature climbs. Scorpions, sun spiders, and cockroaches all forage at night. They eat spores, eggs, or each other and represent the only active resi-

dents through the late dry season.

Most of the larger animals in the area are concentrated around the dwindling water resources. Down in the valley the river no longer flows and it has broken up into a series of muddy pools. Many aquatic creatures have left the area, following the river downstream to the lowland swamps before the flow stopped completely. Above the stagnant pool clouds of insects hover and several Peteinosaurus dive back and forth, plucking their victims out of the air.

The water itself is crammed with phytosaurs. Their spiny black backs writhe over each other in the shrunken pools. Occasionally, fights break out and ripple through the crowded reptiles as they jostle for space. The heavy jaws and long, overlapping teeth reveal that most of them are males. Many of

When the going gets tough: while the dry season drags on, large areas of the uplands turn to desert. Coelophysis survive well in these conditions, and here a hungry young male stalks a whip scorpion that has taken refuge in an old Postosuchus skull.

the females appear to have abandoned the area, perhaps moving downstream to sit out the last of the dry season in the swamps. However, the males are territorial and will not abandon their home patches, making tension high.

This overcrowding is made worse by the presence of a herd of Placerias. Since the ferns disappeared from the scrubland, the herd has been sustained by the dense growth of horsetails and club mosses along the banks of the riverbed. Although the hatchlings are now almost 10 feet long, it is a dangerous time for them. In the heat of the day they need to drink, but the dirty water is alive with phytosaurs. Repeatedly, juveniles stumble over the thick mud and sip at the water's edge, only to end up clamped in a phytosaur's mouth.

The situation with the adult Placerias is completely different. At this time of year they feed mainly at night. During the day, they sit around with their legs and bellies sunk into the deep mud on the edges of the pool. When they get too hot, they simply wander into the phytosaur-infested water to cool off.

This is the only time of the year when the Placerias are forced together in

LITTLE GHOSTS FROM TRIASSIC TIMES

WHEN DINOSAURS FIRST appeared, they did not take over the world. For millions of years they formed only a small part of the reptilian fauna. The earliest fossil remains show that they made up about 5 percent of the animals. For palaeontologists investigating this period, they are rare finds and that is why the discovery made by Edwin Colbert in 1947 is so remarkable. At the aptly named Ghost Ranch in New Mexico, Colbert found the remains of a delicate carnivore called *Coelophysis*. As he and his colleagues dug, they uncovered more and more remains. Ghost Ranch turned out to be the site of a mass death, hundreds of contorted *Coelophysis* skeletons wrapped round each other. There were so many that large blocks of stone had to be cut out and sent directly to museums for investigation. For the last 50 years scientists have painstakingly excavated the tangle of bones. *Coelophysis* was a very early dinosaur, and because of this find we have a huge amount of information about the way it lived. *Coelophysis* means "hollow form" and it is so named because its bones are paper thin, indicating that it must have been very light. Individuals vary from 2 feet 6 inches to 10 feet long, so the change in body shape from a young *Coelophysis* to an old one can be traced. There are clearly two types of adult, a robust form and another more slender form. These probably represent females and males, and although no one can be absolutely sure, many believe the females had the heavier such high numbers and this appears to trigger their mating behavior. The first sign of this is increased tension among the males. They vary substantially in size, with the oldest bulls weighing around 2 tons and measuring well over 10 feet long. Younger males will display and compete vigorously too, but they are rarely successful. Displaying involves a male standing with his mouth wide open, showing off his face horns, and liberally spreading his dung in a patch around him. With such a disparity in size, it is very rare for two evenly matched bulls to meet. However, when they do, their horns can inflict terrible wounds.

The females, who have smaller horns, are attracted to bulls who can defend a large area filled with their strongly scented dung. Once she has chosen a mate, a female lets the male cajole her into what is left of the river, where he mounts her, often pushing her completely under the water. All this takes place among the crowded phytosaurs, who pay no attention.

While the Placerias mate, the forest around the river is slowly filling with

OVERLEAF Dangerous waters: late in the dry season the normally solitary Coelophysis congregate around the last trickles of water. The presence of flocks of these hungry little carnivores makes it impossible for other creatures to come down and drink.

One of 28 blocks removed from Ghost Ranch. Each contains a complex network of delicate dinosaur skeletons. In some cases cleaning and removing these wafer-thin bones from the rock matrix has taken scientists decades.

Since 1947, the cliffs of Ghost Ranch in New Mexico have produced hundreds and hundreds of Coelophysis skeletons, making it one of the world's richest dinosaur finds.

skeletons because they were the ones who had to lay eggs.

The Ghost Ranch site is so well preserved that scientists can even see a glimpse of the sort of Triassic world where dinosaurs first appeared. The Coelophysis skeletons were found in the sandstones and mudstones of an old riverbed. With the bones were the remains of fish, clams, small crocodile-like phytosaurs,

and crayfish. Any of these could have been prey for Coelophysis. There are also clues to the biggest question surrounding Ghost Ranch – why did all these dinosaurs die together? Perhaps the skeletons were deposited there over many years, but Edwin Colbert is convinced that it was a mass death and that the culprit has left its mark. In the rocks, there is evidence of mud cracks and crayfish burrows (something that would occur only in very dry conditions), and some of the skeletons have curved necks reminiscent of animals dried out by the sun. Colbert believes that the Coelophysis were drawn together by dwindling water resources before dying. Then, before they could be torn apart by scavengers, a flash flood buried them in mud, preserving them for millions of years.

Coelophysis. Normally the little dinosaurs hunt alone or in small groups. However, at the height of the dry season they gather in flocks of several hundred and only then can their numbers can be appreciated. When their population becomes denser, their behavior subtly changes. Although there is always aggression between individuals, the flock gradually start to coordinate their activities, moving as one, and hunting together. They lose interest in small prey and instead pursue large animals. Therefore, juvenile Placerias are strangely safe on the banks, but should a bull be badly wounded, he could become a target. In the extreme circumstances of the late dry season, this makes sense. If all the Coelophysis continued to attack smaller prey, competition would become intolerable, and many would die in the squabble for food. However, if

Death mask: the mouth of Postosuchus with its long serrated teeth is the most fearsome weapon in the Triassic. Yet with his body riddled with infection and malnutrition, this male will not be able to hold off an attack from a flock of Coelophysis.

they prey as a flock on larger animals, they open up a new source of food and, after a kill, there is usually enough meat to satisfy them all.

In the haze of the afternoon an oven-hot breeze blows up the valley. On one wide bend in the river, beds of dried-up clams mark a large flood plain. Its surface has been trampled flat by the Placerias herd and the wind has sorted the yellow fern litter into piles. In the center of the plain sits a wounded male Postosuchus. It is the same creature who was chased off the scrubland several weeks before. He is starving, desperately thirsty, and also an infection that has cost him the use of his back legs is clouding over his eyes.

However, he is still aware enough to see a single Coelophysis standing in front of him. The little dinosaur hops from foot to foot and bobs his head, all the time keeping an eye on the old predator. The Postosuchus opens his jaws as a threat but the Coelophysis is unmoved. More Coelophysis appear out of the forest. Soon between 40 and 50 dinosaurs are flocking round the Postosuchus, snapping and barking with excitement. Shuffling around on his front legs, the big predator vainly tries to face his tormentors. His immobile tail and rump present an easy target for the Coelophysis. They dart in and start to bite. Suddenly, the Postosuchus lurches forward, catching a female by the foot. He pins her under his front claws and with one bite severs her neck. When he shuffles around again to defend his shoulders, several Coelophysis drag the female away and start to eat her. The flock are now in a feeding frenzy and will eat anything that bleeds.

The heavy scales on the Postosuchus' back and tail mean that for a long time the Coelophysis bites have little effect. However, eventually they catch his soft underbelly and he starts to bleed. While his movements become less and less frequent, the Coelophysis climb onto his body and feast. With their long snouts they are able to wriggle their heads deep under the Postosuchus' scales, eating the armored creature from the inside out. Over the next few days they will clean out the corpse, slicing the toughest hide with their serrated teeth and then picking the bones and scales clean with their nipping front teeth. The Postosuchus' body will give the flock enough food to last them for two weeks.

A Parched Wilderness

JANUARY—THE RAINS ARE LATE

In such a finely balanced system, even a short delay in the arrival of the rains is a severe test for the resident animals. The dry season has lasted nine months and should have broken two weeks ago, but still there is no sign of rain. It is six weeks since the old Postosuchus died, and his bones are now bleached white by the sun. The scrublands are empty except for the few underground insects and spiders. In the valley there is no longer any standing water, and the river has disappeared. The pools have evaporated and the soft, cooling mud that used to surround them is baked as hard as a rock. Trapped in the center of many of the pools are the rotting carcasses of numerous phytosaurs, mostly large males who stuck by their territories even when the water dwindled around them. Along the banks of the river large holes have appeared in the mud, dug by phytosaurs escaping the drought. Here they are mostly females carrying next season's eggs. In their burrows they can lie dormant for a number of weeks, but it is only a temporary measure, sooner or later they will need food and moisture.

Phytosaurs are not the only animals to perish in large numbers. There are no longer any Placerias in the area. Some of the herd managed to make the long journey north to the coastal swamps, but the drought has claimed hundreds in the process. The dry riverbed is littered with their remains, their huge horned skulls bleached by the sun. The Placerias are specialists in surviving on the dry fern scrublands, but this means they depend heavily on the monsoons. They have evolved over millions of years to thrive in an environment where the rains arrive regularly every year, but global climate changes have made these increasingly unpredictable. Even a short drought can rid whole areas of swaggering herds.

In one of the old Placerias skulls a female whip scorpion has laid her eggs. She stands at the entrance to the eye socket, protecting them from raiders. When a shadow passes over her she raises her powerful pincers in defense. The

DINOSAUR CANNIBALS

THE GHOST RANCH site in New Mexico has turned up hundreds of *Coelophysis* skeletons, but two large adults were of particular interest. Crammed inside their body cavities were collections of smaller *Coelophysis* bones. At first it was suggested that these might be embryos, but their little bones were all jumbled up and belonged to animals far too large and well formed to be unborn. It is now agreed that this was evidence of the *Coelophysis'* last meal.

Cannibalism is not uncommon among animals. It has been documented in 138 different species. When male lions take over a pride, they eat all the cubs, Komodo lizards view both eggs and hatchlings as fair game, and many small mammals commit infanticide under stress. Some research suggests that cannibalism comes so naturally in certain species that it has to be chemically suppressed in order for them to raise their

The tiny collection of bones just visible beneath the ribcage of this *Coelophysis* turned out to be the dislocated remains of a very young *Coelophysis* it had just eaten.

own young. However, since the fossilized contents of dinosaur stomachs are rare, perhaps it is surprising that one of the few cases to have survived should be an instance of cannibalism.

Rather than being proof that dinosaurs spent a lot of time eating their own kind, this could be further evidence that drought caused the mass death of *Coelophysis* at Ghost Ranch. Today, adult crocodiles will readily eat smaller ones and, as a result, youngsters usually grow up far away from their parents. However, in times of crisis,

such as drought, crocodiles of all ages and sizes can be forced into close proximity and then cannibalism becomes more common. This could have happened at Ghost Ranch as the local *Coelophysis* population succumbed to Triassic drought and the large adults turned on the young and vulnerable.

shadow belongs to a Coelophysis. Unfortunately for the whip scorpion he is looking for a meal and the whip scorpion will do nicely.

The dinosaur strikes at the scorpion, but she pulls back into the skull. When the Coelophysis explores further a cloud of acid sprays his face. The dinosaur leaps back, scratching at his snout while his nostrils burn with the effect of the scorpion's defense. He barks and snorts in irritation but immediately returns to the skull, his face pushing in deeper to catch the stubborn prey. His efforts are rewarded with another spray of acid. The dinosaur backs off and wipes his snout in the dust. He has not come across a whip scorpion before, otherwise he probably would not have bothered, but he persists, eventually evicting the scorpion from its shell and eating her. After he has left the foul-tasting abdomen that sprayed him, it seems that the meal was hardly worth it.

Red in tooth and claw: an adult Coelophysis pauses before finishing off one of his own kind. When these dinosaurs crowd around the dwindling water resources, cannibalism becomes more common.

Despite the drought, Coelophysis numbers are still high. They have had plenty of dying Placerias and phytosaurs to feed off of and have even dug up buried lungfish. However, their varied diet is not the only reason they have survived so well. Coelophysis are specially adapted to dry conditions. Most animals need a lot of water, not only for nutrition, but also to help them excrete poisonous nitrogen waste products such as ammonia. However, in dry conditions, passing large amounts of water as urine is wasteful. Coelophysis, like all dinosaurs, have developed the ability to package their waste nitrogen in uric acid, which is less toxic and requires little water to be excreted.

Yet another dry, airless day dawns and still there is no sign of the rains. A small flock of Coelophysis track down an old riverbed and spread out to hunt. Two of them bicker over a dismembered centipede. Further down the bank a lone, immature Coelophysis hides under a cycad. The flock draw nearer. The youngster knows he is in danger. Even in less harsh times, adult Coelophysis will readily cannibalize smaller individuals. Suddenly the tiny dinosaur panics and runs. Immediately, he has two adults after him. The leader strikes and flings the youngster into the air by the tail. When he lands, he tries to regain his footing, but the jaws of his elder swiftly close on his neck. The young Coelophysis goes limp and immediately the second adult tries to snap and tug at the body. Now the killer has to run for the scrub to avoid losing his prey to the rest of the flock. Several others pursue him. He will have to fight hard to keep his prize.

Normally by this time of year the flocks would have disbanded with the onset of the mating season right before the rains. Instead it seems that the females are becoming more solitary, while the males remain in large bands. Several of the females have mated successfully and will wait for the rains to arrive before laying. If the drought is long, they are capable of arresting the development of the eggs inside their bodies for considerable periods and then restarting the process once the rains arrive. Females who have not mated may be subjected to attacks by the various bands of males, and often become badly injured in these confrontations. It is hard to see the evolutionary advantage of this behavior, unless it helps weed out weaker individuals.

Waters of Life

Three hundred and six days after the last rain the wind changes and starts to blow from the south. Gradually the humidity builds and huge gray clouds gather over the Mogollon Highlands. Soon the clouds blot out the sun and distant lightning flashes appear on the horizon. The wind becomes stronger, gusting 95 miles per hour, breaking dried plants, and raising a huge dust storm. A few large raindrops herald a torrential downpour and within minutes water is beginning to run down every dried-out gully or stream. Half an hour after the rain arrives a huge wall of silt and water sweeps down the riverbed, having gathered volume and momentum from the highlands. Few of the Coelophysis have time to escape, and hundreds are swept downstream and buried under tons of silt in the lowland swamps. Some of the phytosaurs are also buried by the silt, but the majority emerged from their retreats when the rain began to fall and, as strong swimmers, survive the flash flood.

High on a bank above the river the pair of cynodonts has made a new burrow. It is accessible only by means of a suspended tree root and, although the floodwater rises toward the entrance, the burrow is too high to be at risk. Despite the large number of Coelophysis in the area, the cynodonts have not been discovered and the pair are breeding again. The female is already wrapped around three tiny eggs in a rough nest. When the rains stop after three days, the male heads out to hunt again.

After fifteen minutes he returns to the burrow with a slim reptile in his mouth. It is a juvenile Coelophysis, probably the most numerous prey available early in the wet season. However, he and his partner will need several of these little creatures to satisfy their appetites, so the male goes hunting again.

Over the next few weeks the river valley fills with life. Horsetails and ferns reappear from deep roots within the red earth. Once dormant insects and crustacea hatch in the fresh water, producing an abundance of food and drawing fish upstream from the lowland swamps. The

only creatures that do not return in the same abundance are the Placerias. A small herd re-establishes itself on the scrubland, but it is only a shadow of what it once was. At the same time, another group of grazing animals increases its numbers to take advantage of the newly vacant niche.

In the river valley the sound of smashing branches heralds the arrival of a herd of Plateosaurus. It is hard to believe that these creatures are related to Coelophysis. They have long tails and walk with an upright gait, sometimes on all fours, but frequently only on their back legs. However, the similarity ends there. Some of the adult Plateosaurus measure up to 30 feet in length and weigh up to 4 tons. To date the Plateosaurus are the largest animals ever to walk on land.

At the end of their long necks is a narrow head with a mouth full of serrated teeth designed for cropping the toughest vegetation. Plateosaurus' size and reach allow them to graze on everything from low ferns to tree branches almost 13 feet off the ground. They also have powerful grasping hands and can easily pull branches down to feed. Their size gives them another advantage. Any food they eat stays in their guts longer, giving them a chance to extract more nutrients from it. Plateosaurus is perfectly designed for the vegetation of Pangaea.

Throughout the Triassic, the conifers have become the dominant trees and shrubs across the continent. Their leaves are tough and often poisonous, and many species grow too tall for existing reptiles like Placerias to graze on.

However, now the dinosaurs have caught up. Plateosaurus can exploit tree branches no large animal has touched before and their huge guts can digest the toughest vegetation. Even trees taller than 13 feet are not immune. If a Plateosaurus wants leaves out of his reach, he will often pull down the whole tree to get them.

There are 20 adults and sub-adults in this herd and their destructive progress through the forest scatters many of the resident animals. A group of Coelophysis flee along the riverbank while a fully grown female Plateosaurus

'Plateosaurus can exploit tree branches no large animal has touched before and their huge guts can digest the toughest vegetation.'

OPPOSITE Triassic titans: two adult Plateosaurus bulldoze their way through a stand of araucaria. These gentle herbivores are the largest land creatures on the planet and, at over 4 tons, their sheer size makes them invincible.

blunders out of the undergrowth. Her size and the long claws on her forearms ensure that the Coelophysis will not bother her. Even if there was a flock of them, it is unlikely that the Plateosaurus would be threatened. She continues across the river and the rest of her herd follow. Their sensitive noses have picked up the smell of a fruiting cycad grove and they are specialists at plucking this nutritious food from the crown of the tree before it falls, thus depriving ground-grazing animals, particularly Placerias, of the annual harvest.

While the sun sets, the only animals visible along the river, besides the phytosaurs, are the Plateosaurus and a few wary Coelophysis. This scene has echoes across the length and breadth of Pangaea. Dinosaurs are coming to dominate the land. Their numbers and varieties have been increasing steadily for the past four or five million years, and Plateosaurus also shows that they are getting bigger. Their light bones and upright gait are perfect for living on land and this continues to give them a huge advantage in the wildernesses of the Triassic.

New world order: a Postosuchus meets his match as a giant Plateosaurus drives him from the river. Plateosaurus herds are becoming increasingly common in the uplands, as are numerous other species of dinosaurs.

Time of the Titans

2

T

HE EARTH 155 MILLION YEARS AGO. It is the late Jurassic and dinosaurs have dominated the land for almost 60 million years. The vast continent of Pangaea has started to break up, with the narrow Tethys Ocean beginning to divide it into two landmasses, Laurasia to the north and Gondwana to the south. Although the climate is still dry and seasonal around the Equator, these continents are much wetter toward the poles. This has allowed the growth of huge conifer forests that stretch for thousands of miles. Inside these forests a bewildering variety of small dinosaurs and pterosaurs inhabit the dense understory. New insects and amphibians, including frogs and salamanders, have appeared. Mammals have evolved full fur coats and give birth to live young, but there are not many species and they are mostly small insectivores.

The forests do not dominate all the moist Jurassic landscapes, however. There is another force at work here, one that

Life on the plains: a herd of Diplodocus passes a lone bull Stegosaurus. They are standing in an araucaria forest, which is kept open like this by the destructive grazing of numerous sauropod herds.

keeps the great trees at bay and artificially maintains huge areas of low scrubland. The Jurassic is distinctive for its herds of giant sauropods, the family name for the largest dinosaurs that have ever lived. They roam across the plains of Laurasia and Gondwana in groups of 30 or more, devouring any vegetation in their reach and crushing the rest. This is the first time in Earth's long history that animals have had such a profound effect upon the environment.

Fully grown, these huge grazing machines could weigh over 70 tons and, from the tip of their tails to the end of their snouts, could measure 45 yards in length. Yet all this bulk had to grow from a hatchling that could fit inside an egg no bigger than a regulation-size football.

A "living fossil" plant: *Ginkgo biloba*, or the maidenhair tree, is the only living descendant of a large group of trees that thrived during the Mesozoic.

TRIUMPH OF THE DINOSAURS

BETWEEN THE TRIASSIC and Jurassic periods there was a significant mass extinction. We still do not know what caused the loss of so many species on land and in the sea, but many paleontologists believe that this was a key moment in dinosaur evolution. Although dinosaurs thrived in the late Triassic, in the early Jurassic they came to dominate every niche on land. After this Triassic extinction, although the climate, landmasses, and vegetation gradually changed, the dinosaurs remained on top.

This period represented a time of transition. In the early Jurassic the global climate was still mostly dry, and the prosauropods were the dominant herbivores.

However, while the era progressed, the world became wetter, especially at the higher latitudes, and the giant sauropod dinosaurs took over. Sauropods were huge four-legged herbivores with long necks and tails, and there was something about the late Jurassic that suited them. Although Pangaea was breaking up slowly, there were still many large landmasses, and, as a result, animal and plant communities remained similar across the globe. However, during this time the first signs of provincialism appeared. China developed a unique range of animals, and northern and southern flora began to look slightly different.

In the steadily moistening climate, ferns

Amphibians evolved almost 400 million years ago, but frogs, with their distincitive hind limbs, and salamanders are advanced forms and did not appear until the Mesozoic era.

and conifers came to dominate habitats and dense forests developed. In the higher northern latitudes redwoods and ginkgos did well, and in the south podocarps flourished. The equatorial regions continued to be dry and seasonal. Among the plants, the

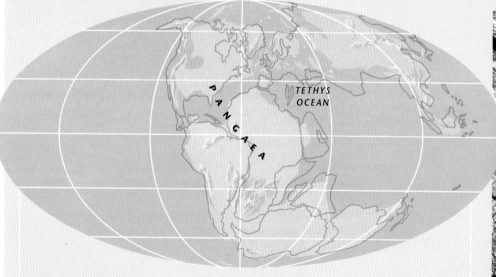

For most of the Jurassic, the giant continent of Pangaea almost remained unbroken from one pole to another, but toward the end of the period, wide cracks opened. In particular, North America began to rotate toward the northwest, away from Africa. Movements deep within the Earth's mantle powered this slow drift, which still continues today, gradually creating a wider and wider Atlantic Ocean. The westward arm of the Tethys Ocean made inroads into the Pangaea coastline, and the continental drift enabled its waters to spread even further, dividing the giant continent into northern and southern landmasses. However, plants and animals across the globe displayed remarkable similarities throughout this period. Increased diversity and provincialism were a feature of the Cretaceous.

bennettites represented a range of plant types, although they never became large trees and were commonly low shrubs. Perhaps the most distinctive species was the short, barrel-shaped *Cycadeoidea*. Its rotund stems were soft and fleshy inside but were surrounded by a tough cover of dead leaf scales. It had a ring of cycad-like leaves on the crown, and around the top of the stem it carried flower-like receptacles for insect pollination. This group became extinct during the late Cretaceous after the arrival of flowering plants.

The Jurassic saw the evolution of many groups of animals that are alive today. Among the insects, the three largest orders, the beetles, wasps, and flies, first appeared. Also,

frogs, salamanders, newts, and lizards can be traced back to this time. The mammal-like cynodonts continued into the early Jurassic, but by the end of this period, most mammals were small, furry insectivores. It is probable that they also took to the trees to increase their foraging range. The Triassic extinction had killed off all the phytosaurs, and, in their place, crocodiles diversified, not only in freshwater habitats, but also on land and in the sea. Out of all of these new groups, perhaps the most significant were the birds. *Archaeopteryx*, the oldest known bird, appears in the late Jurassic but already has feathers and wings (see page 188).

Meanwhile, the skies belonged to the pterosaurs, a group that had produced numerous bizarre species. Beneath them the dinosaurs had also diversified and become much larger. The descendants of *Coelophysis* had grown into powerful predators, but a new group of carnivores that would come to dominate the killers of the Cretaceous had appeared. These tetanurans, as they were called, gave rise not only to the birds and the

Insects, such as this giant lacewing, learned to live with predation from pterosaurs and birds. Fossil lacewings have been found with eyespots that could have distracted attackers.

giant *Allosaurus*, but later to the raptors and eventually to the mighty *Tyrannosaurus*. The predators had to be good because their prey was becoming more difficult to attack. The armored dinosaurs evolved during the Jurassic, as did the stegosaurs, which used a range of lethal spines to protect themselves. Then there were the sauropods, which simply became enormous.

Although all sauropods were similar in shape, there were subtle differences between them. *Brachiosaurus*, *Diplodocus*, *Apatosaurus*, and *Camarasaurus* all had their own distinct grazing styles and appear to have coexisted easily on the Jurassic plains. Their impact on the environment must have been dramatic since they would have shaped the vegetation around them like elephants do today.

In the seas giant reptiles thrived. The ichthyosaurs declined slightly in diversity while the plesiosaurs became successful. Generally, the Jurassic oceans saw a huge change in marine life, but that is discussed in Chapter 3.

At this time conifers were the dominant trees. Redwoods were an early group, and species similar to these Californian redwoods grew large enough to dwarf even the sauropods.

This fossilized or "stone" cone is almost identical to that produced by modern species. Many mature conifers hold their cones in their topmost branches, an adaptation that could have evolved to avoid dinosaur grazing.

Babes in the Wood

YEAR ONE–IN THE FOREST

Sunrise across the vast western plains of Laurasia is greeted with the bark and chatter of a dinosaur chorus. Once this was the bed of an ancient, shallow expanse of water called the Sundance Sea, which stretched hundreds of miles to the north, but now it is dry, and low thicket and scramble ferns, bennettites, and seed ferns cover the plains. Isolated groves of maidenhair, conifers, and cycads grow, especially near the many seasonal rivers.

WHEN SIZE WAS IMPORTANT

THE FOSSIL EVIDENCE for much of the Jurassic period is poor, but toward the end, there are some superb sites in the United States, Tanzania, and China. Most of the animals in this chapter come from the Morrison Formation in the United States (see page 108), one of the most studied fossil groups in the world. The range of creatures shown is typical of the late Jurassic world. The dinosaur herbivores were dominated by the giant sauropods, with various species of armored stegosaurs alongside. Along with a range of small carnivores, a group of giant predators had evolved, presumably to tackle the enormous prey around them. Most of the dinosaurs would have had to live on large, open plains because of their size. Where dense forests developed, a totally different fauna must have existed.

DIPLODOCUS

The longest of all the sauropods, but still lightweight compared to some. Length boosted by an extraordinary whip-like tail. Lived in herds of 20 or more, which contained only adults and subadults. Had large heavy scales on its back, and spines running the length of its body.
EVIDENCE Based on five skeletons without skulls and several skulls with isolated elements of the skeleton. Four species have been identified from the Wyoming and Colorado Morrison Formation.
SIZE Up to a maximum of 100 feet (30 meters) long and weighed up to 20 tons. Height at the hip 16 feet (5 meters). However, larger bones have been found of diplodocids that could have reached 150 feet (45 meters) and 30 tons. In this chapter these have been used as the basis for older *Diplodocus*.
DIET Would have selected vegetation that it could strip with its peg-like teeth. Since it was mostly a low grazer, ferns must have made up a large part of its diet.
TIME 155–145 million years ago.

BRACHIOSAURUS

The real giant among sauropods, not because of its length or even its height, which was considerable, but because of its sheer bulk. Like a giraffe, it was adapted to feed on high plant material and had close-cropping teeth for nipping food.
EVIDENCE Although two partial skeletons come from the Morrison in Utah and Colorado, the best known species was identified from finds in the Tendaguru Beds in Tanzania.
SIZE About 75 feet (23 meters) long, but weighed up to 70 tons and could graze at a height of about 43 feet (13 meters). Its height at the shoulder was about 20 feet (6 meters).
DIET Like Diplodocus, probably not choosy, but its diet would have been biased toward conifer leaves and fruit.
TIME 160–150 million years ago.

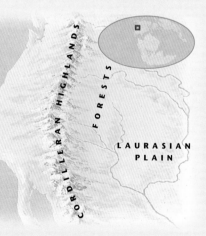

During the late Jurassic, western North America was dominated by wide, open plains left by the retreat of the Sundance Sea. To the far west were the Cordilleran Highlands, later obliterated by the Rockies.

Clearly visible among the vegetation are herds of sauropods, long-necked dinosaurs who have dominated this Jurassic landscape for millions of years. Although all the sauropods look similar, their grazing habits are subtly different, allowing many different species to live side by side on the plains. Trailing the herds, looking for the weak and vulnerable, are large and powerful predators such as Allosaurus, which have evolved to prey on these massive animals.

Out here in the open the success and grandeur of the dinosaurs is easy to see, but there is another side to their story. On the edge of the plains, while the

STEGOSAURUS

Large herbivore with highly characteristic plates that ran down its back and probably flushed when it wanted to display. Its main defense was four fearsome spikes on the end of its tail.
EVIDENCE Numerous finds of three species, including complete skeletons and juveniles in the Morrison Formation.
SIZE Maximum length about 43 feet (13 meters) and weighed about 7 tons. Height at the hip, including the plates, almost 23 feet (7 meters).
DIET A low browser, but the strong beak allowed it to tackle even the toughest plants.
TIME 160–145 million years ago.

ALLOSAURUS

The lion of the Jurassic, the largest and most common carnivore found in the Morrison. A swift hunter with long, grappling hook-like claws on the end of its arms, it would regularly have attacked sauropods.

EVIDENCE More than 60 complete and partial skeletons from all over the Morrison, from Wyoming to New Mexico.
SIZE Up to 40 feet (12 meters) long, with a weight of around 3 tons.
DIET Meat, and lots of it.
TIME 150–145 million years ago.

ORNITHOLESTES

A small, active carnivore with long, grasping hands but a small head and conical teeth. Usually feeding on smaller animals and carrion, it was suited to hunting among dense vegetation.
EVIDENCE A skull and associated skeleton found in the Wyoming Morrison.
SIZE Around 6 feet 6 inches (2 meters) long and weighed about 90 pounds (40 kilograms).

DIET Small mammals, lizards, and insects, but *Ornitholestes* was also an opportunist hunter, who would eat carrion.
TIME 155–145 million years ago.

ANUROGNATHUS

A tiny pterosaur with a short head and pin-like teeth for catching insects. Although it belonged to the long-tailed pterosaur group, its tail was comparatively short, allowing it more maneuverability for hunting.
EVIDENCE Only one skeleton has been found in the Solnhofen limestone of Bavaria. For the purposes of this chapter, it has been moved to the west.
SIZE Although *Anurognathus* had a wingspan of 20 inches (50 centimeters), its body was only 3½ in (9 centimeters) long. It cannot have weighed more than perhaps ¼ oz (a few grams).
DIET A range of insects, although some, such as the dragonflies, might have been too big for it.
TIME 155–145 million years ago.

land climbs to the Cordilleran Highlands, denser forests of maidenhair and conifers take over. Here insects, mammals, and amphibians thrive, as do the smaller herbivorous dinosaurs. Rarely more than 6 feet long, they are often fast-moving bipeds mostly living off the new growth in the understory. Large predators are rare since it would be difficult for them to operate among such dense vegetation. Here the emphasis is on speed and agility, not power.

On the edge of the green forests, the morning sun reveals an elegant Ornitholestes grooming himself after a night of sleep. He is a little dinosaur, only about 8 feet long, and most of that is tail. A hungry predator with a small head full of conical teeth, usually he is found hunting small lizards and mammals among the ferns deep in the forest. His most distinctive quality is his

Cold-eyed killer: this female Ornitholestes, showing off her display scales, is a common predator in the Cordilleran forests. She is only about 6 feet long and lives mostly off mammals and lizards, but she can also be a menace to baby dinosaurs.

body's decorative scales. Down the back of his head and across his shoulders the scales have grown long and narrow, allowing him to puff up during display. This technique is primarily designed to make him look more formidable to larger predators, but he also uses it to impress potential mates.

He stands on the fallen trunk of a giant tree, sniffing the air, his bright blue head decoration flashing in a ray of light that has filtered down from the canopy 70 yards above. The edge of the forest is a dangerous place since the larger of the plains predators could easily spot him. However, experience and his nose have drawn him here in anticipation of a feast. He scampers along the trunk into the shadows and waits, tucking up beside his body his flexible arms, with their long grasping talons.

Below him the forest floor is almost completely clear of plants. Six months ago the nearby river flooded the forest edges, dumping tons of silt over the ground. The mature redwoods have survived unscathed, by pushing up roots through the suffocating layer of mud. However, it will be some time before all the understory plants have re-established themselves. The Ornitholestes watches this apparently lifeless scene with expectation.

Suddenly, on top of the silt, in the middle of a large clear patch, the thin layer of redwood leaves starts to move. At first it is only in one tiny spot, but soon there are several areas twitching. A host of tiny animals is struggling to dig out of the ground. Eventually, the needles part and a head on the end of a thin neck stretches up for its first breath of clean air. This is what the Ornitholestes has been waiting for. He pounces off his trunk and darts toward the hapless creature. His talons flick out and grab his prey by the head. With one powerful tug, he pulls the whole animal out of the ground.

It is a tiny Diplodocus, hatched from an egg laid by one of the longest and most elegant of the sauropods. Even with the comparatively short neck and tail of a newborn, he is already 3 feet long. His green and brown dappled body still has egg membrane stuck to it, but his fight for survival is already over. He has no way of protecting himself against the Ornitholestes, who swiftly kills him with a bite to the neck.

However, the hatchling's sacrifice is part of a survival strategy for the species. While the little predator starts to feed on a substantial meal of sauropodlet, the victim's brood are unearthing themselves across the clearing. Soon nearly 100 sauropodlets fill the forest floor. This glut of food is more than a dozen Ornitholestes could handle. Even though more carnivores will be drawn here by the smell, synchronized hatchings taking place all along the forest edges will ensure that the predators are heavily outnumbered by tiny Diplodocus. Nearly 2,000 sauropodlets will wriggle out of the ground on the same day and, despite each one being vulnerable, local predators will probably claim only about a quarter of them.

Three months ago a herd of Diplodocus laid their eggs here. Though Diplodocus predominantly feed on the plains, they lay their eggs in open areas

on the edges of the forests. The recent flood meant that ground conditions were perfect for laying. Each huge adult female found herself a suitable clearing and laid about one hundred large, round, hard-shelled eggs. Then she abandoned them and rejoined her herd.

Sauropodlets grow inside the eggs, their necks and tails bent to fit, until there is no room left. At hatching time they have to wriggle through 3 feet of soft silt to gain their freedom. Unfortunately, they are not built to burrow and many fail in this first crucial endeavor. Sometimes, if the subsoil in which they are buried has dried out, the whole nest may perish. This is why the mother's choice of laying site is so important. Once the hatchlings have dug themselves out, they have to seek a safer environment. Their short ungainly legs do not allow them to run fast, and in the open clearings they are very exposed.

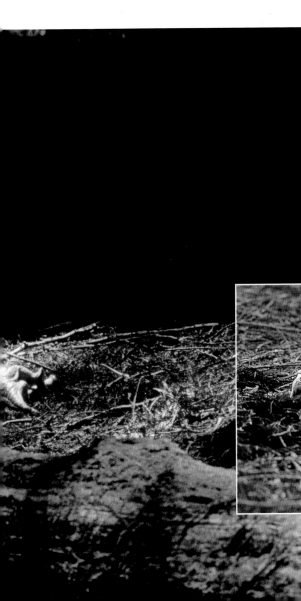

Escape to danger: for baby Diplodocus, the effort of digging themselves out of the hole in which their mother laid them is exhausting. Many newly hatched youngsters sit around the clearing recovering from their exertions. However, this is a dangerous time for them since there are plenty of hungry Ornitholestes looking for an easy meal.

However, they are born with an instinctive desire to seek cover and this, coupled with an apparent preference for running uphill, is usually enough to ensure that they head for the denser parts of the forest. They still have egg yolk in their stomachs, which provides the nourishment and enables them to stay on the move for several days, pushing deeper into the upland forests until they find a safe place. Eventually, they will settle down to life in the dense understory, grazing on new green shoots and hiding from any encroaching predators under the thick layers of fern fronds.

Eating for the future : baby Diplodocus have to grow at a phenomenal rate, putting on about half a ton in weight in the first year. Soon after they hatch, they start a lifelong obsession with eating.

For the first three years of the sauropodlets' lives, the inner forest is home. While there, they stack weight on at the astonishing rate of more than 5 pounds a day. By the end of the first year they will have tripled in length and may weigh close to half a ton. This means that they quickly become large by forest standards and impervious to the attentions of predators like Ornitholestes.

In the silt-covered clearing the morning wears on and two more Ornitholestes appear. After the first few, they no longer eat the sauropodlets. Instead they kill them and leave the bodies. They cannot consume all the carcasses, and it is hard to explain why they continue the slaughter. Perhaps it is useful hunting practice, or simply a form of play.

At the far corner of the clearing a female sauropodlet climbs free of the confines of her egg. She sits momentarily, recovering from the effort, redwood needles and silt plastered on her dappled skin. Her appearance is unusual because her pigmented skin is darker than the rest of her brood. Suddenly, as if she heard a gun shot, she trundles off toward the dark side of the clearing. An Ornitholestes looks up from his kill, stretches out his arms, and runs after her. While he closes in on her, two more hatchlings cross his path. He stalls and partially turns, catching one of the pair with his claws. It is a quick kill, but by the time he looks up, his original target, the dark female, is out of the clearing and has reached the first scrappy ferns on the edges of the flood area.

Following her most basic instincts, the sauropodlet travels uphill, away from light. She stands only about one foot off the ground and soon the huge fronds of king fern form a dense green canopy over her head. Then she picks up a familiar scent, the same smell she encountered in the clearing, the unmistakable odor of a predator. Zigzagging through the ferns, another Ornitholestes is hunting for sauropodlets. He can smell his prey, but he cannot pinpoint her among the dense foliage. He stops and watches, looking for shaking fronds that will betray the presence of a hatchling.

Now that she is under the cover of ferns, the sauropodlet reacts to the predator in a completely different way. When she smells him she crouches down and freezes. She flattens her head and neck to the ground, her dappled back giving her perfect camouflage against the tangle of moss and dead fronds. This behavior is innate since there is no parent there to teach her such successful survival tactics. Even though the Ornitholestes is a forest hunter, relying on scent as much as on sight, and the sauropodlet still carries the aroma of her egg membranes, he passes her by. This is the environment in which such a vulnerable creature can survive. She remains motionless for a few minutes more before scrambling up and continuing deeper into the forest.

This upland Laurasian forest is the nursery for the giant sauropod herds of the plains. When they are small the sauropodlets exploit the lowest ground level vegetation in the forest. Here there is plenty of food including liverworts, club mosses, moss, fungus, and a number of delicate species of small ferns. There are also larger ferns, such as the king fern, that have highly nutritious stems. The sauropodlet will have to learn quickly what is and is not good to eat if she is to gain the weight as fast as she needs to. While she progresses further into the forest and the yolk in her stomach is used up, she begins to pick at the plants around her, starting a lifetime obsession with feeding.

'By the end of the first year Diplodocus will have tripled in length and may weigh close to half a ton.'

Absent Parents

Out on the plains, the sauropodlet's mother is already almost 60 miles away from her hatchling's struggle for survival. She is part of a herd of adult Diplodocus grazing on cycads in the hot Jurassic sun. Of all the sauropods, Diplodocus are perhaps the most elegant. Even the oldest animals weigh only about 25 tons, half as much as the bulkier species such as Brachiosaurus. Yet they can grow to be twice as long as a Brachiosaurus, about 130–150 feet. This is partly due to an extraordinarily long, flexible tail, which for the last 10–13 feet is a long, thin whip.

Diplodocus are also unique because they produce a distinctive range of sounds to communicate with each other while they continue feeding, even with their heads buried deep in ferns. The strangest of these sounds is a low-frequency rumble that travels through the ground and is sensed by other Diplodocus through their feet. This is a way of keeping the herd together. Even if he cannot see them, since each member can feel the others rumbling nearby, he feels reassured. The pitch is too low for most creatures to hear, but close to the herd the rumbles make sand skip across stones and plants vibrate.

The deepest and strongest rumbles come from the females, who dominate Diplodocus herds. They are larger than the males and, because size matters in a predatorial world, they tend to live longer. This particular herd contains one gigantic old female. She is by far the longest creature there and must be at least 100 years old. Many of the spines that run down her back are broken or twisted, and her flanks are crisscrossed with scars from decades of predator attacks, but her sheer size makes her almost invincible. Except for the occasional wandering male, all Diplodocus live in herds, bound together by the need for protection. Large, old females are an extraordinary asset, providing security for many other smaller Diplodocus. There are 40 sauropods in this herd and most are subadults ranging from 6 to 15 years old. There are no really young animals. When the herd is on the move, the smaller animals tend to follow the larger females, walking under their long tails, for protection.

The old female has led the herd to the cycad grove, where they are feeding. Besides the low rumbles, there are other sounds, a range of audible snorts that get deeper the larger the animal is, and the constant eerie swish and crack of their tails.

On the move: the lead members of a Diplodocus herd approach a cycad grove. The trees are just starting to flush with new growth, and the giant herbivores will tear the grove apart to get at the fresh, new leaves.

DIPLODOCUS MAKE OVER

THE OLD AND FAMILIAR image of *Diplodocus* shows it dragging its long, snake-like tail along the ground. Its skin is smooth with small wrinkles, like an elephant's, and its neck curves up to crop the trees. However, as a result of a number of finds, this picture has changed. Now it is believed that massive ligaments down *Diplodocus'* back helped hold its long body horizontal, like a suspension bridge. Its neck vertebrae did not articulate much, therefore it could move its head around only in long, sweeping curves. This gave it a wide feeding arc, but would have made it impossible for it to bring its head around more than 90 degrees. At the end of the long neck, the head was orientated downward for grazing.

The tail was held aloft, and in the late 1980s it was pointed out that this appendage bore an uncanny resemblance to a bullwhip. The base was heavily muscled but flexible, and the end tapered to a long thin tip. Some 40–50 small vertebrae continued for about 12 feet with no obvious function. The last 6 feet 6 inches (2 meters) of this massive creature's tail was only 1¼ inches (32 millimeters) across and weighed about 5 pounds (2 kilograms). Computer studies have shown that if the sauropod swished the base of its tail, the far end would

move at supersonic speeds and probably produce a crack similar to a bullwhip, but 2,000 times louder. Pathological damage has been found in the bones at the base of the tail, suggesting it was heavily stressed by repeated movment. It is unlikely that *Diplodocus* used its tail to whip predators, because that action would cause it too much damage. However, they could have used it to threaten, or for courtship or communication.

The final part of the transformation of *Diplodocus* involves its skin. Faint traces in the rock around the best-preserved skeletons suggest that their backs were covered in skin spines. These were not made of bone, like

For many years the *Diplodocus* skeleton in the main hall of the Natural History Museum in London showed the dinosaur dragging its tail along the ground. Recently it has been reset with its tail held aloft.

those of the armored dinosaurs. They were more like the skin structures that run down the back of a modern iguana. The flat scales across the surface of *Diplodocus'* back were actually humps about 4 inches (10 centimeters) long, and down the midline of its back ran spines up to 7 inches (18 centimeters) high. The "new look" is more like a medieval dragon than a lizard, but it is unmistakably reptilian.

Diplodocus balanced its enormously long body over its legs like a suspension bridge. Tall spines on its vertebrae provided attachment points, and huge ligaments running down its back helped take the strain of the neck and tail.

Diplodocus use their whip-like tails as highly sophisticated communication devices. Similar to the rumbling, the tail carries on a conversation while the head is buried in vegetation 30 yards away. With a gentle flick of the base the thin end of the tail can be accelerated so fast that it whistles through the air and produces a supersonic crack. If several members of a herd perform the same trick, the noise can be considerable, and this is the first line of defense when they are threatened by predators. Although they avoid making direct contact with attackers, the aggressive cracking is often enough to scare off all but the most determined. The tails also maintain a tactile communication within the herd, constantly exploring the backs of other members. In fact, it often appears that the more tails an individual can feel, the calmer he is. If a Diplodocus begins to feel isolated, he will swish his tail or snort to attract attention before he bothers to lift his head from feeding.

A background to all this snorting, rumbling, swishing, and cracking is another noise, the deep gurgle and grind of active stomachs. The Diplodocus' gut is one of the secrets of its success. Indeed, all sauropods benefit from having this huge food processor, which allows them to feed and extract nutrients from some of the most unpalatable food imaginable. The stomach of a Diplodocus can hold over a half a ton of vegetation. In addition, it contains several pounds of stones, used to digest the food and grind it down further. This digestive activity is audible outside the animal and adds a particular character to the sound of a Diplodocus herd.

This herd has been attracted to the cycad grove by the flush of new leaves. Cycads are unattractive plants to the majority of grazing animals since their bark is as tough as armor, their leaves are thick and spiny, and they produce poisons to make themselves even more unpalatable. However, their new leaves are soft and more easily grazed. These grow from a central crown on top of the plant and are protected by a ring of older leaves around the outside. However, the Diplodocus reach over with their long necks and pluck at the crown within. Securing each long leaf stem with their peg-like teeth, they strip upward, removing and swallowing all the soft new growth. The older spiny leaves have little effect because the Diplodocus' soft nostrils are placed well out of the way

on top of their heads. Cycads have evolved to overcome this threat by growing their flush of new leaves quickly, and they are less likely to be discovered by a grazing animal during their vulnerable period. Unfortunately this grove of cycads has been unsuccessful and the Diplodocus are feasting.

When they feed, the herd smashes their way through the grove, disturbing clouds of insects. Leafhoppers, shield bugs, sawflies, and thrips all live among the cycads and fern understory and are temporarily evicted by the herd's passage. This is exactly what a small companion of the Diplodocus wants. Sitting on the back of each one of these huge herbi-

Forbidden fruit: cycads use some of the most formidable defenses of any plant, armor, spines, thick cuticles, and even poisons to protect their fruit. However, none of these will stop a determined sauropod.

vores are up to a dozen pterosaurs called Anurognathus. With a wingspan of only about one and a half feet and a tiny mouth less than an inch long full of needle-like teeth, they are voracious insect eaters. Anurognathus use the Diplodocus' backs as hunting platforms and spend the entire day swooping back and forth after the prey flushed out by the destructive feeding of their giant traveling companions.

Anurognathus spend their entire lives on the backs of sauropods, leaving only to lay eggs. Otherwise they feed, mate, fight, and grow up on the Diplodocus spines. In any herd of sauropods, flocks of these tiny blue and green creatures can be seen flitting from back to back. When the Diplodocus are feeding on low ferns, the Anurognathus line up in rows along their necks, bickering and snapping at each other for the best position. Along with insects, Anurognathus will eat the Diplodocus' dead skin scales, parasites, and even its blood if it is wounded. It is hard to see what the herbivores get out of this relationship, except removal of the occational parasite. The Anurognathus can frequently make wounds worse, and most adult Diplodocus are covered in pterosaur droppings. However, the giant herbivores seem utterly oblivious to their activity, not even registering the hundreds of tiny sharp claws that cling to their thick hides.

Through the afternoon the herd works their way into the grove, destroying two and a half acres of cycads in four hours. When evening approaches, predators start to appear from the cool places they have been hiding, avoiding the hottest part of the midday sun. This is a daily ritual and the Diplodocus are well prepared. The larger of them feed on the edges of the herd, presenting a formidable wall of flesh to all potential assailants. On these plains there are many predators large enough to bring down young Diplodocus, but none would attack a fully grown adult.

Today, when the sun drops lower and the shadows lengthen, no large predators appear. Instead, a small group of Coelurus stalk in among the feeding giants. They are about 6 feet long and effective hunters of small reptiles, especially since they often join together to hunt in groups. However, they are far too small to threaten even the youngest Diplodocus. They are probably after Anurognathus, or other insectivores or herbivores attracted to the destruction the herd produces, but when these sleek little creatures crawl deeper into the grove, one of the subadult Diplodocus picks up the smell of meat. He starts a long hollow alarm call. Other members of the herd hear the call and wave their tails in agitation.

Strange traveling companion: the tiny pterosaur Anurognathus spends most of its life on a Diplodocus' back, feeding off the insects the giant dinosaur disturbs while grazing.

The grove suddenly becomes a dangerous place for the Coelurus. When they try to escape, they run into the path of the huge female, who is swinging her neck and tail in defense. The first Coelurus is caught when a huge Diplodocus neck sweeps toward him out of the evening gloom. The blow sends him tumbling back into the cycads and he is killed instantly. The other Coelurus scatter into the undergrowth, leaving the herd calling rest-

lessly. By nightfall they are calmer. Some sleep where they stand, and others continue to feed in the moonlight. The plains can be as dangerous at night as during the day, therefore some members of the herd are always alert. The sound of cracking wood and tearing leaves continues in the darkness.

By morning the Diplodocus have destroyed almost half the cycads. Having finished with one tree, they move onto the next, frequently crushing underfoot the one they have just left. Some of these trees are decades, even centuries, old and it is unlikely that the grove will recover for some time. This is typical of sauropod grazing and it is what has shaped these plains. Repeated cropping by

DINOSAUR DUNG

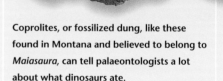

AMONG THE MATERIAL left behind by dinosaurs are items we would not expect to find after so long, such as coprolites, or fossilized dung. This might seem merely amusing until you consider how much a modern zoologist can tell about an owl from its pellets. The dinosaurs must have produced a lot of waste but, as with most trace fossils, it is astonishing that any survive. Immediately after the dung was dropped, it would have started to decompose, then it could have been trampled, eroded, dried out, or even eaten. Nevertheless, coprolites have been discovered all over the world. In Yorkshire a collection of small pellets has been found, each measuring just under ½ inch (1 centimeter) across and containing diced bennettite leaves. The clue that they might have belonged to a dinosaur is in their volume. There is over 10 square feet (a square meter) of them.

In Montana, near a collection of large Cretaceous herbivores called *Maiasaura*, paleontologists have discovered bulky coprolites containing plenty of woody conifer debris, which suggests that these dinosaurs were used to a tough diet. Even more interesting are the short columns of dung found in the sediment nearby. These were left by dung beetles, who would have carried away pieces of dung and buried them in tunnels with their eggs. When the eggs

Coprolites, or fossilized dung, like these found in Montana and believed to belong to *Maiasaura*, can tell palaeontologists a lot about what dinosaurs ate.

hatched, the young would have fed on this material. Dung beetles do the same today on the plains of Africa, where they play a vital role in recycling the tons of waste dropped every year. The Montana coprolites prove that early dung beetles carried out the same essential task for the dinosaur herds.

Findings like this are part of a trend among paleontologists to study the areas around fossil finds. Once they would have simply pulled the bones out and walked away, but now people wonder how the bones ended up where they were and what other discoveries can be made in the vicinity.

Dung beetles are an essential part of the ecosystem on the plains of Africa, clearing the tons of dung dropped by large mammals. There is evidence that similar beetles first evolved during the age of the dinosaurs.

these huge creatures prevents the growth of all but a few mature forests and encourages the spread of faster-growing low plants. The cycad grove has been lucky to survive this long. In some areas too much grazing has had a disastrous effect, especially around the salt lakes to the east of the forest. Intensive feeding and dry weather have loosened the topsoil, creating drifting sand dunes. It is almost impossible for plants to colonize these areas since the sauropods have turned them into deserts.

However, the effect of the herds is not all bad. Besides destroying vegetation they also fertilize the plains, dumping tons of dung on the ground in the course of a year. This is an important source of nutrients not only for the plants, but also for the insects. One type of beetle lives on sauropod dung.

It takes the herd only three days to complete the destruction of the cycad grove. Eventually, the old female takes the lead and they start to move on. While she makes her slow but steady progress, two males and a young female follow immediately behind. The old female's tail constantly explores this small group at her rear and they, meanwhile, jostle for prime position. Although this might look like a close bond, it is highly unlikely that there is any genetic link between the old female and the smaller Diplodocus. Rather, the whole herd is a marriage of convenience. The young join the herd when they are about five or six years old and too large to stay in the forest. They benefit from the protection of the larger individuals and, since they are smaller, rarely compete for food with the adults. The adults' acceptance of these unrelated youngsters appears at first glance to be an extraordinary act of altruism, but it is not. The plains are full of predators, and when they attack Diplodocus herds, they usually pick on the smaller, more vulnerable members.

Shaping the landscape: huge sauropods, such as this Diplodocus, require so much food that there are no large trees across vast areas of the Jurassic plains, since the browsing herds prevent them from reaching old age.

81

Growing Pains

YEAR THREE—IN THE FOREST

Deep in the forest a giant redwood has come down, dragging several smaller trees with it. Its trunk now lies across a large clearing on the side of a hill and sunlight pours through the opening in the canopy above. Low ferns have covered the floor of the clearing and the air is thick with insects. Among the fronds, a group of 20 or so juvenile Diplodocus are feeding. Since they settled in the deep forest as sauropodlets, they have started to associate in small groups. Again, this is for defense, providing more eyes and ears for spotting predators, but these crèches are dynamic arrangements. Sometimes, when there is a lot of food, crèches will join together, forming huge grazing groups that can quickly clear all the vegetation between the trees. However,

Heads down: a juvenile Diplodocus strips the leaves off newly sprouted horsetail ferns. Meadows of these plants grow around the rivers in the forest and are a favorite feeding ground for the young herbivores.

when targeted by predators, which they often are, so many are killed that a crèche can dwindle to almost nothing.

There is roughly an even mix of males and females, but the latter are already slightly larger and one female is noticeably darker in color than the others. In her three years of life she has increased her length tenfold and now weighs a little under 3 tons. She is large for her age, a sign that she has done well in the forest. Her body shape has changed with the increase in size. Her neck and tail are much longer and her legs are comparatively thinner. The small horny plates that will eventually cover her back are beginning to appear and a line of small spines has developed down her back.

Her method of feeding has also changed. Instead of nibbling selectively at new growth, she now feeds in bulk, like an adult Diplodocus. Her neck has grown enormously and she has developed peg-like teeth. Most of the time she uses these to strip low fronds. Occasionally, she will rock back on her hind legs, plant the base of her tail on the ground, lift her head 20 feet into the air, and graze on leaves. She tends to avoid conifers, either because of the taste or because her teeth cannot cope easily with the woody branches. Most mature conifers lose their lower branches naturally and escape dinosaur grazing. On the other hand, sapling maidenhair trees offer more attractive foliage and, despite their high toxin content, they are a favorite with the young sauropods. Increasingly, the dark female and her crèche mates stick to more open areas. Their bulk prevents them from exploiting areas of new growth where the trees are too close together. They are developing some of the range of noises of the adult herd, but they do not yet have the bodies for the rumbling and tail cracking.

The crèche's feeding fills the clearing with dust and spores while they slowly and methodically strip the entire area of fern fronds. Flitting from one sunlit back to another are several Anurognathus, frantically harvesting the feast of forest insects thrown up by this activity. Some of them already have mouths crammed with food. These are young Anurognathus, some with wingspans of as little as one foot long, and they have been living with the crèche for only a few weeks. However, every day their numbers increase. Like the sauropodlets, they hatch on the forest fringes. Then some will then fly to the plains and look for host herds, and others will spend their first few weeks searching the clearings on the edge of the forest for crèches. There are almost always too many pterosaurs for the number of juvenile Diplodocus and competition between these little creatures is fierce. Once established with a suitable host, the Anurognathus will transfer with the crèche to the open plains. However, the relationship is never close. Anurognathus are always willing to abandon one back for another.

The dark female's feeding takes her right to the edge of the clearing where she disturbs an Ornitholestes. Much has changed since three years ago when this creature terrorized the sauropodlets. The herbivore is now huge compared to the slim little predator, and under normal circumstances the Ornitholestes would have avoided the clearing altogether. However, this is a female and she is guarding her buried nest since the movements of the crèche could accidentally crush her brood. She snaps at the Diplodocus and puffs up her long scales. What she lacks in size she makes up for in aggression. The startled herbivore rocks back on to her hind

Changing roles: juvenile Diplodocus grow so fast that by the time they are three years old, once-formidable predators, such as Ornitholestes, are no longer a threat.

legs and pulls her head away from the confrontation. From her considerable height, she watches the antics of the little animal below. The Ornitholestes is lucky because while as the Diplodocus rears up, the crèche starts to move out of the clearing. When the predator backs off a little, the dark female returns onto all fours, and turns to follow the others away from the Ornitholestes' nest.

The group of young sauropods follow the path of a small stream, plucking at vegetation while they go. The stream leads steeply down to a shallow valley under the trees and joins a larger river. While they crop the horsetails, the crèche continues to move down the bank. Only a mile or two further down, the river leads out of the forest onto the plains, where it starts to meander, creating wide open marshy areas. Here, rising out of a dense stand of horsetail is the

distinctive bulk of a Stegosaurus. His 40-foot-long, 7-ton, dark brown body and the light-colored plates running down his back label him as an animal from the plains. He has wandered up the river valley in search of lush vegetation.

His scent signals to the crèche that he is a herbivore and therefore not likely to be a threat. However, they will not know from experience that a Stegosaurus can be very aggressive in defense and will frequently damage quite innocent animals if he feels stressed. A careful look at a Stegosaurus reveals why other animals learn to give him a wide berth. His neck is heavily armored and down his back runs a series of huge plates, but the real cause for concern is at the end of his tail, four spines each a yard long. The tail itself is fairly short and muscular, and the Stegosaurus can use these spines very effectively.

Strong features: Stegosaurus, like this magnificent bull, have very thick skin. To protect their necks they have rows of pebble-like bones held in an impregnable sheet.

Although his limbs are not designed for speed, they do allow him to turn his vast body rapidly, presenting his lethal spines to anything that surprises him.

When the crèche filters out onto the marshy flood-plain, the Stegosaurus pays little attention. He is busy working his way through a tough bennettite stem, and in any case, he is used to feeding in the company of sauropods. However, his sensitive nose soon picks up a smell that sets off alarm bells in his brain. Since the crèche started to move down the river valley, they have unwittingly attracted the attention of a predator. A subadult bull Allosaurus has been stalking the Diplodocus for the past hour. He is 30 feet long and could easily

HOW THE STEGOSAURUS GOT HIS PLATES

IN 1877 CHARLES Marsh described a very bizarre dinosaur dug up in Colorado. It was a large, four-legged herbivore with a small head, a line of plates running down its back, and four long spikes on its tail. He called it *Stegosaurus*.

Stegosaurus was the largest of a group of armored herbivores that spread all the way from the United States to China during the Jurassic. They all had spiny tails, but none seem to have had plates as large as Marsh's creature. From the beginning it was clear that the tail was a powerful weapon of defense, but the plates were more of a puzzle. At first it was assumed that they were

armor, but they were in a strange position, too high on the back to be effective. Close examination also revealed that they were made of thin honey-combed bone full of blood vessels, the last type of structure grown as a means of defense. Another theory arose, suggesting that they helped control body temperature. On cold mornings the *Stegosaurus* could face the sun and warm its plates quickly. The blood running through them would then help raise its temperature. During the hotter part of the day, a breeze through the plates would cool the dinosaur, performing a similar function to an elephant's ears today.

Defensive armor, heat exchanger, or display board? All have been suggested as an explanation for the stegosaurs' plates. Although they might have performed all three roles, it is now thought that they were for display.

Recently, scientist Ken Carpenter has suggested another role for the plates – display. With such a rich blood supply, they could have been flushed at will. Therefore during sexual display, they could have been used to advertise. They might also have been important in defense, but not as armor. When a predator approached, the *Stegosaurus* could flush its plates, and accentuate its size. If this made the predator stop and think, the spiked tail would quickly make up its mind.

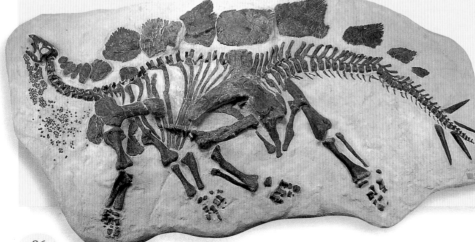

A flattened *Stegosaurus* from the Morrison Formation. This display clearly shows the animal's distinctive throat armor, back plates, and tail spikes.

kill a juvenile, but he has been wary of attacking the whole crèche in case they panic. If that happened in the closed environment of the forest, he could be injured or crushed. However, in this open marshy area he has grown bolder and is gradually moving nearer.

Allosaurus are the most successful carnivore on the plains, a constant menace to the Diplodocus herds, whether in groups or singly. In this time of titans, they are also the largest predators ever to evolve. Allosaurus are ambush hunters. They prefer not having to chase food down, even though they have a terrifying turn of speed. They use their three-clawed hands like grappling hooks to hold on to prey, while their powerful jaws and serrated teeth deliver the killer blows. With strong prey like Diplodocus, they will frequently attack, tear their prey with their teeth, and then back off, waiting for the victim to show signs of weakening. If several Allosaurus adopt this tactic with a single animal, the creature can die quickly of shock and blood loss.

Unfortunately for this Allosaurus, once the Stegosaurus picks up his scent he loses the element of surprise. The large herbivore embarks on a pre-programmed set of defense maneuveres. First he bellows, pounds his front feet, and swings his tail vigorously. Then he scans for the attacker. His sense of smell is better than his eyesight, and this movement will continue for some time until the predator makes himself more obvious. However, this time he spots the Allosaurus in the open, behind the crèche. Immediately his plates flush a deep red-brown and he turns giving the Allosaurus the full benefit of his display.

The Stegosaurus' general attitude of alarm disturbs the crèche and they start to move around and swing their tails. The predator

Stalemate: a bull Allosaurus faces a 7-ton Stegosaurus. When confronted with a predator, the Stegosaurus goes through an aggressive pattern of defense, bellowing, flushing his plates, and swiping his lethal tail from side to side. Despite his hunger, the Allosaurus is unlikely to attack.

knows from experience that it would be dangerous to attempt an attack with a belligerent Stegosaurus nearby. He avoids the marshy area and heads down the river.

The Stegosaurus' aggressive state lasts for some time, but slowly, as the scent of Allosaurus clears from his nose, his plates return to their normal color. The Diplodocus are quicker to calm down, especially once the Stegosaurus' alarm calls cease. On the plains these two species frequently graze together, not only because they crop the vegetation in different ways, but also because their senses complement one another, allowing them both to pick up predators quicker than either would do alone.

With the disturbance over, the crèche continues feeding in the marshy area. Although they might return to the clearings occasionally, from now on they will tend toward areas like this, and inevitably that will lead them onto the plains.

A New Home

YEAR FOUR–THE FOREST EDGE

The crèche is smaller now. Several attacks by lone predators have reduced their number by a third. They are mostly feeding on the forest edge, and this exposes them to attack by larger predators without giving them the advantages of being part of an adult herd. There has been a particularly long, dry period and the plains' vegetation is suffering from drought. Therefore, the members of the crèche have remained in the open to seek out the adult herds.

A lightning storm to the south starts a fire in the Cordilleran Highlands. Fires are not uncommon in this area, but it quickly becomes apparent that this is going to be a big one. In tinder-dry conditions, warm southerly winds fan and drive the fire north. A firestorm starts among the conifers, and within a few hours, floating pieces of burning vegetation spawn a thousand more fires. Soon a 60-mile stretch of forest is an inferno, completely incinerating the understory. Huge columns of fire leap up through the canopy.

Thousands of sensitive dinosaur noses pick up the scent of smoke long before the fire reaches them, but many will perish either because they flee in the wrong direction or because they are not fast enough to outrun the advancing flames. Few sauropodlets will survive, and those that do will be easy pickings for the predators. A fire like this comes along only once in every few hundred years, but when it does, it can wipe out whole generations of animals.

When the conflagration reaches the edge of the forest, it starts smaller wild fires among the open scrub, but the drought has left the vegetation here sparse and these blazes quickly burn themselves out. The crèche pick up the smell of smoke early and are finally driven out of the forest and onto the plains. They are followed by a pair of huge Brachiosaurus. Even by Jurassic standards, these are gigantic dinosaurs, dwarfing the Diplodocus. They are only about 70 feet long, but they are enormously heavy, weighing over 70 tons, more than twice as much as other sauropods. Their upright stance and elevated necks mean that they can graze at heights of almost 43 feet. They have evolved as specialist tree feeders and their strategy is different to that of the Diplodocus. They do not strip leaves and rarely touch low-lying vegetation. Instead, they have sharp, chisel-like teeth for nipping off cones, fruit, and new growth from a height no other sauropod can reach. They feed along the forest edges, seeking out the trees in fruit and cropping all but the tallest branches. Although they can cause considerable damage because of their sheer bulk, they only push trees over if they have grown too tall. This makes sense because they are adapted to cope with food at tree height.

While the two Brachiosaurus pull away from the burning forest, the members of the crèche amble aside to let them through. With a very stately walk, the pair head for a small knot of araucaria 8 miles from the main forest. There are other ways in which these animals are different from Diplodocus. They are mostly solitary, occasionally forming small groups, but not for protection since their sheer size leaves them with little to worry about, even from the largest predator. Despite this bulk, they make little noise. Without other herd members to "talk" to, they call only to attract a mate.

'Brachiosaurus have sharp, chisel-like teeth for nipping off cones, fruit, and new growth from a height no other sauropod can reach.'

OVERLEAF Titanic harvesters: this pair of Brachiosaurus are searching the top branches of araucaria trees for their nutritious cones. Although some of the trees can grow too high even for these giants, the dinosaurs can always flatten them, like they have done with the tree on the left-hand side of the picture.

With their long strides, the pair quickly remove themselves from the burning forest, their ponderous footsteps shaking the ground as they move. The crèche heads off in the same direction, but they are more confused and panicked by the fire. They wander much further than the Brachiosaurus, eventually stopping at nightfall by a shallow river to drink. Along the distant horizon a line of orange flames marks the destruction of their previous habitat. The forest will recover and, despite the enormous heat, many of the largest trees will survive, but there will be little for the Diplodocus to feed on for another

GIANTS AMONG DINOSAURS

SAUROPODS WERE TRULY enormous even by dinosaur standards. Most other large herbivores, such as *Triceratops* and *Iguanodon*, might have weighed as much as two or three elephants, but a single *Brachiosaurus* would tip the balance against 15 or 20 elephants. Their long neck and tail design was supremely successful. Sauropods evolved some time in the early Jurassic, dominated the late Jurassic, and continued until the end of the dinosaurs as a group known as titanosaurids. Even paleontologists cannot be sure how large they grew. There is a history of tantalizing pieces of skeleton and single bones that suggest gigantic creatures still only dimly described. These finds jostle to become the biggest dinosaurs ever and have been given evocative names, such as *Ultrasaurus* and *Seismosaurus*. However, since sauropods probably grew throughout their lives, it is possible that one or two of these may simply be older versions of well-known species.

The complete skeleton of Diplodocus shows it to be about 80 feet (25 meters) long, but two bones, a shoulder-blade and neck vertebra, from a similar animal called *Supersaurus*, suggest a creature more than 120 feet (36 meters) long. In South America a collection of huge back bones suggests that the titanosaurids were not small. They were wider bodied than their ancestors, so *Argentinosaurus* might have been only slightly shorter than a large *Diplodocus*, but could have weighed a staggering 100 tons.

This still does not claim the prize of largest dinosaur ever found. That belongs to a very mysterious find indeed. In 1878 Edward Cope described a 5-foot (1.5-meter) portion of a vertebra from the Jurassic sediments at Green Park in Colorado. The complete bone could have been about 8 feet 6 inches (2.6 meters) high. Unfortunately, it is not possible to check because it has been lost. Cope named the find *Amphicoelias fragillimus,* and modern scientists have attempted to calculate its size. It is possible that it was almost 200 feet (60 meters) long, stood 30 feet (9 meters) at the hip and weighed almost 150 tons. This is certainly longer than, and almost as heavy as, a blue whale.

With all these finds, the most obvious question that emerges is "why?" For marine creatures, such as whales, weight is less important than it is for land animals, and as long as the waters are rich in krill, there is no problem with size. However, sauropods had to have legs and a skeleton strong enough to support tons of flesh, and they also had to feed on land off fairly poor-quality plant food.

Perhaps no one will ever know enough to solve this mystery entirely. Certainly, there are many advantages to being big since giants are

Diplodocus had a small skull for its size, and weak jaws, given the amount of food it must have had to eat. However, its peg-like teeth were very efficient at stripping the leaves off plants.

The giant *Brachiosaurus* skeleton on display in the Humboldt Museum in Berlin could have belonged to a dinosaur that weighed almost 70 tons. It is believed that sauropods could have grown much larger even than this.

year or two. Their best chance of survival now lies in finding an adult herd to join on the plains.

By first light the fire has moved to the north and a dark pall of smoke hangs over the smouldering forest. The crèche has remained by the river and with the morning sun start to feed on some new growth of horsetails. The smell of burning hangs in the air and mixed with it is the faint scent of scorched carcasses. All through the night this has attracted many predators looking to scavenge an easy meal.

very difficult to attack, and a giant herbivore could have a long gut enabling it to digest any food it wanted. Most experts agree that sauropods fermented their food since they had no chewing teeth to break it down. Estimates about the size of their stomachs vary, but it is possible that the larger animals could hold half a ton of vegetation in their stomachs. All this was ground down and mixed up with the help of stomach stones. Evidence for this has come from collections of highly polished stones that have been found with sauropod fossils. Sauropods may also have grown so large simply because they were the first land animals to be able to. With the efficient upright stance of the dinosaur adapted with four column-like legs, huge weights could be supported.

However, none of these points really answers the question "why?" because they all apply to animals that are already big. Sauropods originally must have been smaller, and gradually evolved longer necks, longer tails, and bulkier bodies. Something along the way must have rewarded each step up in size. This is probably a function of how they interacted with the environment around them, and here lies the real key to their size.

Polished pebbles found among the bones of fossilized sauropods suggest that they used stones in their stomachs to help digest tough vegetation, just as some birds do today.

The Jurassic plains were not dominated by one plant like grass. There was probably a great mixture of vegetation. To exploit a variety of different tough plants at different heights, the best design might have been a large feeding platform that did not have to waste too much energy moving around to find suitable food. A longer neck would have made a wide area of grazing available to a static animal. Sauropods probably worked their way methodically across miles and miles of vast country, their shape being ideal for coping with unpredictable and very poor-quality vegetation.

On the other side of the narrow river a lone Allosaurus watches the crèche. He is a huge beast, at 40 feet and 3 tons, about as large as a member of his species gets. He is the king of the plains. The bony red crests on his head flash when he turns to focus one eye on his prey. Despite their numbers, the crèche is very vulnerable. In the open this Allosaurus could catch and drag down any one of them, and they are not fast enough to flee from him. He flexes his talons and watches them. The Diplodocus become increasingly nervous and move upstream. A pair of smaller Allosaurus appear in front of the crèche and move toward them. The juveniles bunch together and head across the river toward a stand of maidenhair. When they reach the other side, the large Allosaurus darts forward and launches himself at the leading member of the group. The pterosaurs on her back flee in all directions. Despite the blow, she manages to stay on her feet, but the Allosaurus sinks his teeth into the flesh over her rump. The shock of the bite makes her legs buckle and she collapses in a cloud of dust, with the predator riding her back as she falls. He then shifts his bite to her neck. She tugs and pulls to get free, dragging the Allosaurus along the riverbank, but his bite is well aimed and he succeeds in severing her spinal cord. Her fight is lost.

The predator stands back as his prey's body spasms. For all his power and ferocity, he is wary. Allosaurus are built for speed and agility. Their bones are light compared to the massive weight-bearing limbs of the sauropod. A stray kick from even a dying Diplodocus could cause serious injury.

By now the other Allosaurus have attacked one of the juveniles at the rear of the group, in the river. The Diplodocus lets out a series of honking alarm calls and succeeds in flattening one of his assailants with his tail. However, the second predator leaps on to his flank and tears at his flesh. Yet another Allosaurus appears and bounds across the river, attacking from the other side. Soon the Diplodocus drops to his knees amid a spray of water and blood.

The surviving members of the crèche are now in full flight, leaving several of their number dead or dying by the river. Behind them a disorganized flock of Anurognathus try to cope with their loss. Diplodocus are not capable of running quickly since their column-like legs are designed to support tons of flesh. The best they can manage is a steady amble that gradually takes them away from the killings. Fortunately, the Allosaurus are engrossed in the several tons of flesh lying by the river, and do not pursue them. The smell of the kill and the sound of Diplodocus alarm calls draw even more predators to the area, but they too head for the carnage by the river. This allows the panic-stricken young sauropods to make their escape. Soon the river is teeming with predators of all sizes and ages. There is some fighting over the bodies, but the size of the largest Allosaurus ensures that they eat their fill first.

The dark female is lucky. She has survived the attack. However while the remaining members of the crèche flee across the plain, she soon finds herself alone. Nearby there is a small group of female Stegosaurus, therefore she heads for them, perhaps remembering how effective these armored herbivores were against the Allosaurus. A short distance from them, she stops and begins to look for food. This is difficult because the Stegosaurus are feeding in a small field of scrub juniper, not a preferred item on the Diplodocus menu. Her head swings from side to side, cropping the odd fern as she searches for softer vegetation. For the first time in her life she is alone, without the reassurance of other members of her species.

The dark female shadows the Stegosaurus for several days, with both species ignoring each other. Eventually, through her feet, she picks up low-frequency vibrations. She watches as the dust dances over the leaves on which she is feeding. Then she rocks back on her hind legs and scans the horizon. About a mile

Easy kill: young Diplodocus are defenseless against fully grown Allosaurus unless they are protected by a herd. Here a female Allosaurus brings down a yearling Diplodocus on the edge of the forest. She will consume most of the carcass herself, and has little desire to share her kill with her rival.

away to the north she spots a herd of adult Diplodocus. The sight of their large bodies, coupled with the vibrations she has instinctively recognized, attracts the young female to the herd. She leaves the Stegosaurus and heads across the plains. When she approaches, a range of other noises reach her and she acknowledges them with a series of low hoots. Gradually, her calling becomes more insistent, as if demanding some sort of response. The herd seems to have a high proportion of smaller animals, and it has been known for adults to reject new juveniles if there are already too many in the herd.

However, after a few minutes of nervous calling, a large bull moves out and round the other adults, lifting his tail and swishing it vigorously. The female responds to the obvious display of a large adult rump and falls in behind him. After four years' fending for herself, she has been accepted as a member of an adult herd and her chances of survival have increased enormously.

High plains drifter: a Stegosaurus grazing on the dry highlands of equatorial Laurasia. Recent rains have created a flush of new growth on the conifer scrubland around him and lured many large herbivores up from the plains.

FOOTPRINTS IN THE SAND

AS SPECULATION ABOUT dinosaur behavior increases, paleontologists have turned to trace fossils for clues. Trace fossils are objects created by living animals such as nests, burrows, dung, and teeth marks, which by extraordinary luck have been cast in rock to be studied millions of years later.

Perhaps the most significant traces left by dinosaurs are their footprints. Surprisingly, dinosaur tracks have been found all over the world, sometimes in huge quantities, and these can provide an enormous amount of information. In fact, footprints proved beyond doubt that dinosaurs had an upright gait and did not sprawl. Single tracks can reveal stride length, size, speed, and stance. Groups of tracks can suggest herd structures, migrational movement, different species that might have grouped together, and even growth rates. Sauropod footprints from two sites suggest a group of 20 or more creatures, either with the large animals traveling on the outside of the herd or with the smaller individuals following the big ones. Small sauropod tracks are rare and never found with the larger tracks. However, in the Jindong Formation in South Korea footprints made by a group of dog-sized sauropods have been described.

Rarely tracks appear to have captured specific moments. In 1940 at the Paluxy River in Texas Roland T. Bird described a set of tracks which, he suggested, were evidence of a large predator attacking a sauropod. At the time, few people believed him, but now scientists have revisited his work and confirmed his findings. Along the riverbed a set of predator prints fall into step with those of a large herbivore. The pair even lurch to one side together. Then the carnivore hops twice on its right foot and the sauropod stumbles and drags its foot. This appears to have been the moment when the predator struck its prey and, if so, its method of attack was similar to the tactics of modern mammals. Unfortunately, then the Paluxy River tracks end, and we will never know the outcome. Despite all this information, it remains almost impossible to identify the exact species that made the footprints.

Low sun picks out a series of fossilized sauropod tracks revealed by the erosion of the river in Colorado. In this light it looks as if the herd passed by only yesterday.

The tracks of a giant predator found in Utah. Prints left by carnivorous dinosaurs showed that they placed one foot in front of the other, confirming their upright stance.

The Next Generation

YEAR TWELVE – ON THE PLAINS

It has been raining all night, creating a beautiful dawn. Layers of mist hang above the wide plains and wash up along the sides of the highlands. Above this sea of white the dark green forest is found by the morning sunlight. When the sun rises, the mist burns off and some of the prominent features of the plains appear like a copse of maidenhair, a cycad grove, and the rounded backs of a Diplodocus herd. When the sun hits their huge sides, they glisten with condensation. Rows of Anurognathus line up on the sunny flanks to warm themselves after a cold night and chase the first insects of the day.

Most of the herd are feeding. The plains' vegetation is rich and green after an unseasonably high rainfall. A large, dark female lifts her head out of the mist to look around. There are two Anurognathus mating right behind her nostrils and they must be clawing a particularly sensitive spot because she shakes her head in irritation, sending up a spray of water. She is now 12 years old and almost an adult. Although her growth rate has eased in the last few years, she has still doubled in size since joining the herd and no longer follows under the tail of a larger guardian. She is now about the size of the biggest males. Along her back she has a fine row of horny spines, and she hosts a large flock of Anurognathus, which have left her covered in droppings. About 90 feet away her tail gently caresses two other members of the herd.

While the last of the mist lifts from the plains, the herd stops feeding and moves toward a wide, shallow river to drink and graze on water plants. A small group of Coelurus scatter when they arrive. The Diplodocus swing their long

Male pride: three bull Diplodocus compete for the attentions of the female on the far right. They will stomp, flash their tails, bellow, and even fight, but there is no guarantee that she will decide to mate with any of them.

A HOT-BLOODED DISPUTE

OTHER THAN THE ORIGIN OF birds (see page 188), no issue in paleontology has been so hotly contested as the question of whether dinosaurs were warm- or cold-blooded. This is partly because the conclusion affects our basic perception of these animals, but it is also because the subject is so complicated. Dinosaurs are extinct and we have virtually no direct evidence about how their bodies worked, so the arguments revolve around inferences. Furthermore, the two conditions are not simple and clear-cut. Some cold-blooded lizards maintain higher body temperatures than warm-blooded mammals. We know that dinosaurs evolved from creatures that could not generate their own heat, similar to crocodiles, and that they left behind birds, which keep high body temperatures.

The theory used to run along these lines: all modern reptiles are cold-blooded, dinosaurs were reptiles, therefore dinosaurs must have been cold-blooded. However, in the 1970s scientists such as Bob Bakker pointed out the absurdity of this position.

The graceful, upright skeletons of dinosaurs were built for speed and agility, closer in design to birds than to crocodiles. There were many other arguments in favor of warm-bloodedness, including dinosaurs' rapid rate of growth and the structure of communities, in which the ratios of herbivores to carnivores were similar to those found in modern mammal populations. Other paleontologists countered that if the largest sauropods were warm-blooded, they simply would not have been able to lose all the heat their bodies produced; that their brains were consistently small, like those of reptiles; and that there was no evidence that they had the insulation needed to conserve heat. It seemed that the metabolic requirements of a giant sauropod were so completely at odds with the needs of a small

At one time cold-blooded crocodiles were thought to be the best model for dinosaurian metabolisms. However, it is now believed that dinosaurs had a variety of different ways for maintaining body temperature and that the small carnivores were much closer to warm-blooded birds.

carnivore that both sides were wrong.

Three decades of studying bone growth rings, nasal cavities, oxygen isotopes, and many other indirect lines of inquiry have produced a sort of consensus, even if there are still many dissenting voices at either extreme. The current view is that dinosaurs were probably neither warm- nor cold-blooded. They were a mixed group that showed a range of metabolic solutions to maintaining their body temperature. They probably had four-chambered hearts to ensure efficient distribution of blood, and very active metabolisms, which crocodiles do not. They also probably used their bulk to help keep warm.

There remains a big question surrounding the small carnivores. At their size, which most experts agree was probably about that of a turkey, a warm-blooded creature with no insulation would die of hypothermia during a cold night. Although a few rare fossils from China have shown small dinosaurs with some sort of pelt, the majority provide no evidence either way. Since we will never study live dinosaurs, it is unlikely we will ever know.

necks over the water, and the Anurognathus line up along the necks ready for a glut of freshwater insects. Besides the tiny pterosaur, many predatory insects also use the Diplodocus' back for a hunting platform. Damselflies and dragon-flies rest on the herbivores' flanks, providing dots of iridescent color on a huge slab of dappled brown flesh. One Anurognathus spots a predatory lacewing set-tling near a spine. Slowly the pterosaur crawls toward the large insect, fixing it with his beady red eyes. When he is about one foot away, he flicks out his wings and jumps at his victim. The lacewing immediately extends its own wings, revealing a pair of bright red eye dots. The pterosaur stalls, momentarily con-fused by the display, and before he can resume his attack, the lacewing drops off the Diplodocus' back, escaping into the horsetails. Insects are evolving ways of combating predation by pterosaurs.

Tension has been building in the herd for some days now and the general level of tail swishing is increasing. A clue to this behavior lies in the abundance of vegetation that has become available because of the recent rains. The herd has fed exceptionally well and their vast crops are full of fermenting food. Although other seasonal stimuli are also involved, this is the single most important factor in inciting the Diplodocus to mate.

'The bulls attempt to attract the females with frantic tail displays and by rearing up on their hind legs and stamping down with their front feet.'

To the casual observer the first indication that mating has started is the break-up of the tight herd structure. The females stay in a group, while the bulls separate and take up individual positions away from the herd. This will be the first year the dark female has mated since she has only just grown large enough to take the weight of an adult bull on her back. For the smaller members of the herd, mating can be a dangerous time. When the herd breaks up, the juveniles are left vulnerable and on their own.

Once clear of the herd, the bulls attempt to attract the females with frantic tail displays and by rearing up on their hind legs and stamping down with their front feet. The vibration from this stamping can be felt many miles away and frequently attracts the lone bull Diplodocus who wander between herds. If the

OPPOSITE Framed by the new sun: an adult Diplodocus warms himself in the first light of day. Only mature bulls travel alone outside the herd, but they have little to fear since they are too large even for an Allosaurus.

bulls get too close to each other and do not have enough room to display, fights can break out. A fight between two 15-ton bulls is an awesome sight, usually involving a trial of strength. After much tail thrashing and snorting, the two combatants stand next to one another, each leaning all his weight against his rival. In this sort of challenge, size is everything, and a small bull pushing above his weight could be badly injured, with broken ribs or even shattered limbs. If the bulls are evenly matched, they might start exchanging blows with their necks. Again, this is dangerous for such large animals, but the reproductive rewards are worth it. Though the bulls rarely outnumber the females, many of the females will not mate every year. Female Diplodocus can store semen for over a year, therefore they can fertilize and lay their eggs even in the absence of males. Given the perilous life the bulls lead, having to fight for a mate and being smaller and more vulnerable to attack, this is a very useful adaptation. However, in evolutionary terms, unless a bull manages to reproduce, all his years of survival will have been for nothing. As a result, the rivalry between bulls is intense during the short period of mating.

During the long, still afternoon, nine bulls whip their tails and stomp their feet in display until the air hangs heavy with dust. Distressed Anurognathus flit back and forth from one host to another. The tail display can be an important measure of age and fitness in a male. Most Diplodocus, if they live long enough, develop stiffness in their whip tails. Some even suffer painful arthritic conditions. Consequently the younger males try to compensate for smaller size with more vigorous displays.

Night falls and the females still have not moved from the edge of the river. Through the warm Jurassic night, the bulls display sporadically, even though it is unlikely that the females will mate in the dark. At dawn the largest female starts to move toward the tired bulls, and others follow her. Only about half the females appear to be interested in mating, yet it is probable that, given their ability to store semen, all the mature ones will lay this year.

With the movement of the female group, the bulls start their frantic displays again. The dark female singles out a male her same size. When she walks up beside him, he stops stomping and waving his tail. She passes down the

length of his body, rubbing her tail over his head, neck, and back. He uses his tail in the same way and they walk past each other like this several times. Then the female signals her receptivity by lowering her head and neck close to the ground. The bull moves behind her and rears up on his hind legs, using the base of his tail for support. He then puts his front legs on either side of her spine, digging his long front claws into the horny plates on her back to steady himself. Male sauropods have evolved a long penis with plenty of muscular sup-

THE MIGHTY MORRISON

THIS CHAPTER IS based on finds in the Morrison Formation, a vast and highly productive fossil bed that covers 600,000 square miles (1.5 million square kilometers) of the western United States. It runs from New Mexico in the south up to Canada, from Idaho in the west across to Nebraska. The first bones from the formation were discovered in 1877, and ever since, it has been producing literally tons of material. *Diplodocus, Apatosaurus* (*Brontosaurus*), *Brachiosaurus, Stegosaurus,* and *Allosaurus* have all been found in the Morrison, along with numerous crocodiles, mammals, lizards, and fish. This has allowed us a very detailed vision of the late Jurassic in

North America. The fossil bed is so rich that the first two palaeontologists who studied it, arch rivals Edward Cope and Charles Marsh, competed to extract the most fossils. Later, the American Museum of Natural History and then the Carnegie Museum used the Morrison as the basis of their collections. By the early twentieth century, America's dinosaur exhibits were the best in the world.

The Morrison itself dates from the late Jurassic, between 155 and 148 million years ago, and represents the low plains left by the retreat of an ancient waterway called the Sundance Sea. In its northern reaches, where Montana is now, the climate must have been wet and swampy because there are coal

deposits. Toward modern Colorado there were flood plains with vast, meandering rivers and seasonal lakes. This is where the richest finds have been because periodic wet seasons must have flooded the low-lying landscape and dumped animal bones in large numbers. This is beautifully illustrated at Dinosaur National Monument, where 1,500 bones remain in their substrate, forming a wall of giant bones for visitors to view. To the west, in Utah and Arizona, there was higher ground, covered in redwood forest. Finally, down south in Arizona, the Morrison turned much drier, suggesting that a desert formed its southern borders.

Many of the dinosaur bones in the Morrison are well preserved because they were deposited by one of the many rivers that crossed the ancient landscape.

The formation, a huge treasure trove of Jurassic remains, stretches from Canada almost down to the Mexican border. Since 1877 it has produced literally tons of fossils.

port to help them curve it under the female's body and make contact with her cloaca. Eventually, the pair mate, a process that is usually over in a few minutes. She returns to the river and he continues to display. Sometimes a female will visit many bulls and each male will try to mate several times.

Over the next two months the herd stays on the move, feeding constantly. Gradually they drift closer to the highlands, where the forest is beginning to recover from the devastating fire that ripped through it eight years ago. When the herd graze closer to the forest edge, the dark female leaves and heads for the trees. She is carrying nearly 100 large round eggs inside her and, acting on instinct, she pushes through the low trees on the fringes of the forest where even now she can pick up the smell of burning, the smell that drove her away all those years ago. Deep inside some of the large redwoods, slow fires still burn years after the event, eating out the center of the tree while it grows. The Diplodocus continues, searching for a clearing and crushing saplings as she goes. Soon she finds an opening where there are few ferns and a dense layer of conifer leaves covers the ground. For a while, she tests it with her feet and then she tastes the litter with her tongue. Perhaps she has distant memories of the earth into which she hatched and is trying to find a similar mix of silt and humus in which to lay her eggs. Once she is satisfied that she has found the right spot, she starts to excavate a huge, circular trench a yard deep, using her long front claws to tear up vast quantities of litter and soft sand. When she has finished, she turns around, lowers her rump over the hole, and starts to lay her eggs. She holds her neck high and steady, as if in a trance, but as each large white sphere rolls into the trench she shifts a little to make sure the next is laid beside and not on top of its brood mate.

After she has completed this task, she gently refills the trench, pressing on the earth with the delicacy of an animal a fraction of her weight. Finally, she steps out of the clearing and returns to the herd, leaving her future sauropodlets to their fate. If she lives to a ripe old age, she could repeat this activity as many as 50 times, laying over 5,000 eggs. What she cannot know is that her mother laid a similar number and she is almost the only one of them who has survived to produce her own eggs.

A Cruel Sea

3

T

HE EARTH 149 MILLION YEARS AGO. While titanic movements in the Earth's crust break up the old continent of Pangaea, the Jurassic coastlines are being shaped by a steady rise in sea levels. Thousands of square miles of low-lying land have been flooded, creating huge shallow, or epicontinental, seas and these sunlit waters have supported a revolution in marine life.

Coral reefs pepper the sea floor and above them armies of spiral-shelled ammonites feed in water thick with plankton. Squid and sharks thrive as they have done for millions of years, but their prey has become faster. The bony fish have become swift swimmers and have escaped the predators long enough to create a blizzard of silvery new species.

With such a profusion of potential prey, many land animals have adapted to live in the water. After taking over on land and in the air, the reptiles have completed their domination of the

Sunlit waters: a 26-foot-long Ophthalmosaurus glides through a swarm of jellyfish in a shallow Jurassic sea. These bright waters are rich in life, supporting everything from meadows of sea lilies to giant predatory marine reptiles.

Mesozoic world by becoming top predators in the oceans, too. These marine killers are not related to dinosaurs, but they are still giants. Although they all breathe air, they have developed into a variety of forms. Sleek, fish-shaped ichthyosaurs chase squid through the depths, marine crocodiles crunch armored ammonites, and long-necked plesiosaurs ambush fish shoals out of the gloom. The largest of all the marine predators are the pliosaurs, animals such as Liopleurodon, which, at almost 80 feet long, is the biggest carnivore that has, or ever will, exist. Its mouth alone is nine and a half feet long and is designed simply to tear its prey apart. These denizens of the deep are every bit as terrifying as the dinosaurs.

Although corals and sponges evolved in the pre-Cambrian era, they were badly affected by the Permian extinction. Those that recovered in the Mesozoic were different from their ancient ancestors.

AN AGE OF SUNLIT WATERS

ALL OVER THE JURASSIC world the sea was more significant than it is today. Despite the break up of Pangaea, the Panthalassa Ocean still occupied the other half of the planet. Sea levels have fluctuated, but at times were at least 330 feet (100 meters) higher than they are now, and vast areas of low-lying land had become submerged beneath warm, sunlit waters. These areas were called epicontinental seas and at times drowned a quarter of the land surface. In places where the currents were weak the water stagnated. However, in many places these shallow waters teemed with life.

Corals, which had been recovering as a group since the Triassic, formed extensive reefs. Most corals need light to grow and are killed by sediment. However, with less land to dump material along its coastlines and large areas of shallow water to grow in, coral spread across the epicontinental seas. Reefs made of sponges and bacteria bloomed down to depths of 300 feet (90 meters). Sea lilies, sea fans, sea pens, and sea mats are just some of the creatures that colonized any vacant hard surface in these rich waters. In areas of soft sediment bivalves burrowed, and clams and oysters formed massive beds. New predators evolved to take advantage of this novel type of prey. Snails drilled into their shells, starfish pulled them apart, and lobsters developed claws to snip them open.

In the water above, the fish were going through what has been called the Mesozoic Marine Revolution. This involved the spread of a swift new group of fish called the teleosts. In the early Jurassic most fish were either sharks or primitive bony fish with heavy scales, related to modern creatures such as the sturgeon or gar. The most important adaptation shown by the teleosts was a jointed jaw that could be pushed out like a tube and snapped back again, a feature seen in goldfish. This one development opened up a whole new range of feeding possibilities for the teleosts because it allowed them to suck prey into their mouths. It gave them an advantage over their competitors and, during

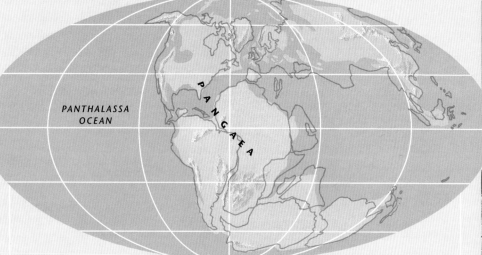

PANTHALASSA OCEAN

PANGAEA

With the break-up of Pangaea, the ancient coastlines began to change rapidly. This was due not only to the movement of land, but also to a rise in sea levels. Huge areas that we know as land today were flooded, especially in Europe and Asia. Siberia and China effectively became island continents, while Europe was a collection of small islands, some of them very low-lying. Warm currents ran around the Equator, but what remained of the vast landmass of Pangaea still diverted them toward the poles. Consequently, most water lay in tropical or sub-tropical zones, and there was no icecap at either pole to restrict the movements of marine or land animals. Through these extensive seas large fish and reptiles could roam freely around the globe.

the late Jurassic and early Cretaceous, they completely replaced most of the older bony fish species. Today most fish are teleosts, whether they are pikes, eels, herring, cod, tuna, or seahorses. The sharks, being larger and fiercer, were less threatened by the teleosts and, in parallel with this, evolved sleeker, more modern species to stay in touch with their faster prey.

A very important part of these marine ecosystems were the cephalopods, a group represented today by squid and octopus. In the Jurassic, ammonites and belemnites were the most common cephalopods. The ammonite's coiled shell protected its soft body and was used to control its buoyancy. Inside

Sturgeons are an ancient type of bony fish. Unlike most of these fish, they lack the specialized sucking mouth that has helped teleost fish to dominate today's seas.

the final chamber of the shell sat the ammonite itself. Over millions of years, thousands of different species of ammonites came and went, ranging from tiny creatures less than ½ inch (1 centimeter) long to some the size of a quarter, but they were all extinct by the end of the Mesozoic, leaving behind a very distant cousin in the *Nautilus*. Belemnites disappeared at the same time. These creatures looked like modern-day squid, except that they had hooks on their tentacles instead of suckers, and inside their bodies they had delicate skeletons similar to those of cuttlefish.

Belemnites were built for speed and probably lived in shoals.

While reptiles had been the dominant life form on land since the Carboniferous period, comparatively they were newcomers in the Mesozoic seas. After first entering the ocean sometime in the Triassic, they had evolved by the late Jurassic into a range of predators. The dolphin-like ichthyosaurs, pursuit predators who preferred the open water, continued to flourish, but were not as diverse as they had been in the late Triassic. Sea-going crocodiles were also common.

Since slipping off the land, they had developed deep tails and paddle-like limbs, and hunted by ambush. However, the most successful marine reptiles of this time were the long-necked plesiosaurs and the short-necked pliosaurs. Both propelled themselves under water with four large flippers and grew to great sizes. The plesiosaurs specialized in catching fish and squid, using their long necks to pluck them out of shoals. The pliosaurs occupied the top predator position and the larger forms mostly hunted other marine reptiles. Their spectacularly large jaws and messy feeding habits have left their mark in the fossil record. Half-eaten ichthyosaurs and teeth marks in plesiosaur flippers are evidence of their voracious appetites.

Araucaria trees were common during this period. Very few species of these conifers survive today, and one, the column pine, grows wild only around New Caledonia.

Feather stars like these are typical filter-feeding echinoderms. They belong to a group of animals that has thrived on the sea floor since the Cambrian era.

Some crustacea, such as the crayfish, had been around since before the time of the dinosaurs, but during the Jurassic true crabs and lobsters made their first appearance. Both predatory groups developed powerful claws for snipping open the tough shells of their molluscan prey.

The Gathering Begins

At the southern end of the long seaway that connects the Tethys and Boreal oceans lies a wide expanse of shallow epicontinental sea dotted with thousands of islands. From a pterosaur's view, each lonely spot of green land is framed by pale coral reefs and divided by deeper tracks of blue. Occasionally, rivers spill off the larger islands, pushing wide silt fans into the azure waters. Millions of years ago this whole area used to be dry plains with the occasional upland. While the sea rose, the uplands became large islands cut off from the continents to the east and west, and when these flooded, they formed groups of tiny islands. To the south a continental shelf falls off into the deeper waters of the Tethys, and here lies one such group of islands, the Vindelicischs. In some parts of the epicontinental sea there are so few currents that the waters are almost stagnant, but around the Vindelicischs the upwelling of cooler, oxygen-rich water from the ocean makes conditions perfect for marine life.

On the coast of one of the smaller, nameless islands a sleek brown plesiosaur suns herself on a warm coral shelf. She is a Cryptoclidus, about 22 feet long, and her four elegant flippers lie spread out on the rocks. At the end of a long neck her small head protrudes over the glittering waves that rise and fall against the coral beneath. She is asleep. It is early in the day and the temperatures have not reached a level that would cause her to overheat. She has probably been here all night, safe on an island where there are no predators large enough to threaten her. Another Cryptoclidus is basking on the shelf about 50 yards away, but the two show no interest in each other. Cryptoclidus are lone marine hunters living off a diet of fish and squid, and although a dozen or so are around the island, they interact only during the mating season.

While the sun begins to strike the coral directly, the female Cryptoclidus wakes and, with a couple of cumbersome movements, launches herself off the shelf into the cool sea. Once in her element, she glides effortlessly. Like all plesiosaurs, she propels herself with four large flippers that move like underwater wings to help her fly through the water. While she pushes down with the front

MONSTERS FROM THE DEEP

THE SHALLOW EPICONTINENTAL seas have often proved ideal for preserving the skeletons of marine creatures. Where the bottom was covered in thick mud, any animals that died above floated down, became buried in the sediment, and stood a good chance of "surviving" as a fossil. In the late Jurassic a large island stretched from London across the English Channel and into Belgium. Just off its coast the waters were rich in life and the sea floor was made up of deep mud. This now forms the Oxford Clay (see page 131), which stretches like a sash across the center of England. All the animals in this chapter have been found fossilized in this formation and many have also been found elsewhere in the world.

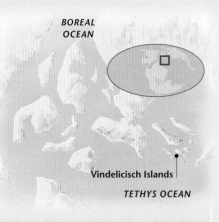

BOREAL OCEAN

Vindelicisch Islands

TETHYS OCEAN

The Vindelicischs were a group of islands on the edges of the Tethys Ocean. To the east lay Siberia, to the west the opening Atlantic. The current ran predominantly north from the warm Tethys to the colder Boreal Ocean.

OPHTHALMOSAURUS

A very common ichthyosaur in the late Jurassic. It had the largest eyes of any vertebrate, which helped it hunt for squid at night or at great depth. Its snout was long and thin, perfect for snapping after fast, maneuverable prey.

EVIDENCE Several beautifully preserved skeletons, ranging in age from juveniles to adults. Remains have been found in Europe and Argentina.
SIZE Around 16 feet (5 meters) long, with a skull 3 feet (1 meter) long.
DIET Fish and squid.
AGE 165–150 million years ago.

CRYPTOCLIDUS

Medium-sized plesiosaur with a slightly flattened skull and upward-facing eyes. Its long, slender teeth may have been used for piercing squid, but could also have helped sift burrowing animals out of the mud.
EVIDENCE Several complete skeletons, including juveniles. Most have been found in England and northern France, but there are also reports of finds in Russia and South America.
SIZE Maximum length of 26 feet (8 meters) with a 2-foot (60-centimeter) skull. Possibly weighed as much as 8 tons.
DIET Fish and squid.
AGE 165–150 million years ago.

LIOPLEURODON

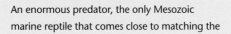

An enormous predator, the only Mesozoic marine reptile that comes close to matching the size of the largest modern whales. The teeth in the distinctive rosette at the front of its snout were twice as long as those of *Tyrannosaurus*.
EVIDENCE Complete skeletons and several fragments, found mostly in England and France, but also possibly in Chile.
SIZE Adult length of about 80 feet (25 meters) with a skull an incredible 16 feet (5 meters) long. *Liopleurodon's* weight is difficult to estimate, but it may have been 150 tons.
DIET Anything else in the ocean.
AGE 165–150 million years ago.

EUSTREPTOSPONDYLUS

Not much is known about this European carnivore. Given the maritime environment in which it was found, it could have been a beachcomber, as well as an active carnivore.
EVIDENCE Based on a single skeleton found in the Oxford Clay, north of Oxford. This was probably a carcass that had drifted out to sea.
SIZE Around 16 feet (5 meters) long and weighed about half a ton.
DIET Carnivore and scavenger.
AGE 165–160 million years ago.

RHAMPHORHYNCHUS

A common marine pterosaur of the late Jurassic. The shape and orientation of its teeth suggest it could have fished by flying low over water and scooping out prey.
EVIDENCE Range of skeletons from the Oxford Clay and Solnhofen in Germany; also Tanzania.
SIZE Wingspan of almost 6 feet (2 meters); skull of 8 inches (20 centimeters). Including tail, total body length was about 3 feet (1 meter).
DIET Fish.
AGE 170–145 million years ago.

pair, the back ones are raised by the water, and then when she pushes the back pair down the front ones rise. Gently repeating this cycle, she moves above the coral meadows in search of prey. Each flipper has powerful muscle attachments and is capable of working together or independently. This means that the Cryptoclidus can use just one flipper to make herself turn very fast, or all four together if she wants a burst of speed.

About a mile from the island she encounters a massive Perisphinctes methodically working his way over a coral meadow. Perisphinctes are ammonites, a common group of shelled marine mollusks, and this is one of the largest in the area, with a heavily–armored, coiled shell measuring about a yard across. He is a predator, and issuing from the end of his shell are several power-ful pink tentacles that regularly pluck small animals off the coral and pass them back to his crushing jaws. While the bright Jurassic sun filters down through the water, the ammonite picks out the magnificent red and white stripes that wrap around his shell. He has built this beautiful structure chamber by cham-ber as he has grown. Now his soft body occupies only the last, largest chamber of the whorl and the vacated sections are filled with air for buoyancy. Although out of the water he weighs around 220 pounds, here he hangs weightlessly above the coral. Under his tentacles lie a small siphon which he can point in any direction and through which he can jet water, enabling him to move around in search of prey.

A sweep of the Cryptoclidus' flipper sends the Perisphinctes tumbling away from the coral and she turns to inspect his defenses. He has withdrawn within his shell and pulled shut the hood that covers the end. The Cryptoclidus knows her teeth are not strong enough to break in, so after nudging him a couple of times, she moves on, searching for softer prey.

There is no shortage of food for either animal. Beneath the Perisphinctes is a bewildering array of marine life. The sea here is perhaps richer and more varied than it has ever been in Earth's history. Besides the tiny organisms that actually build the coral meadow, it supports other filter feeders, such as oysters, clams, and sea lilies. Sponges sprout from the coral, forming large, plate-like structures and tall, elegant baskets. Among these crawl shrimps, crabs, snails,

OPPOSITE Settled on the seabed: a curious young Cryptoclidus comes to inspect an empty ammonite shell. Cryptoclidus teeth are long and thin, best suited to catching slippery prey such as fish and squid. They rarely attack ammonites because their spiral shells are too thick.

and predatory worms. Above them swim numerous species of fish, rays, sharks, and squid. Although each of its inhabitants occupies only a tiny patch of coral, this reef stretches for hundreds of miles, forming a complete patchwork across the shallow sea. It varies in form depending on the depth of the water, from shallow meadows to deep sponge banks with massive flat reefs built by bacteria. The only areas without coral are those where the water drops below about 250 feet and the coral

LIVING FOSSILS

THE IDEA THAT dotted around our modern world there are a few animals that have managed to survive since prehistoric times and escape extinction is extremely attractive. However, this is an inaccurate concept, since no individual species lasts more than a few million years. It is the families or groups of animals that keep producing new species, each one varying only minutely from a basic plan and therefore giving the impression that they are ancient.

With the exception of jellyfish and corals, which are much older, most major groups of animals can trace their origins back to the Cambrian period 550 million years ago when, during the Cambrian explosion, hundreds of new animal designs evolved. Worms, sponges, crustaceans, mollusks, and, even our own group, the animals with backbones, called echinoderms, appeared then. However, humans could not be classed as living fossils and bear little resemblance to the tiny fish-like creatures that first developed

Ammonites died out at the same time as the dinosaurs. Today their nearest relatives are the rare *Nautilus*, found in the Pacific.

Once a year horseshoe crabs reproduce by gathering on beaches and laying their eggs in the sand. This group of animals is over 400 million years old.

a primitive neural chord. If we wind forward in time, creatures with a striking similarity to animals that are alive today start to be found in the fossil record. Horseshoe crabs appear 430 million years ago from the group that also gave rise to spiders. Lungfish first evolved 400 million years ago, sharks 300 million years ago, and sturgeons 200 million years ago. Evolution flows through time, creating and losing species.

Perhaps the only creatures that can genuinely be described as "living fossils" are

those left behind once a large and diverse group is driven to extinction. *Coelocanths*, discovered in the early twentieth century off the coast of Africa, are the only species alive today from a group of lobe-finned fish that were extremely common 300 million years ago. The ginkgo, or maidenhair tree, is the only representative left of a group of trees that used to forest the Mesozoic. After the ammonites were cleared out of the sea 65 million years ago, a related group of mollusks somehow survived, and descendants called *Nautilus* can still be found in the Pacific.

Hard evidence of the antiquity of creatures such as horseshoe crabs comes from fossils like this. It even shows the last tracks the creature made before dying.

stops because there is not enough light to support growth. It also does not survive near islands where the silt run-off from rivers can smother it.

Above the Perisphinctes other ammonites feed nearer the surface. Disappearing into the blue gloom, hundreds of their coiled shapes float suspended in the water, occasionally bobbing after prey with their tentacles. A shoal of squid slip among the ammonites. Although both these animals are mollusks and both use jets of water to propel themselves, their approach to life in these rich seas is completely different. Unlike the ammonites, the squid have no protective shells and are always on the move. Their soft bodies form the staple diet of many large predators and their speed is their only chance of escape.

Several yards below, the squid are being stalked by the Cryptoclidus. She is about to use the ambush technique for which she is designed, gliding across the coral to position herself directly below the shoal. Despite her size, the squid are oblivious to her presence. Her mottled brown back is a perfect camouflage against the coral meadow below. Also, of her 22-foot body, more than 6.5 are feet, and this is where it comes into its own. These plankton-rich waters enable her to approach her prey while her large body remains a crucial 6 feet out of sight. When she comes up under the squid shoal, she halts and prepares for attack. Her eyes are located on top of her head, which helps her keep her prey in view. Slowly she starts to rise, her back flippers positioning her while her front flippers lift in readiness for a powerful downward stroke. When she moves toward the squid, her back flippers also rise. This is her attack posture.

'When the Cryptoclidus comes up under the squid shoal, she halts and prepares for attack. Her eyes are located on top of her head, which helps her to keep her prey in view.'

Suddenly the shoal turn and start toward her. This is what the Cryptoclidus was waiting for. Squid move backward through the water and have a blind side behind and below. The Cryptoclidus is ideally positioned. She drives down both pairs of flippers and shoots forward. While she meets the oncoming shoal her head darts from side to side, snapping at the squid. At the same time the shoal scatter in all directions, filling the water with clouds of ink. The encounter lasts only a few moments, but as the Cryptoclidus bursts free of the inky curtains, she has three squid skewered on her long, pin-like teeth.

She rises to the surface and lifts her head out of the water to flick the squid into her mouth before taking a gasp of air. While she does, she watches a pterosaur glide close to the water. It is not unknown for Cryptoclidus to pluck pterosaurs from the air while they are fishing, but this time the flyer steers well clear of the predator and soon she slips back below the surface. Before positioning herself for a new ambush, she dives to the bottom and digs her mouth into a patch of soft sand and pebbles. Then, pulling it out again, she swims forward with sand streaming out between her teeth. Soon all she has in her mouth is a collection of stones, which she swallows. Though odd, this behavior is

Ambush predator: this Cryptoclidus, like most plesiosaurs, uses speed and surprise to catch her prey. Her head is on the end of a long neck, which means that her large body and flippers may not be visible to a fish when her comparatively small head is ready to strike.

essential if she is to continue hunting. Like all reptiles, she is an air breather and if she wants to dive deep she has to compensate for the buoyancy. The stones weigh her down and stop her having to struggle against her natural tendency to float. Once the stone ballast is on board, she returns to gliding across the coral in search of squid and fish.

While she scans the yards of water above her, she spots a new shape slipping through the rays of sunlight filtering down from the surface. It is another reptile, a little smaller than she is but far too large to be prey. When she turns to look, more of these creatures appear out of the depths. Soon the sea above is full of these reptiles, hundreds spreading across the shallow coral. The Cryptoclidus turns and gives up her hunt. She has encountered the annual arrival of the Ophthalmosaurus and knows it is pointless to linger.

Ophthalmosaurus are beautifully streamlined marine reptiles. The origin of their group, the ichthyosaurs, lies somewhere back in the early Triassic period, even before the dinosaurs evolved. While other reptilian predators chased prey with paddle-like limbs, the ichthyosaurs developed long, fish-like bodies, sleek fins, and powerful crescent tails. The easy side-to-side beat of these tails allowed them to cruise effortlessly through the Mesozoic seas, becoming top predators long before animals like Cryptoclidus appeared. Now, although their glory days are over and they face stiffer competition from other reptiles, they are still extraordinarily successful, which becomes obvious at this time of year.

Cutting through the blue waters, the Ophthalmosaurus race over the coral, exploring the reef while giving the retreating Cryptoclidus a wide berth. At regular intervals they steer up to the surface, take a breath, then return to the coral, streaming bubbles behind them. Ophthalmosaurus usually live in small pods of unrelated individuals, hunting fish and squid in the deep waters of the Tethys. Their distinctively large eyes are a special adaptation to help them spot prey at depth or at night. However, during early summer, females break away from their pods and migrate for hundreds of miles, gathering in the shallow waters around the Vindelicischs to give birth. Over the space of a few days the area around the island will see the arrival of well over 10,000 Ophthalmosaurus, each heavily pregnant with pups. It is another adaptation to marine life that ichthyosaurs do not lay eggs. Instead they give birth to live young at sea. The need to crawl out of the water every year and bury eggs, as turtles do, must have prevented the ichthyosaurs' ancestors from exploiting

the water fully. However, once they evolved live birth, they no longer needed their limbs, and were free to take on their present sleek, fish-like shapes.

Several weeks before converging on the Vindelicischs, the female Ophthalmosaurus conceive and hatch tiny eggs within their birth canals. Then, as the mothers-to-be continue to hunt and feed, their babies grow inside them, supplied with food and oxygen through the mothers' blood supply. Eventually,

the pups become too large to remain inside their mothers, and this stimulates the females to swim to shallow waters and give birth. Also, the pups are now large enough to survive on their own. Having given birth, the mothers abandon the young to fend for themselves, and that is why the pups gather above the coral. Although they are large, at a foot and a half long, the newborn pups are still vulnerable to a number of predators in open waters. They would also starve trying to chase fast, ocean-going squid and fish. However, among the coral and seaweed of the epicontinental sea, there are plenty of places to hide and no shortage of slow-moving food for them to eat.

Having arrived in the vicinity of the Vindelicischs, the Ophthalmosaurus will give birth as soon as possible. Despite the abundance of food, the adults find it hard to fish here. They are not adapted for the sundrenched waters. Their hunting technique relies on speed and endurance, best in open areas of deep water where there is plenty of room for pursuit. These shallow waters cramp their style. Packed into this comparatively small area, they also find it harder to escape large predators. While the sun drops toward the horizon, the still waters around the island are alive with countless Ophthalmosaurus. Their fins cut through the surface as they chase squid, occasion-

LEFT Mother's day: in mid-June female Ophthalmosaurus arrive from the Tethys to have their pups in the seas around the Vindelicischs. Each of these females is carrying several young and will give birth in the shallow waters so that their babies can seek protection among the coral. The mothers themselves will leave the area the moment the pups are born.

ally leaping out of the water in pursuit.

The island is typical of the Vindelicisch group. This whole area is regularly hit by violent winter storms that roll in from the east and, since most of the Vindelicischs are low-lying, they have become accustomed to being flooded. Having been isolated for millions of years, the islands have developed a unique range of plants and animals that can cope with periodic flooding. The most obvious greenery is provided by groves of column pine, but in between the thin trunks of the conifers most of the island is covered in dense thickets of stunted podocarp. These small trees are found nowhere else in the world and have specially–thickened trunks that resist the effects of flood. They grow extremely slowly and there are some that are only 6–9 feet high and are well over 200 years old. The insect population is also unusual, including a large predatory beetle that scavenges the mud-flats in search of stranded marine creatures. Unfortunately, because sea levels are rising steadily, in a few thousand years this island will probably disappear permanently beneath the waves, and with it, the unique ecosystem.

'In a few thousand years this island will probably disappear permanently beneath the waves, and with it will go its unique ecosystem.'

Many of the larger animals here are not so unusual. The island supports a large colony of Rhamphorhynchus, red-faced marine pterosaurs that are common along the Tethys coastline. The adults live entirely on fish from the sea, but the younger animals will also prey on insects on land. These smaller islands in the group are an ideal habitat for pterosaurs because they are usually safe from large predators. In the evening light hundreds of Rhamphorhynchus gather along the old coral ledges to roost in large bickering groups. They crawl all over the rocks looking for suitable sites and signaling aggressively to each other with their stiff little tails. At this time of year the females in the colony are getting ready to lay. They will soon start constructing small nests made of anything from leaf litter to seaweed. Although in most areas Rhamphorhynchus lay eggs all year, on this island there is a definite nesting season and this is connected to another unique feature of the island. Every year on one particular night, when the tides are high and the moon is full,

MESOZOIC MARINE MONSTERS

FOR MORE THAN a century paleontologists have been finding fossilized ichthyosaurs with tiny embryos preserved within them. Over the years almost a hundred have been identified, most from one site near Holzmaden in southern Germany. Here the Jurassic ichthyosaurs have been exquisitely preserved in what were deep silt layers at the bottom of the seabed. Most fossils contained between one and four embryos, and some as many as twelve. For a long time it was thought that these were examples of cannibalism because this was easier to accept than the thought that such early marine reptiles had evolved live birth. However, all the embryos were found inside the body cavity, not the stomach, and their skeletons were in perfect shape, rather than jumbled up as if half-digested. Scientists now agree that ichthyosaurs must have given birth to live young, and there are even fossils of embryos half out of their mother's birth canal. These are not examples of the

moment of birth being caught in stone, but rather the unfortunate consequences of a mother dying in the process of giving birth and the baby then being partially expelled after the build-up of gases during decay. From the Holzmaden finds we know that ichthyosaurs were born tail first, like modern whales, because they are air-breathing animals. If they were born mouth first, they would have drowned.

It is unlikely that these live births led to any close bond between mother and offspring. In fact, there is some evidence that ichthyosaurs were also cannibalistic. Because of the large number of mothers and embryos found at Holzmaden, it has even been suggested that this must have been some kind of birthing area, where generations of ichthyosaurs came to give birth, protecting

This beautiful German fossil shows an ichthyosaur apparently at the moment of birth. This is irrefutable proof that at least one Mesozoic reptile developed live birth.

themselves from predators through sheer force of numbers. At what point ichthyosaurs gave up laying eggs is not known, but it does explain how they managed to evolve such sleek, fish-like forms. Without the need to crawl back on to land to lay, they could afford to let their limbs and body become completely aquatic.

In other marine reptiles the question of live birth is less clear. No embryo has ever been found in the plesiosaur or pliosaur fossils, and their hefty skeletons might have been designed to help them drag themselves on land. However, all four of their limbs were dedicated paddles (turtles have retained stumpy hind limbs for digging holes to lay eggs) and no plesiosaur or pliosaur eggs have been discovered. Also, the truly gigantic pliosaurs, which could have weighed many tons, would have faced a major problem climbing out of the water and hauling themselves up a beach. Today no one knows how other marine reptiles reproduced, but we know that live birth is possible.

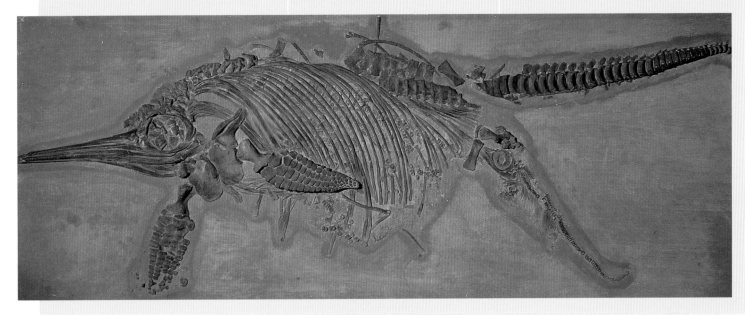

thousands of horseshoe crabs crawl up on to its beaches to mate and lay their eggs. For a few days the beaches themselves become an abundant source of protein, as millions of tiny, pearly green eggs develop just below the sand. This is an important source of food for the hatchling pterosaurs.

While the sun finally sets, the calm water becomes thick and dark. Along the beaches two large, clumsy shapes rise out of the shallows and draw themselves uncomfortably on to the sand. The Cryptoclidus are preparing to spend the night out of the water. With their huge flippers they have to strain and twist to drag themselves clear of the water. However, this effort is worth it for a safe night's sleep. Somewhere out in the dark waters are bigger predators, such as the fearsome Liopleurodon that can devour even a 22-foot-long Cryptoclidus.

OPPOSITE **Colonial life: several Rhamphorhynchus colonies are found around the edges of the island. These are colorful and noisy places, especially as the adults come and go on fishing trips.**

High and dry: a male Cryptoclidus hauls himself on to the beach for the night. Although his four flippers enable him to move swiftly and elegantly under water, on land they are cumbersome.

Danger from the Deep

It is a breathlessly hot day on the small island. There is no wind and the tall thin conifers at the far end of the island twist and contort in the heat haze. Most of the Rhamphorhynchus have taken cover under the podocarps, except for those tending the more exposed nests. A number of the inexperienced mothers have built badly, placing their piles of vegetation too near the water or in the open on dark rocks. With temperatures well into the 100s even in the shade, their tiny clutches of eggs are in danger of overheating. Without cloud cover, many of these mothers will be unable to stand the heat and will soon abandon their nests.

On the coral headland several pterosaurs suddenly whistle in alarm. About 100 yards out, bobbing through the water, the grotesque head of a Eustreptospondylus has appeared. This is the largest dinosaur predator on the Vindelicischs and he has developed the ability to swim in order to island-hop in search of food. Beneath the waves his back legs paddle quickly as his tail helps him stay upright and on course. Because of the dangers of marine predators he has no desire to be in the water longer than necessary, and the draw of the island is too much for him to resist. Except for other Eustreptospondylus, he will face little competition for all the small pterosaurs, lizards, and mammals that live on the Vindelicischs, and there is always a plentiful supply of marine creatures washed up on the shore. Despite his size, Eustreptospondylus is primarily a scavenger and will eat anything he finds on the beach, from jellyfish, sharks, and fish to the odd stranded marine reptile.

The Eustreptospondylus strikes for shore. This has been a long swim and his head is beginning to sink low in the waves. When he reaches a shallow, white-sand bay he draws himself out and pauses on the beach to recover. He is about 16 feet long and as he looks around the water streams off his gray, blotchy flanks. He stretches his arms,

THE LAND OF SEA DRAGONS

ALTHOUGH BRITAIN DOES not have the vast dinosaur beds of the US, in one respect it is rich in finds. Stretching from the Yorkshire coast near Whitby across central England and down to Dorset, together with patches in south Wales, are the exposed remains of Jurassic seabeds known as the Oxford Clay. The ichthyosaur and plesiosaur skeletons in this formation have been studied in Britain for over 300 years.

Most of the first attempts at reconstructing what life might have looked like "before the Flood" were dominated by vivid drawings of monstrous creatures, which were simply described as sea dragons.

The first illustration of a plesiosaur bone was made in 1604, and while the new study of natural sciences grew, collections of these fossils were made. In 1706 the Ashmolean Museum in Oxford even published a handbook for their identification. At the time most people believed in the biblical version of prehistory and thought the finds were fossilized fish bones. In 1719 the first complete ichthyosaur was found and identified as an extinct dolphin or crocodile killed in the Flood. It was not until the early nineteenth century that these creatures were acknowledged as fish-like reptiles.

In Lyme Regis in Dorset early Jurassic seabeds form soft cliffs and are constantly being exposed by the sea. Collecting in the 1820s was so popular that many locals made a living out of finding and selling fossils. One of them, Mary Anning, found her first fossil when she was 11 years old and went on to discover some of the finest marine reptile skeletons ever to be displayed. By the time dinosaur remains were correctly identified and science acknowledged their role in evolution, the general public was already familiar with "sea dragons" from prehistory. At the end of the nineteenth century brick pits were opened up around Peterborough, cutting into late Jurassic seabeds. Once again, marine reptiles tumbled out and more are found every year.

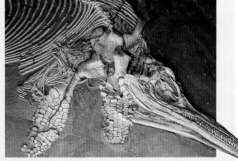

Fossil marine reptiles were so common in Britain that their existence was well known long before anyone had heard of their terrestrial cousins. The name "ichthyosaur" was coined 20 years before "dinosaur."

extending the long dark talons on the end and shaking vigorously. His tail flicks from side to side. It is badly deformed with a heavy callus bending it in the middle, probably a souvenir of an attack by a marine predator. In the hot sun he quickly dries and warms up. He barks as if to greet his new residence and starts to move around the bay toward the headland, scanning the beach litter for anything edible.

A decaying feast: a scavenging Eustreptospondylus cleans out the inside of a turtle shell. Even though the carcass was probably rotting by the time he picked up its scent, he will still eat every bit of it.

The whistling alarm calls spread through the Rhamphorhynchus colony. Several adults circle around the predator's head, flapping and screeching to distract him. He snaps occasionally, but he is not listening to them because he has caught the scent of food in the air and he is hungry. To a crescendo of whistling, he stalks past the headland that holds many pterosaur nests and steps gingerly down the rocks to a small cove on the other side. He is already drooling. There, in the middle of the beach, is the decaying body of a huge turtle. The Eustreptospondylus bends down and pushes his head into the half-empty shell. With a tug he draws out a large blob of meat and starts to feast.

No more than 200 yards from where the Eustreptospondylus is feeding, the last few mother Ophthalmosaurus are giving birth just below the surface of the water. One slows down and stops cruising over the reef. Her body convulses a couple of times as her abdomen prepares to push out the large occupant. Visible beneath the pale skin of her underbelly is the writhing form of the baby. The mother paddles slowly to the surface for air, then hangs motionless as her body readies itself for birth. She twitches and a small cloud of red drifts away from her cloaca. This is followed by the tiny limp tail of the baby. For a moment she remains like this, then convulses again and turns to dive down to the coral. When she does, she leaves behind a large plume of blood and a startled baby Ophthalmosaurus. Immediately, the little female heads for the surface to take her first breath of air. She is an only pup, but her mother will no longer play any part in protecting her. Instead the adults will soon join the long list of predators that would be quite happy to eat the young Ophthalmosaurus. Fortunately for this pup, her mother quickly leaves the birthing area and heads back out to the deep water to rejoin a pod.

After filling her lungs, the baby dives down to hide among the corals. She is only about a foot and a half long and can easily use the caves and weeds as cover. However, even when she is sheltered among the rocks, she is not entirely safe. The birth of so many ichthyosaurs has attracted the local population of hybodont sharks. These predators are now patrolling the coral in large numbers, their yellow-tipped fins visible on the surface as they circle the birthing

Hide and seek: baby Ophthalmosaurus are quick and highly maneuverable. With a beak full of sharp teeth, they hunt a range of small prey in the cracks and crevices of the corals.

Ophthalmosaurus. Although they would not touch a large mother, they frequently take the pups before they can even draw their first breath.

Nearby, in the slightly deeper water just beyond the reef shelf, another mother is giving birth, but it is not going well. Her body convulses repeatedly but there is no sign of the small tail. The baby is stuck further up the birth canal. The mother returns to the surface for air and her body is hit by another wave of muscular contractions. She is releasing blood now, but is still unable to give birth. She is clearly exhausted, and again she returns to the surface.

THE FOUR-FLIPPER PROBLEM

Like a terrifying echo from the past, this complete *Liopleurodon* skeleton clearly shows the distinctive features of the pliosaurs. Note the plates on the underside that help turn its body into a reinforced box.

ONE LOOK AT a plesiosaur skeleton shows that they must have had a unique method of swimming that has no modern equivalent. Although many marine creatures have flippers, none have two equally powerful pairs as these marine reptiles did.

Figuring out how these limbs work has tested scientists since the early part of the twentieth century. The first detailed study suggested that they rowed through the water, using their tapered flippers like oars. However, this would have made them poor swimmers who would have also found it difficult to dive. In the 1970s American palaeontologist Jane Robinson studied the muscle attachments of the flippers and concluded that they worked like underwater wings, powering the reptiles through the water the way the flippers of penguins and turtles do today. However, more recently it was realized that plesiosaurs could not raise their flippers as high as these creatures, and the sea lion was suggested as the nearest equivalent because it moves through the water in a sort of backward rowing way.

It was also noted that plesiosaurs had very strong muscles for pulling their flippers down, but relatively weak ones for the return stroke. This suggested that while one pair of limbs was pushed down, the second moved up passively, setting up an alternating stroke cycle between the two pairs. This cycle would have propelled the plesiosaurs at an even rate, but it would not allow for bursts of speed. However, the reptile might have used both flippers together if it was able to "porpoise," moving up through the water on the power stroke, gliding down on the passive return, and producing a characteristic undulating motion through the water.

Plesiosaur skeletons support this theory. The flippers were attached to a rigid body whose backbone was curved like an archer's bow and held in position by reinforced ribs. This would have allowed the body to absorb the stresses of a double stroke and might even have enabled plesiosaurs to use each flipper independently. If so, they could have cruised comfortably, turned quickly, and accelerated with ease. Considering how long they prospered in the oceans, the system must have been productive.

Watching her struggle from below is a fully grown male Liopleurodon, all four flippers raised in attack posture. He is 80 feet long and weighs almost 150 tons. Each flipper measures more than 10 feet and at the end of his huge mouth he carries a crown of dagger-like teeth for impaling prey. He could have been drawn to the birthing Ophthalmosaurus from as far as 150 yards away because he has a highly sophisticated method of smelling and tracing prey in the water.

He raises his massive head slowly and then drives his flippers down. When he lurches forward, ammonites are sent tumbling through the water and fish are dragged off the coral in his wake. His mouth opens and snaps firmly shut around the mid-portion of the struggling Ophthalmosaurus. The power of the attack carries both his head and his prey clean out of the water, where they hang for a moment before he brings both down with explosive force. Among all the spray and blood, his victim dies instantly, her body punctured by his long teeth and her back broken. He adjusts her limp corpse in his mouth, repeatedly biting and shaking it. Eventually it breaks into three pieces and, grasping the front portion, he rises to the surface, flicking it to the back of his gaping pink throat and swallowing. He returns and picks up the second portion repeating the process. Meanwhile, the Ophthalmosaurus' elegant crescent tail quickly sinks, passing the coral wall and dropping 100 yards to the bottom of the sea. The Liopleurodon turns to chase it, but then decides to let it go.

While he resumes his hunt, he slides through the water, moving his head from side to side to help him detect potential prey. His huge flippers displace so much water with each stroke that they only have to move slightly to propel him forward at cruising speed. Only when he is ambushing prey do these flippers beat together.

Like all Liopleurodon, this male is beautifully bi-colored, with black markings on top and white underneath. However, he is old and these patterns are no longer as visible as they once were. His flippers and head are covered in deep scars from frequent encounters with other Liopleurodon, the only marine creatures capable of inflicting such wounds. Also, he has collected the usual range of "squatters" during his decades at sea. Along his ridged back bry-

OVERLEAF Out of the deep blue: a giant male Liopleurodon launches an attack on an Ophthalmosaurus. The ichthyosaur is more than 10 feet long, yet it is dwarfed by the predator. Using his four massive flippers, the Liopleurodon can produce a terrifying turn of speed in pursuit of prey.

ozoans, anemones, seaweed, and even corals grow, and among them lampreys, leeches, and shrimps feed. His eyes are encrusted with lice, but this does not concern him. However, all Liopleurodon occasionally suffer from heavy infestations of worms in their nostrils and ears. These ailments can compromise their ability to hunt, and in the worst cases stop them catching anything, effectively starving them to death.

While the light from above gradually fades with the coming of night, the Liopleurodon continues to hunt. A hundred yards below, by the coral wall, the remnants of his last meal provide a bounty for numerous bottom-dwelling creatures. In particular, within an hour of the tail reaching the seabed, the first hagfish slithers out of the gloom. Eyeless and colorless, these scavengers have been trawling the deep sea for carrion since the very first fish evolved and they are still as successful as they were more than 200 million years earlier. As long as there are messy predators like Liopleurodon in the waters above, these scavengers will continue to thrive.

A Precarious Home
SEPTEMBER–A RACE FOR LIFE

At first light the female Cryptoclidus is woken by the scent of dinosaur. She has attracted the unwanted attention of the hungry Eustreptospondylus 100 yards down the beach. When she lifts her head, the predator runs forward. The Cryptoclidus is larger and bulkier than the dinosaur and he would probably not attack unless she were visibly weakened through injury or disease. However, she reacts with alarm and drags herself back into the water as quickly as her flippers can manage. The predator slows even before he reaches the place where she has been sleeping. Then he stalks forward and sniffs the depression she has left behind in the sand. Meanwhile, the Cryptoclidus is gliding through a shoal of ammonites far out to sea.

The waters around the Vindelicischs are now completely free of birthing Ophthalmosaurus. The mothers have returned to deeper water, but they have left the reefs full of their pups. With the danger from sharks, marine crocodiles, and the occasional Cryptoclidus, only a small proportion of these youngsters will live to enjoy the wide expanses of their parents' domain. However, they have adaptations to help them survive among the rocks. They are more mottled than their parents, which helps them hide against the coral, and, unlike adults, they have prominent teeth. Fully grown Ophthalmosaurus have long, thin, elegant snouts ideal for snapping at small, soft prey while swimming at speed. Teeth would add weight and offer more resistance. However, the reef presents the pups with much more varied food, which their short-toothed jaw is better able to deal with. Those pups who have survived the first hazardous weeks of life have done well on their seafood diet, doubling in size in a month.

Under a huge, spreading fan coral a male pup is tormenting a small ammonite. Somehow he has succeeded in cornering the shelled creature so that it cannot escape into the open water where the pup would not dare put up a sustained chase. However, the ammonite has drawn in the hood that covers the opening of its shell and presents the young Ophthalmosaurus with an impenetrable defense. He tries butting up against the rock and nibbling at the

Drawing up the defenses: an ammonite pulls its hood over the opening in its shell as a baby Ophthalmosaurus approaches. Behind the hood lie a pair of calcified plates that can be drawn together, providing an almost impenetrable barrier to attack.

Sheltering sky: while the baby Ophthalmosaurus grow, the caverns and tunnels of the coral are an ideal place for them to hide from predators' eyes. Within a few months, however, they are large enough to survive in the open water.

closed hood. Each time, the ammonite simply bounces around the coral and floats back upright. Eventually, the pup turns and darts up to the surface for a breath. On his return he finds the ammonite slowly squirting itself away from its coral prison. He snaps hold of one of its tentacles. The ammonite immediately retracts inside its shell and draws its hood back. The pup, however, does not let go and thrashes as the ammonite attempts to free its appendage. Finally, the ammonite jerks free and the pup returns to the coral with a small tentacle dangling from his mouth.

The Vindelicisch island chain is split in the middle by a long, deep water channel that runs up from the Tethys for about 400 miles. Here, within a few hundred yards, the depth drops from about 50 yards to almost a mile. Coral reefs decorate the rim of this channel, but at the bottom of the abyss there is nothing but a thick layer of mud full of creatures such as hagfish, which survive on the rain of dead animals from the sunlit waters above. This was the route favored by the Ophthalmosaurus as they arrived to give birth, and now it brings other ocean-going creatures high up into the shallow seas.

The channel runs close to the island, and on its eastern side large ocean breakers crash against the coral outcrops. Standing on these rocks, a Eustreptospondylus stalks among the spray looking for dead fish. He stops to sniff a smashed ammonite and foolishly turns his back on the ocean. Suddenly, a bow wave sweeps through the dark blue water toward the dinosaur. While it explodes, the mouth of a huge Liopleurodon erupts out of the water and clamps on to the Eustreptospondylus' tail. The dinosaur thrashes around, screaming in terror, but its fate is sealed. Effortlessly, the huge marine predator slides back into the water, dragging the luckless scavenger to his doom. Only a few minutes later the Liopleurodon resurfaces off shore and there is no sign of the dinosaur. His wide flippers hold him steady in the water as he scans the surface. Because of his bulk it is often difficult to appreciate him in his entirety under water. However, on the surface the true size and power of this predator become apparent. His black and white head is almost 13 feet long, with a mouth only 3 feet shorter. At the end of his snout his ring of crown tusks are so long that they overlap. These tusks mean that even if he does not grasp his prey cleanly, a glancing blow is enough to disembowel it. This fearsome structure is held up by a massive neck strong enough to wield the head like a precision weapon.

Terror from the deep: a moment of carelessness and a Eustreptospondylus is plucked screaming from the coral by a giant Liopleurodon.

OPPOSITE In the shadow of a killer: this male Liopleurodon is unrivaled in these Jurassic seas. At 80 feet long, he is the largest and most powerful of predators. The only threat he faces is a confrontation with another male of his kind.

After a moment the giant predator slips back under the water, moving slowly over the coral until he spots the bright red and white swirls of a Perisphinctes. He twists his head to one side and plucks the huge mollusk from the reef. Manipulating it to the back of his mouth, he suddenly tenses his jaw muscles, producing a cloud of shell fragments. He releases the Perisphinctes and inspects his work. With another snap of his jaws, the giant ammonite disappears into the Liopleurodon's throat and he heads off, leaving the shattered pieces of shell still settling on the coral below.

On the surface a pterosaur flock is oblivious to all this. They have been fishing and are returning to their roost on the island. Each pterosaur catches only one fish at a time. Despite a wingspan of almost 6.5 feet, their bodies are less than one foot long and can hold only a small amount of food. On the low-lying island the Rhamphorhynchus nests are empty. Within the last few days, all the eggs have hatched. Each tiny pterosaur has immediately started flapping its wings and attempted to fly. For a while the yolk left in their stomachs has nourished them, but now they need food and they are still not strong enough to fish for themselves. However, the sea is about to produce enough food for all of them, which is why they have all been born at precisely this time. Down on the beach, in the late evening light, two small, dome-shaped creatures, one riding on the other's back, shuffle out of the surf onto the land. They are the first of thousands of pairs of horseshoe crabs crawling toward the island, preparing to mate on its white sands.

The tide is now at its highest, and as the full moon rises, the two long beaches on the southern and eastern sides of the island fill with copulating crabs. The few Cryptoclidus waiting out the night on the sand find themselves surrounded by one of life's oldest spectacles. Horseshoe crabs are not true crabs. They are more like marine scorpions and are ancient creatures with ancestors going back 200 million years. They, or animals like them, have probably been visiting beaches near here since before this land was flooded. Once a year at the full moon they must have drawn up on to the waterline of long-forgotten coasts that existed before the giant continent Pangaea formed. They survived the great killing before the dinosaurs emerged and have been

unaffected by the age of the reptiles. The mating ritual continues, an unstoppable primeval urge driven by the waxing and waning of the moon.

The Cryptoclidus have no desire to eat these creatures, so they shift up the beach, their large flippers sending the crabs skittling in all directions. In the moonlight the smooth sand is covered with glinting domes stretching from one headland to another. On the waterline each female crab digs a hole and lays several hundred pearly eggs. The males fertilize these, release their partners, and return to the sea. Since more and more horseshoes arrive, the sand becomes too full with eggs and the females start to dig up each other's nests.

By morning, most of the horseshoe crabs have returned to the sea. One or two litter the beach, exhausted or stranded after their night's exercise. Some are upturned and hopelessly wave their ridged tails in the air. Dawn also brings out the baby Rhamphorhynchus, who swarm over the beach hunting for food. They feast on the exposed crab eggs that have formed a gelatinous line at the high-tide mark. There are also thousands more eggs right beneath the surface, and some pterosaurs scoop the sand in search of these.

All the activity on the beach draws the Eustreptospondylus out of the podocarps, where he has been hunting lizards. He ignores the horseshoe crabs, since they have little meat on them, and instead strides along the beach, snapping up the pterosaurs. Many are able to fly away, but a large proportion are still too immature and cannot crawl fast enough to escape. It is not long before the predator is swallowing whole mouthfuls of spindly little bodies. Before the sun has fully risen, he has gorged himself, and still the beach is crawling with young pterosaurs.

The crab eggs give the surviving Rhamphorhynchus just what they need, a boost of easy protein while they learn to fly and feed. While youngsters they will have a varied diet of insects and seafood. Not until they are fully grown will they become specialists at fishing. This avoids competition between adults and young on the small island, and prevents the adults preying on the young, which occurs in other reptilian species.

The Storms Arrive

Around the middle of October the young Ophthalmosaurus start to flee the reefs. These nurseries have now served their purpose. Many of the pups are three to four times the length they were when they were born. The hybodont sharks still patrol the coral, but the Ophthalmosaurus are now strong enough swimmers to escape them. They are leaving the shallow waters just in time because this is the beginning of the storm season. Although the passing of the Jurassic seasons is marked only by small variations in temperature, the center of the huge eastern landmass of Laurasia becomes colder. The Tethys Ocean next to it remains warm all year, while the winter takes hold in the east. The temperature difference between the two is enough to generate stupendous storms.

While a stream of Ophthalmosaurus pups head over the coral walls and down into the deep-water channel, the clouds start to pile up on the horizon. The thudding of distant thunder becomes audible and the tranquil sea turns a dull gray. This is the sort of storm that has shaped the Vindelicischs. Plants and animals that cannot survive this onslaught do not inhabit these islands. The Cryptoclidus head for deeper water and the Rhamphorhynchus settle on the trunks of the column pine and podocarps. The pterosaurs are particularly vulnerable to the high winds. Their light-framed bodies do not survive long aloft in 60-mile-an-hour storms and their only chance is to cling on to the trees.

The waves begin to ride higher up the beach, and white spume gathers over the shallower corals. Already the water has turned opaque with silt and the sand drawn up from the bottom. Even though it is mid-afternoon when the storm hits, the clouds have made it as dark as twilight. The rain swipes at the pterosaurs huddled on the tree trunks and the waves ride up between the podocarps, tearing the ferns and club moss

Nursery food: a young Rhamphorhynchus probes the column pine bark for insects. Juveniles tend to have a more varied diet than the adults.

145

and draping them over the lower branches. At the highest point on the island the Eustreptospondylus squats down close to the rocks as the howl of the winds rises. He has sat out storms like this before and, although this is a dangerously low-lying island on which to stay, he knows better than to take to the water in search of a larger refuge.

Out at sea the waves roll across the coral, plucking at the sea creatures. Most of those attached to rocks can resist the physical effects of the waves, but with all the sand that is being moved around, many will have been buried by the time the storm is over. Some of the larger ammonites, such as Perisphinctes, cling to the rocks, but the others ride the waves back and forth, jetting frantically to hold themselves in place.

It is a bad storm and it continues to pound the shallow sea for three days. By the time it finishes and the sun once again warms the land, the small island is a mess. Except for a patch about half a mile square in the middle, the sea has swept the entire understory away, piling it up in large rotting heaps. The lower parts of the trees are festooned with a mixture of fern, seaweed, and the occasional piece of coral. Along the top of the beaches dead pterosaurs lie crumpled up with smashed ammonites and stranded fish. The Eustreptospondylus shakes himself and basks in the tropical sun. Soon the gentle breeze, which is all that remains of the storm, draws a pungent smell from the beach to the south. The Eustreptospondylus picks his way across the battered island, lured by the promise of carrion. When he reaches the coast, he finds plenty of small animals lying up and down the beach, but there is another smell in the air. He heads once again for the cove where he found the rotting turtle, and while he crosses the headland, the source of the new odor becomes apparent.

Lying with his tail just in the water and his head and front flipper tangled among the podocarps is the male Liopleurodon. From his position about 150 yards away the Eustreptospondylus can hear his desperately labored breathing. Occasionally a deep bellow of pain rolls out of the giant's mouth as his lungs are crushed under the weight of his own body. He swings his head and tries to shift his flipper. Mature podocarps shatter like twigs, but the Liopleurodon is stuck. At some point during the storm he must have become confused and

OPPOSITE Underwater flight: a Cryptoclidus dives to the sea floor to pick up stones, which he uses for ballast. In the background a second glides to the surface for a breath of air. During the storm, both seek shelter in deeper waters.

OVERLEAF Flash point: Eustreptospondylus are solitary scavengers, surviving by swimming between small islands for food. However, the huge Liopleurodon corpse on the beach has drawn several of them to the same island and, despite the plentiful food, fights are frequent.

147

The end is nigh: a giant bull Liopleurodon lies stranded on the beach after the storm. Nothing will touch him while he still lives, but after his weight crushes his lungs, the Eustreptospondylus will tear him to pieces.

ended up stranded. Now he is too heavy to crawl back into the sea and he has a short time to live. Not only are his lungs collapsing under the pressure, but in the warmth of the sun his body temperature is soaring.

Another bellow tears from his lungs and he starts to bleed from the corner of his mouth. The Eustreptospondylus creeps forward slowly. He can smell that the huge creature is dying, but it is still capable of crushing him or tearing him in half should he be foolish enough to get too close to those mighty jaws. The dinosaur holds back, waiting for the giant to die, intoxicated by the stench of 150 tons of meat.

Despite the Liopleurodon's terrible condition, it is four more hours before his head crashes to the ground for the last time. As the patient Eustreptospondylus edges forward, he notices two scarred gray faces bobbing through the waves toward the cove, more of his own kind drawn by the scent of death. By now this huge carcass is probably attracting every Eustreptospondylus in the Vindelicischs. The two new arrivals draw themselves out of the water quickly. They are exhausted after the long swim and would not usually dare to challenge the incumbent scavenger, but with a mountain of flesh stretching across the whole beach the usual hierarchy before a carcass is irrelevant and the first dinosaur ignores the intruders. While he pulls at the head, the other two tear at the rear flippers.

Large, stranded reptiles are not unusual, especially after a big storm. However, to have such a giant creature on a small island is rare, and the delicate balance of its inhabitants may be affected for some time. Within days, there could be as many as 50 Eustreptospondylus crowded around the corpse. They will stay there, fighting, eating, and mating, for as long as the food lasts, which could be six months. Worse still, when the meat runs out, the Eustreptospondylus will probably strip the island of everything they can catch before another scent tempts them off.

By evening there are seven Eustreptospondylus standing or sitting around the corpse. They have gorged themselves and this has made them lethargic. On a nearby headland the female Cryptoclidus draws herself out of the water for the night. She raises her head and sniffs the breeze. Her island is cloaked in unfamiliar smells: decay rising from the corpse, the musty odor of the predators, and, most of all, the smell of blood. For a while, the lure of the Liopleurodon will keep her safe from attack, but sooner or later the scavengers will have to hunt again. Ironically, the Cryptoclidus' salvation is likely to be another storm. Such a large number of Eustreptospondylus would not be able to shelter here and would either be swept away or have to swim for safety elsewhere. With several months of winter to go, another storm is almost guaranteed. This will probably refloat the Liopleurodon carcass and return it to the sea, where animals such as the hagfish will be the eventual winners again. For now the Cryptoclidus must simply steer clear of the unwelcome visitors to her island and wait for the storm clouds to gather once more in the east.

Beneath a Giant's Wings

4

THE EARTH 127 MILLION YEARS AGO. The Cretaceous period has taken over from the Jurassic and the world's continents are on the move. From Laurasia right down through Gondwana a new ocean is opening up slowly, cleaving what will become South America from its giant partner, Africa. Sea levels are high and the once-great landmass of Pangaea is unrecognizable. The climate is becoming wetter and, along with the isolation of continents, a huge number of new plants and animals are appearing.

The most significant newcomer is not another type of dinosaur. Instead, for the first time on earth, flowers have started to bloom. For millions of years plants have defended themselves against grazing animals in as many ways as possible. Now flowering plants have adopted a new strategy. They grow fast, reproduce fast, and recover faster after being eaten. In essence, plants have found a new way to live with herbivores.

King of the sky: a giant Ornithocheirus soars effortlessly through the air, suspended by the warmth of a late evening thermal. Sometimes he can travel for over 30 miles with a single wingbeat.

At the same time, the destroyers of so much Jurassic flora, the massive sauropods, are in decline and their place has been taken by smaller herbivores. In particular, the ornithischian dinosaurs, that until now had been relatively unsuccessful, have come to dominate the plant-eating populations and move in vast herds across the lush Cretaceous landscape.

Other reptiles are changing too. The old, "long-tailed" pterosaurs have disappeared, replaced by flying leviathans, some of which have wingspans of up to 38 feet. These huge gliding monsters are the pinnacles of pterosaur evolution, and as a group they have never been so diverse. However, formerly the sole masters of the air, they now have to make room for competitors, birds, a new group of feathered dinosaurs, which is quickly proving itself to be more adaptable than the pterosaur group.

Although flowering plants evolved during the early Cretaceous, conifers continued to dominate the landscape for millions of years.

WORLDS APART

N THE EARLY Cretaceous period the movement of the continents radically remodeled life on Earth. Driven by movements deep in the Earth's mantle, a volcanic ridge that ran down between Europe and North America, South America and Africa, and around between Africa and Australia started to unzip the old landmasses. All this activity in the crust periodically pushed up sea levels and allowed the Tethys Ocean to flood land to both the east and west, finally isolating Laurasia to the north and Gondwana to the south. In all these new lands the animals and plants diversified and took on local characteristics. In particular, the north/south divide was strong. In Laurasia the

redwoods and cedars became more common and a new conifer group, the pines, thrived. To the south the ancient podocarps and araucaria continued to do well and excluded other types of conifer.

With the changing shape of the continents global weather also changed. The world became wetter. The moist polar climates spread and the ocean currents running through the Tethys brought a mosaic of wet microclimates to previously dry equatorial regions. This led to a decline in some plants, such as the cycads, but a boom in those that thrived in marshy, damp environments. In particular, the early Cretaceous saw the emergence for the first time of flowering

plants. The impact of this group on both plants and animals cannot be overestimated (see The Arrival of Flower Power, page 182). The advent of flowers is probably the single most important evolutionary event of the Mesozoic era. However, their initial appearance as small shrubs in the Laurasian marshes gave little indication of their later success. It was not until the late Cretaceous period that they began to dominate the planet's flora.

Insects were finding new and varied ways of preying on plants. Aphids and leaf miners appeared during the early Cretaceous. The evolution of flowers was paralleled by the success of one of today's largest groups of insects, the hymenopterans (bees and wasps).

Elsewhere, the feathered dinosaurs had evolved into birds and spread across the globe. They appear initially to have thrived around lakes, and probably did well in dense forests. The bird's wing, made up of separate feathers, was more resistant to damage by twigs and branches than the stretched skin of the pterosaur's wing.

Among the dinosaurs there was a radical change in dominant groups, especially in the

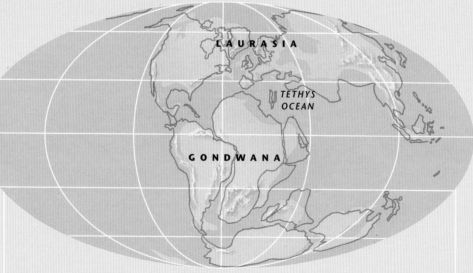

LAURASIA

TETHYS OCEAN

GONDWANA

The continents unravel: during the Cretaceous period the world's major landmasses continued to subdivide into smaller continents. This break–up was driven by movement deep within the Earth's mantle, which weakened the crust and created a volcanic ridge

that ran down between Europe and North America, Africa and South America, and around the southern-most tip of South Africa. Over millions of years this movement opened the Atlantic Ocean, isolated Antarctica, and drove India north on a collision course

with Asia. A rise in sea level split the North American continent in half and allowed the Tethys Ocean to separate the northern and southern continents. This division led to the evolution of subtly different flora and fauna in the two hemispheres.

Fossils from Brazil show that the pterosaur *Tapejara* had a sail-like head crest three to four times taller than its skull.

north. Stegosaurs declined, but their distant ornithischian cousins became incredibly successful and went on to dominate the Cretaceous herbivores. First there were the iguanodontids, such as *Iguanodon*, which gave rise to the duck-billed dinosaurs, then the armored dinosaurs, such as *Polacanthus*, and finally the horned dinosaurs which, although non-existent at the beginning of the Cretaceous, formed vast herds by the end of this era. Among the carnivores, the allosaurs started to die out, but were replaced by a variety of new designs. The dromaeosaurs, or raptors, were small, active hunters, while later the tyrannosaurids evolved as giant meat-eaters. The ostrich-like dinosaurs, or

ornithomimids, fast-running omnivores, also appeared at about this time. The only group who suffered from this fragmented world were the giant sauropods, who went into sharp decline, except in South America.

In the warm seas, the Jurassic plesiosaurs disappeared, and different species evolved. These new, four-flippered marine reptiles looked very similar to the old, except that some took the long necks to even greater extremes, with the elasmosaurs having as many as 70 vertebrae in their neck. In the sea specialized predators appeared to take advantage of the abundance of sedentary bivalves, the mollusks that took sanctuary between two hard shells. Crabs and lobsters

Hungry beauty: starfish are active predators that specialize in eating mollusks such as oysters. They pry open their victims' shells, slip their stomachs inside, and digest the creature where it lies.

had powerful claws to snip them open. Starfish used their arms to force the shells apart and inserted their stomachs to digest the inhabitant within. Finally, marine snails developed the ability to drill small holes through the shells and lick out the insides. It is not surprising that bivalves learned to burrow.

Above all this, the early Cretaceous was the heyday of the pterosaurs. The older, long-tailed species died out and many developed into huge gliders. Some of these had wingspans in excess of 33 feet (10 meters) and were specifically designed to gain lift from the smallest of air movements. What is most extraordinary about these gigantic pterosaurs is not how they flew but how they managed to stay on the ground, especially if it was windy. Their wings were feeding platforms which held aloft a small body and a large head. Palaeontological finds suggest that most of the pterosaurs, large and small, were marine species with a number of novel feeding techniques, including one that used combs on its beak to filter-feed, like modern day flamingos. However, this may just be bias in the fossil record because delicate fossils are almost always found around lakes and seas, rather than in uplands that were subject to erosion. Again, the lack of finds does not prove that a creature did not exist.

Wasps are part of a group of insects, Hymenoptera, whose development appears to have been closely related to the evolution of flowering plants.

Conifers dominated the age of the reptiles, but it was not until the Cretaceous that the pine family evolved. While many species died out with the success of flowering plants, pines continued to flourish.

A Long Journey Starts

THE TIP OF BORBOREMA

On the northern coast of Borborema a huge granite outcrop juts out into the deep blue of the ocean. Rain and thousands of years of pounding waves have carved this dark rock into a series of spectacular pinnacles. From a distance they are clearly visible, bristling at the end of a long headland, but close up they are even more impressive. Hundreds of small pinnacles are mounted on taller outcrops and these in turn build to the highest peaks, towering almost 200 feet into the air. Here and there among the rocks large blowholes periodically send spouts of water up among the pinnacles and the waves make

THE SECOND FLOWERING OF DINOSAURS

SINCE THE NINETEENTH century, most fossil finds have been made in North America and Europe, but new digs on other continents are now challenging this emphasis. Sauropods were once thought to have virtually disappeared by the early part of the Cretaceous period, but recent work has shown that they continued to thrive in South America. Research in China has demonstrated how successful the early birds were, and Africa may yet reveal large

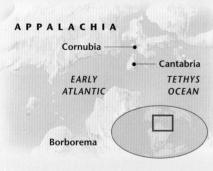

APPALACHIA

Cornubia

Cantabria

EARLY ATLANTIC

TETHYS OCEAN

Borborema

The Ornithocheirus migrated across the Atlantic to Appalachia, and then followed the coastline to reach Cornubia (now Cornwall) and Cantabria (now Iberia).

carnivores that could dwarf *Tyrannosaurus*. Evidence about the creatures in this chapter comes mainly from the Americas and Europe, but each represents a group which appeared and became successful in the early Cretaceous.

ORNITHOCHEIRUS

Very large marine pterosaurs probably able to migrate huge distances. Their long, keeled beak could pluck fish from the water during flight.

EVIDENCE Numerous fragmentary finds in Europe and South America, mostly the Santana Formation in Brazil. Different finds were initially identified as separate species, leading to some confusion about the naming of giant pterosaurs. Many names have been suggested, but *Ornithocheirus* (the name given to the earliest find) seems likely to prevail. The huge size attributed to the pterosaur is based on several wing-digit fragments found in the Santana Formation and Europe.

SIZE A maximum wingspan of 40 feet (12 meters), but a total body length of only

about 11 feet (3.5 meters). *Ornithocheirus'* weight is difficult to calculate, but he was almost certainly extremely light for his size, around 220 pounds (100 kilograms) is possible. His head was about 5 feet (1.5 meters) long and when standing on all fours he would have been about 10 feet (3 meters) tall.

DIET Mostly fish and squid.

TIME About 125–110 million years ago.

TAPEJARA

Medium-sized Cretaceous pterosaur with a huge display crest on its head. *Tapejara* lived on the edge of lakes and inland seas, and was probably a slow flier, not traveling large distances.

EVIDENCE Beautifully preserved skeletons in the Santana Formation in Brazil.

SIZE Wingspan of around 17 feet (5 meters), with a body around 3 feet (1 meter) long. Although the head was only 12 inches (30 centimeters) long, with the crest on top it was three times that length.

DIET Mostly fish.

TIME 120–110 million years ago.

a constant dull booming as they rush along the tunnels and caves that have been carved out beneath.

It is late afternoon and the warm winter sun throws an orange light across the water. A pterosaur appears, gliding effortlessly on the updraft from the waves, slipping from one swell to another with no perceptible movement of his wings. When he draws nearer, it is clear that he is an Ornithocheirus, light gray on top with a black, flecked pattern breaking up his outline. His long yellow beak has a wide, keel-like crest at the end. However, the most distinctive thing about Ornithocheirus is his size. He is the largest pterosaur in the world, measuring 38 feet from wing tip to wing tip, a true giant of the air.

IGUANODON

Herd-dwelling herbivore found on almost every continent, but the largest, distinguished by long thumb spikes, thrived in Europe. Walked on all fours, but could run on two legs if necessary.
EVIDENCE Numerous bone and footprint finds from Mongolia to the American Midwest. The best-known species, *Iguanodon bernissartensis*, was identified from several skeletons found in a coal mine near Bernissart in Belgium.
SIZE The largest species grew to over 30 feet (10 meters) long, standing 10 feet (almost 3 meters) at the hip and weighing about 7 tons.
DIET Ate most large plants, like cycads, conifers, or ferns, and could browse on vegetation up to 16 feet (5 meters) off the ground.
TIME 132–100 million years ago.

UTAHRAPTOR

Possibly the largest of the dromaeosaurs, a group of raptors distinguished by a vicious sickle claw on each foot. A very successful carnivore that probably hunted in packs.
EVIDENCE One find in Dalton Wells Quarry near Moab, Utah, but since America and Europe were close together during the Cretaceous, it seems likely that *Utahraptor* would have been found on both continents. New evidence from South America suggests the raptors might have grown even larger than was previously believed.
SIZE About 21 feet (6.5 meters) long, it stood 6 feet 6 inches (2 meters) tall. An adult would have weighed almost a ton, and the toe claw was about 12 inches (30 centimeters) long.
DIET Probably specialized in attacking large herbivores.
TIME 112–100 million years ago.

POLACANTHUS

A heavily armored herbivore with a thickened plate over its hips, spines running down the side of its body, and long spikes over its shoulders. Although probably solitary animals, they frequently grazed with *Iguanodon* herds.
EVIDENCE Three fragmentary skeletons and many armor plates have been found in southern England, particularly on the Isle of Wight.

SIZE About 13 feet (4 meters) in length and 3 feet (one meter) high at the hip, this relatively small herbivore could still weigh up to a ton.
DIET Probably not choosy, but perfers ground vegetation.
TIME 132–112 million years ago.

IBEROMESORNIS

A small bird that retained the dinosaur features of teeth in its beak and a claw on its wing. This feathered, strong flier may have lived in forests.
EVIDENCE A well-preserved skeleton found in lake deposits in Las Hoyas, Spain.
SIZE A wingspan of about 8 inches (20 centimetres) and weighing perhaps 1–2 ounces (a few tens of a gram), approximately the size of a goldfinch.
DIET Omnivorous, feeding on any high-energy food it was big enough to tackle. The fact that remains were found in lake deposits suggests that aquatic crustaceans may have formed part of its diet.
TIME 115 million years ago.

159

When he reaches the outcrop, the air currents rise and sweep over the rocks. Suddenly the pinnacles erupt into life. They are home to a colony of Tapejara, an ornate species of marine pterosaur. Although Tapejara are not small, they are dwarfed by the Ornithocheirus while he sails over them. He poses no threat, having a diet of nothing but fish, but Tapejara are excitable and his presence makes them nervous. Just behind the outcrop there is a wide open shelf area. Here the Ornithocheirus stalls his flight and hangs in the air

before dropping clumsily on to his feet. For a moment he is an ungainly heap of limbs and membranes, then he contracts his wings and flips his long wing fingers over his back to adopt a more comfortable sitting position. With his light blue eyes, he looks back at the chaos he has caused among the Tapejara and lets out a series of loud throaty clicks.

Ornithocheirus is a wanderer. His kind can be found in every corner of the globe from north-eastern Laurasia to south-western Gondwana. Some have even been spotted in the middle of the Panthalassa Ocean, although they prefer to stay near land in case they encounter storms. Like all giant pterosaurs, Ornithocheirus is a master of the air currents. Although he can flap, his whole body is designed to exploit contours of the air enabling him to stay aloft with little effort. Despite his size, he weighs under 220 pounds. Most of his bones are no more than paper-thin tubes designed for maximum strength and minimum weight. Some are even filled with air. His wing membranes cover an area of nearly 200 square feet and are filled with tiny muscle fibers that help him control their shape in flight. All this gives him an incredible lift. He does his best to avoid flapping at all and spends most of his life hunting for warm air rising off the land. Then, with the help of these "thermals," he can soar, circling slowly upward to heights of over four miles. At this altitude he can glide without using any energy for almost 50 miles in search of other thermals.

Below the resting Ornithocheirus, the Tapejara are calming down. This colony has about 1,000 members and it is mostly the males the giant pterosaur can see sitting on the pinnacles. Fully grown Tapejara have a wingspan of about 16 feet. They live mainly on fish and, although they often catch food at sea, they specialize in combing the nearby lagoons for washed-up carrion. What makes this

LEFT Unwelcome visitor: an old male Ornithocheirus glides over a Tapejara colony on the northern coast of Borborema. Although he means them no harm, his sheer size causes panic and a flurry of red display crests.

pterosaur unique is its spectacular head crest. In the male a hard sail of bone and keratin rises up almost a yard from the front of his beak, and in full mating colors it is flushed with black and red. The crest is so large that it has a profound effect on the way Tapejara behave. They are very slow fliers and when the wind starts to gust, the whole colony turn toward it to stop being caught in the crosswinds.

Although the immensity of these crests may seem like a handicap, when it comes to mating and display it is clear that size matters. This is the Tapejara's breeding season and each male is fighting to occupy the flat top of a pinnacle, where he shows off by waving and bucking his head. The taller the pinnacle, the more sought-after the site because the females fly over the outcrop looking for a mate, and the more obvious the male is, the better his chances. There is relentless competition between the males for these little theaters of display. The older and youngest Tapejara frequently have to make do with sites close to blowholes and near the waves. Not only are they nearly invisible to the females here, but also they may be swept away by a wave in mid-display.

The Borborema granite is an extraordinary sight as the females circle before sunset. The whole outcrop is a frenzy of exhibitionism. Each dark pinnacle is adorned with a black Tapejara flashing his brilliant crest and issuing piercing calls clearly audible above the booming of the waves beneath. The females are in no hurry to choose their prospective mates, who continue to display while keeping an eye out for competitors who may try to knock them off their chosen pinnacle. This spectacle continues for about an hour, until sunset draws a curtain on the proceedings. Tapejara are creatures of the day, and they do not function in a world without color. When darkness arrives, the females, who spend most of this time of year feeding, land further down the cliff, away from the display area. Meanwhile, the males sit tight on their hard-won pinnacles. Then the whole colony goes quiet.

Twelve hours later, when the sun rises once more, hundreds of green eyes open and spot the red crests of their competitors. The male Tapejara instantly start displaying again. It will be a while before the females take to the air, but the males react instinctively to the sight of the colors. One male starts bucking

his crest and those around him respond. Soon waves of red flashes are sweeping through the colony.

In the morning light, the male Ornithocheirus grooms himself, running his fearsome-looking teeth delicately through the light gray fur on his belly. He has been heading north along the coast of Gondwana for days and will use the granite outcrop as a thermal springboard while he continues toward the Tethys Ocean. His usually aimless wanderings are becoming directional as the mating season approaches. Ornithocheirus may roam the planet at will, but they mate only on the island of Cantabria, about 1,860 miles to the north of Borborema.

Face-off: two male Tapejara size each other up across the Borborema rock. Each male fights to occupy the top of one of the pinnacles on the outcrop. Although the confrontations are loud and aggressive, there is hardly ever any physical contact between the rivals.

GREAT GIANT GLIDERS

FLIGHT IS A HIGHLY specialized activity and those animals, such as frogs, snakes, and certain mammals, which take to the air only occasionally in order to move from tree to tree, tend to glide. Full-time fliers, such as birds, insects, and bats are more usually flapping fliers, capable of powered flight. It may seem strange that pterosaurs should first have evolved as small flapping fliers and, millions of years later, have developed into giant gliders. The explanation is that theirs was a sort of gliding that we can hardly imagine today. Giant pterosaurs could still fly anywhere they wanted. They simply abandoned the need to flap. The nearest modern equivalent is probably something like the stork, but this still does not come anywhere near what an animal such as *Ornithocheirus* achieved.

Gliding ability depends on a feature called wing-loading, the ratio of the wing area to the weight of the animal. *Ornithocheirus* had the wing area of a small airplane, yet because of its hollow bones and tiny trunk, it probably weighed less than a human. The best gliding aircraft design can travel forward 13 feet (4 meters) for every yard it falls. Giant pterosaurs probably did considerably better than that. Coupled with this ability to fall slowly, they would also have been able to capture any rising air and rise very fast. If you know what you are looking for, it is possible to find rising air all across the countryside. It

is either pushed up by a hill or cliff, or generated by the heat of the sun as a thermal updraft over sun-facing slopes or dark patches of ground. Pterosaurs might deliberately have looked for cumulus clouds, which are a sure sign of a thermal updraft, and then could have soared to heights of 3 miles (5 kilometers), enabling them to fly for more than 30 miles (50 kilometers) without flapping their wings once. Even over water, an experienced glider can use the dynamics of the air above the waves to remain airborne with little effort. It has been

Ornithocheirus had a wingspan of nearly 40 feet (12 meters), so had almost 200 square feet (20 square meters) with which to catch the lifting air currents. This, together with their lightweight bodies, made them consummate gliders.

suggested that taking off and landing could be a problem and that pterosaurs would have had to leap off cliffs to become airborne. However, with the lift their huge wings could give them, a light breeze would have been enough for them to take off.

Despite all they sacrificed to be lightweight, they maintained large heads and long, strong legs. Their big beaks were often on the end of long necks and were probably essential if they were to catch food, especially fish, on the wing. The legs were obviously used for walking but might also have allowed them to leap and become airborne with a few lazy flaps if there was no wind. Neither before nor since has Earth seen such consummate gliders, creatures that viewed the world around them in terms of moving air masses that took them, like elevators and conveyor belts, anywhere they wanted to go.

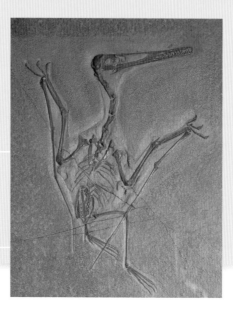

The new model: at the beginning of the Cretaceous the short-tailed pterosaurs took over from the long-tailed varieties, and the shape of their wings changed. They also started to grow much larger.

BENEATH A GIANT'S WINGS

This male is old, about 40, and after spending the first year of his life on Cantabria, he has probably revisited it about 20 times. He is well past his reproductive peak, but still he is driven back once every two years to do battle with other males for his right to mate. Although there are no outward signs, over the last few weeks his body has been getting ready for this. Soon he will also display his bright mating colors, most noticeably his beak crest will flush red.

He waits, watching the Tapejara's extravagant mating displays, while the morning sun climbs higher in the sky and the thermals around the outcrop grow stronger. About mid-morning he rocks back on his legs and opens his wings by extending his arms and flicking out his long wing fingers. In almost the same movement he leans into the breeze and jumps off the granite shelf. Conditions are perfect. He immediately starts to climb, leaving the screeching Tapejara far below as he banks into a tight circle and soars higher. In the distance further down the coast other large pterosaurs are also lifting off. Eventually, as the rising air weakens, the Ornithocheirus peels off and starts to glide north again.

Over water there are no thermals, but the giant pterosaurs can still cross open seas. If the Ornithocheirus cannot island–hop or glide all the way across from a high coastal thermal, he will use what the water has to offer. He can get lift by riding the windward side of waves and, by remaining very low,

'On a good day an Ornithocheirus may fly for 300 miles after flapping his wings only once to become airborne.'

can exploit "ground effect," compressing a cushion of air in front of and below him to help keep himself aloft. He can also take advantage of the wind gradients over the ocean. Friction with the water means wind speeds are lower the closer they are to the surface. An Ornithocheirus flying near the surface can rise into the faster air and the increasing lift will drive him still higher until he loses momentum. Then he glides down at an angle to the wind, building up speed and ready to repeat the entire process. All this means that on a good day an Ornithocheirus may fly for 300 miles after flapping his wings only once to become airborne.

Shelter from the Storm

THE COAST OF APPALACHIA

It is a blisteringly hot day and the Ornithocheirus is fishing off shore. He flies low over the waves, looking for flashes of silver or surface distur-bance. He holds his long beak right above the water and when he sees some-thing he dips it in quickly, snapping it shut the moment it makes contact with prey. In this way he traps fish with his long, sharp teeth and then, with a flick of his head, throws them into his throat pouch, where he starts to digest them even before they get to his stomach. The keel-like crests on his beak are impor-tant because they help keep it moving straight ahead when he dips it into the water. In such a delicately balanced hunter, a force working sideways, against the direction of flight, can be extremely dangerous, either tipping him into the water or damaging his neck.

The Ornithocheirus makes contact with a squid. While he clips it out of the water, its tentacles writhe and it blushes a deep red. Then, in a blink, it is gone, adding to the fish soup in the pterosaur's pouch. He turns toward the shore and starts to flap. The extra weight of fish has upset his usual effortless gliding. While he manages a long slow climb to the nearby cliffs, it is also clear that the heat is affecting him. His wings are paler than usual, indicating that he has reduced the blood supply to his membranes. With so much surface area exposed to the sun, overheating is one of the biggest problems for these huge creatures. Reducing the amount of blood flowing through the wings helps, as does his fine pale fur. The air sacs throughout his body also help him lose heat from his internal organs. However, when temperatures are high, he cannot fly or fish for extended periods without seeking shade. Smaller pterosaurs splash water on their wings and quickly cool down, but this is more difficult for the cumbersome Ornithocheirus.

He lands at the end of a long bay on top of the heavily eroded sandstone cliffs. After he has stowed his wings, he gently wafts his giant wing fingers to create a cooling breeze around his body. He is on the southernmost tip of Appalachia, several hundred miles nearer his breeding ground than Borborema. Dark red mating colors are just beginning to stain the rim of his

Snap shot: an Ornithocheirus beak plucks a fish from the water. The keel crests at the tip help guide the beak through the water, preventing twisting while the pterosaur strikes.

beak crests. He is nervous since the area behind the cliff is dense cycad and tree fern forest and could be hiding all sorts of predators. From somewhere beyond the forest he picks up the distant rumble of a giant herd of herbivores.

At the far end of the beach a river spills out, and where it meets the sea, the swirling currents have dragged the sand out into a long spit. On either side the cycads give way to low thicket fern and lush riverbank plants. While the Ornithocheirus watches from its elevated position, a single adult Iguanodon strides out of the ferns onto the beach. She weighs about six tons and is 22 feet long, a fine example of an extraordinarily successful group of animals. The brown and white stripes down her back mark her as an Appalachian Iguanodon, but her relatives can be found on most continents and sometimes in herds of thousands.

She turns and rocks back on her hind legs, rising to her full height of about 16 feet off the ground. She calls and then heads toward the river. Soon the rest

of the herd appear from the forest edge. One by one they file out on to the beach. Walking slowly on all fours, they vary considerably in size from 6-foot-long yearlings to old males almost 16 feet in length. The juveniles try to keep up with the adults by trotting around on two legs. All Iguanodon are capable of walking on two legs, but the adults do this only when fleeing. Unlike the young, they spend most of their time on all fours, grazing. Some of the larger animals have detached themselves from the main herd and wander alone as outriders. Perhaps they are there to give the herd early warning of danger, or perhaps because they are less vulnerable than the smaller animals and do not need the protection of the herd, they can get a better choice of plants by foraging away from the others. Soon the single file becomes a mass of white-and-brown-striped bodies gently rocking from side to side as they walk.

The herd is using the beach because the river is at its shallowest here, and on the other side lies a large expanse of lush grazing. When more animals cross, the estuary is increasingly churned up and the sand starts to liquefy. Soon the smaller animals are in trouble since they do not have the strength to pull their legs out of the quicksand. Though the bray of worried juveniles fills the air, the adults continue walking, dragging their limbs through the sticky mud, seemingly oblivious to the mounting number of drowning youngsters. It takes about an hour for the whole herd to cross, and by the end, a dozen young Iguanodon have lost their struggle with the sand. While the flow of the river smoothes over the beach, it obliterates all the evidence of the herd's passing and the youngsters are slowly buried.

The rest of the herd head for the lush flood-plain vegetation. Iguanodon are extraordinarily adaptable herbivores, which partly explains their success. They have a wide, horny beak that can crop low plants or pick at higher shrubs and trees. Unlike other dinosaurs, they have evolved batteries of teeth at the back of their mouths, which allow them to chew. Chewing means the plant food is processed before it goes into the stomach and this speeds up the whole process of digestion. Iguanodon hands are also a miracle of adaptability. The middle three digits are wrapped together by a fleshy pad and provide a strong, load-bearing base to the front limbs. This is especially important in this species

OPPOSITE In the late evening light an Appalachian Iguanodon stops for a drink. This is a fully grown female and her long, defensive thumb spikes are clearly visible.

OVERLEAF The herd thunder by: Iguanodon move along the beach in search of new grazing. When moving slowly, adults usually walk on all fours, but if they need to hurry, they can rise up on two legs.

because they spend so much time walking on all fours. Their little finger is held off the ground and is highly flexible, helping them grasp food. Finally there is the thumb, which has evolved into a long spike that can become a fearsome weapon in defense.

The herd will have a profound effect on the flood plain, eating or crushing most of the available plants. In fact, there are clear signs that this herd, or one

TO CHEW OR NOT TO CHEW

EVER SINCE ANIMALS first crawled out of the sea and onto the land, plants have been a difficult source of food, especially when compared to meat. Vegetation was full of indigestible cellulose, frequently protected by armored bark or spines, and could often produce a range of poisons to deter the herbivore. Over millions of years animals have had to show endless adaptations and innovations to overcome these plant defenses. Eventually their guts had to become complex processors, extracting nutrients from fairly unpromising material. Sauropods, the giants of the Jurassic, succeeded because their stomachs were vast stone-containing fermentation tanks, but they did nothing to help prepare the food for digestion.

In the early Cretaceous the ornithopods, the group of dinosaurs that included *Iguanodon*, took food-processing a stage further. They learned to chew. An *Iguanodon* skull shows a beak at the front for cropping and ranks of teeth at the back for shearing, similar to that of a modern–day grazing mammal, such as a horse.

Although this may sound obvious, for many years the question of how dinosaurs chewed baffled scientists. In order to chew you need cheeks, otherwise the food falls out

In order to chew, *Iguanodon* must have had some kind of cheek, otherwise the food would have fallen out the sides of their mouths. This baffled scientists for years because no modern reptiles have cheeks.

of the side of the mouth. Crocodiles, lizards, and turtles, for example, have no facial muscles. Mammals are unique in having such expressive muscular faces, of which cheeks are an integral part. However, the *Iguanodon* skull shows that its teeth were set on the inside of the jawbone, leaving room for some sort of cheek, even if it was just skin drawn between the jaws.

The second problem was the grinding movement of the jaw. In mammals the lower jaw is free to move from side to side, enabling them to chew. Dinosaur jaws could move only up and down. A careful study of the *Iguanodon* head by paleontologist David Norman revealed how the herbivore coped.

Running along the length of the skull was a hinge, which allowed the upper jaw to flex. Checking with the wear patterns on the teeth, Norman suggested that *Iguanodon* chewed by pushing its lower jaw up inside its upper jaw, which then flexed outward to allow the teeth to grind together. Watching an *Iguanodon* idly chewing on its food, you would have seen the bottom jaw moving rhythmically up and down, and the sides of its head gently expanding and contracting. Although there are many theories about why the ornithopods were so successful in the Cretaceous, it is highly probable that their secret was as mundane as they learned to chew their food well.

Beautifully preserved skulls have allowed scientists to recreate the way *Iguanodon* jaws must have moved to enable them to slice up their food.

172

like it, has been here before. The plain is dominated by a shrub called Protoanthus, which is distinctive because from its stems hang small, white flowers. Flowers and flowering plants have recently evolved and are widespread only in the equatorial regions. However, in a short time they have proved extremely successful, especially in lush lowland areas. Their secret is not some new poison or extra spines to make them unpalatable to dinosaurs. Instead, they seem to thrive on being grazed. Protoanthus produces many seeds, each with enough nutrients to give the seedling an early boost. That means that if grazing flattens an area, Protoanthus is often the first plant to reappear. Even if substantial parts of a Protoanthus shrub are eaten or damaged, it can still grow back from different points on the plant, recovering better than other plants. Finally, it grows fast and is quick to produce seeds. Protoanthus have found a unique way to live with the impact of herbivorous dinosaurs, and wherever these appear in large herds, you are likely to find plants such as Protoanthus. Perhaps the most distinctive aspect of this plant is also the most obvious, the color of its flowers. In a world dominated by the greens and browns of ferns, conifers, and cycads the pale white blooms of Protoanthus light up the landscape.

'In a world dominated by the greens and browns of ferns, conifers, and cycads, the pale white blooms of Protoanthus light up the landscape.'

The Iguanodon herd fan out onto the flood plain to graze. Before them is a haze of white Protoanthus. Insects are thick in the air, attracted to the pollen on the flowers, and angry clouds of them rise and fall as the giant reptiles work their way from plant to plant. To the Ornithocheirus, sitting on the cliff a mile away, the mass of striped dinosaurs seems to float on a sea of white froth. He watches the herd while he strums his enormous wings to cool down.

On careful examination another type of dinosaur is visible mixed in with the Iguanodon. There are only a few of them and they are smaller than the Iguanodon and heavily armored. These are Polacanthus, and almost every centimeter of their backs is covered in huge thick spines, except for an area over the rump, which is one solid bony plate. Even the tail has spines running down either side of it. All this makes Polacanthus a formidable prospect for any

AN OLD FRIEND OF PALEONTOLOGISTS

WITH THE ARRIVAL of the new millennium, *Iguanodon* will have its own celebration. It is 175 years old. This early Cretaceous herbivore has a special place in the history of palaeontology since it was only the second dinosaur to be named. In 1825 surgeon Dr. Gideon Mantell identified teeth found in waste rubble in Sussex, England, as belonging to a new species of reptile. It looked as if they came from some giant lizard like an iguana. Mantell called their owner *Iguanodon*, or "iguana tooth," 16 years before the term dinosaur was even invented. *Iguanodon* became famous as a pre-Flood monster and in 1851 had pride of place in the Great Crystal Palace Exhibition.

The brick model still exists in London and shows the limits of scientific knowledge at the time. What was later proved to be *Iguanodon*'s thumb spike was placed on its nose like a rhinoceros horn and the creature is posed as a heavy quadruped.

The first reconstruction of *Iguanodon*, by surgeon Gideon Mantell, was based on the skeleton of a modern lizard. Mantell placed the thumb spike on the nose, like a rhino horn.

In 1878 an extraordinary discovery down a coal mine in Bernissart, Belgium, produced more than 30 fully articulated *Iguanodon* skeletons. It took three years to remove 130 tons of fossil material from the mine. Work by the paleontologist Louis Dollo completely changed the Crystal Palace look. Dollo

After several skeletons were found down a coal mine in Belgium in 1878, *Iguanodon*'s look was revised. The scientist reposed him in an upright stance, but to do this the tail had to be dislocated.

placed the spikes on *Iguanodon*'s thumbs and made it into a giant biped. This became the classic image of *Iguanodon* for most of the twentieth century, standing upright next to its favorite conifer, giving artists the thumbs-up with its spikes. However, in fact, Dollo had broken *Iguanodon*'s tail in order to get it to stand like this.

In the 1970s *Iguanodon* went through another makeover and is now reconstructed into something between a four-legged and a two-legged creature. Its spine is believed to have been held parallel to the ground, and although It was capable of moving around on two legs, while it walked and grazed, it would have been on all fours. This is a unique form of locomotion that has no modern counterpart.

The first bit of *Iguanodon* found was its tooth in 1825. Gideon Mantell identified its similarity to a modern–day iguana, hence the name "iguana tooth."

During the Great Exhibition of 1851 in London, dinosaurs were the star attraction, with several life-size models being built for the occasion.

predator and explains why they are principally solitary. However, it does not explain why they are frequently seen mingling with Iguanodon herds. The two species pay little attention to each other and it is difficult to understand what advantage the association has for both animals. One theory maintains that together they are better at spotting predators because their senses complement each another. An Iguanodon can rise on his hind legs and has good eyesight and hearing. A Polacanthus, on the other hand, stands low to the ground, and has an exceptional sense of smell. Often they can sniff out predators that are hidden from the Iguanodon in the undergrowth.

While the hot day wears on, the humidity rises and the air becomes very still. On the horizon dirty gray and white clouds build. The Ornithocheirus has a keen eye for clouds and an innate ability to judge the currents of air that drive them. He recognizes instantly that these are storm clouds which to him

Eating alone: a Polacanthus grazes on the edge of the river. These armored dinosaurs have a formidable array of defenses. Not only do have they rows of spikes along their sides, but also their rump, a favorite target for predators, is covered in a thick, bony plate.

represent serious danger. Tropical downpours and high winds can knock pterosaurs out of the sky and even on the ground they need to seek shelter from these conditions. The Ornithocheirus defecates the remains of his morning catch, flicks his wings out, and leaps into the sticky air. He drifts along the cliff edge, his huge wings lifted by the tiny breeze rising from the waves below. After a few minutes, he finds what he is looking for, a long overhang in the sandstone rocks. It is high enough to be clear of the waves but not easily

accessible from the land, an ideal spot for sitting out a storm.

Right after sunset the storm rolls in from the east, pushing giant waves before it. Rain hammers down on the cliff and torrents of water sweep over the sand-stone. The Ornithocheirus ducks his head and clings on in the darkness, his wing fingers drawn down tight over his back. While the wind and rain scour the cliff, the pterosaur is quickly soaked and the fine gray fur across his back and wings becomes sodden. Although the rain is warm, with all the wind his body tempera-ture drops and he faces the opposite problem to the one he had a few hours before. Once again he controls the blood flow to his wings, this time to reduce heat loss, and he twitches his massive flight muscles rapidly, which helps maintain a core body heat. He is shivering, and just audible over the rage of the storm is the sound of his beak chattering.

By morning the storm has blown out and a cool breeze wafts in off the sea. After such a violent night, the huge pterosaur is cold and bruised. While the sun rises over the sea, he opens his wings to welcome it, desperately accepting any warmth in its thin early rays. Fortunately, the sun strengthens rapidly, warming the rocks around him. Soon he relaxes and starts to groom himself, repairing the storm damage. It is clear from his movements that the old pterosaur is suffering from arthritis. Having become so cold in the night, his huge finger joints must ache badly. He inspects each wing closely and runs his long beak over their surface like a rake. Like most large pterosaurs, he almost certainly has parasites hanging on to his wings. One in particular, called Saurophthirus, lives only on pterosaur wings. Saurophthirus is a colorless little insect about an inch long. It has no wings, long legs with hooks on the end,

LEFT Dangerous games: a young Iguanodon plays with a Polacanthus. These two species seem to have a great tolerance for each other, which could be based on mutual protection. Iguanodon have good vision and Polacanthus a superb sense of smell.

PARASITES ON THE WING

AMONG SCIENTISTS WHO study fossilized insects from the Mesozoic, there is little doubt that the giant reptiles were plagued with mites, ticks, and all sorts of biting creatures. Despite the dinosaurs' tough, scaly skin, these parasites regularly sought out the soft spots around their eyes, in their ears, and between their scales in order to extract the blood on which they fed. Unfortunately, short of finding a mite fossilized in dinosaur skin, it is difficult to prove the link. However, from an old lake bed in Russia comes one fossilized insect whose odd physical appearance can be explained in only one way. It must have been a pterosaur parasite.

This 1-inch (2.5-centimeter) -long creature comes from the Cretaceous rocks of Transbaikalia in eastern Russia and has been called *Saurophthirus*. It has no wings, long legs ending in hooks, a long proboscis, and a soft body that could have been distended for fluid feeding. For an insect, all these are adaptations to a parasitic way of life. Although not related, *Saurophthirus* also bears an uncanny resemblance to the modern nycteribiid parasite that specializes in feeding on bat wings. This little creature's long legs help it remain steady on a moving surface as it probes the sparsely-haired bat's wing for blood vessels to drain. It does not venture near the hairier parts of the bat because its legs are too long and would become tangled up in the hairs.

The wing of a pterosaur would have offered exactly the same opportunities to *Saurophthirus*. There would have been very little fur and an enormous expanse of skin filled with blood vessels. If this link is correct, then it is highly likely that grooming to get rid of these unwanted parasites was an important part of pterosaur behavior.

At the bottom of a lake in Russia this mysterious fossilized insect has been found. In form it is similar to a common type of bat flea, but there were no bats in the Cretaceous, only hairy pterosaurs.

Pterosaurs, especially the large ones, would have found it difficult to fly in the rain. While grounded, they might have spent time grooming, since flight, and possibly success at mating, depended on their delicate wings being in perfect condition.

and sharp sucking mouthparts. Its entire life is spent hooked on to a pterosaur, drilling the wing membrane for blood vessels. It is important for Ornithocheirus to keep himself well groomed, because large populations of Saurophthirus can seriously weaken him and impede his ability to fly. Even worse, badly infested pterosaurs are rarely picked as mates during breeding displays. By running his teeth through his fur he can break the legs of these parasites and, although he will never eliminate them, this keeps the numbers down.

Methodical grooming occupies the old male until mid-morning, by which time the sun's heat is driving invisible thermals high into the air all along the coast. The sight of large numbers of pterosaurs soaring above him tempts the Ornithocheirus off the cliff and into the warm air. Immediately he starts to rise. Dipping one wing, he turns his flight path into a tight spiral upward and soon he is ready to continue his migration toward his breeding ground.

Cornubia is like a massive fortress in the middle of the Tethys. All along its western coast, sheer cliffs rise out of the ocean, sometimes as high as 1,300 feet. The waves that batter these cliffs have to run the gauntlet of hundreds of jagged black rocks, and the waters of the Tethys are churned up into a thick froth.

The Time is Near

THE ISLAND OF CORNUBIA

Despite its forbidding appearance, Cornubia is a sanctuary for migrating giant pterosaurs. Its warm black cliffs create huge thermals that give the pterosaurs a lift as they island–hop between continents. Thousands crowd onto its ledges and fish in its violent waters.

Toward the center of the island is a string of dark, freshwater lakes from which the pterosaurs drink. From his position high on a coastal thermal, the old Ornithocheirus can see them and he slowly starts to descend. His migration is almost complete. Cornubia is only a few hundred miles from Cantabria and his body is preparing to breed. The crests on the end of his beak are bright red and inside he is weighed down by the growth of his testes. He needs to feed these changes, and one way to do this without expending too much energy is to get other pterosaurs to do the hunting for him.

Below him the lakes are well stocked and a number of smaller pterosaurs are busy fishing, in particular groups of juvenile Ornithocheirus. When they skim above the glassy lake, the old male slows his descent. One of the young Ornithocheirus strikes the water with her beak and then flaps quickly to rise up. In her mouth is the silvery glint of a fish. The male tucks his wings slightly and drops toward the laden pterosaur as she heads for the shore. Showing remarkable agility for his size, the male sweeps in front of the surprised juvenile, issuing a series of aggressive hisses. She drops the wriggling fish on the beach and the male swiftly claims his prize. He will spend most of the day doing this and, although bullying smaller pterosaurs consumes energy, he has a much higher success rate than if he were fishing alone.

Being cut off from the marine environment by the cliffs, these lakes have developed unique residents. In particular, they are dominated by large, predatory turtles. Most of the time these unlikely killers litter the beaches, sunning themselves, and seem somewhat slow and cumbersome compared to other aquatic predators. However, in the dark waters of the lakes they are highly effective ambush hunters and only a few fish escape their powerful jaws.

The island itself is big enough to support large numbers of dinosaurs. In its uplands there are thick forests of Huon pine and cycad. Huon trees have an unusual way of colonizing new areas. Low branches grow from the trunk and, where they touch the ground, roots sprout down into the earth. Over many years a new tree is established and then reproduces itself in the same way. On Cornubia some of these forests are very old, and in some places one original tree and its clones cover whole hillsides. The lowland areas are filled with ferns, bennettites, and large patches of flowers. Through these meadows small herds of Iguanodon

graze. They are a different species to the ones in Appalachia. They have deep green scales and are less bulky around the neck, but fully grown they are larger, weighing about 7 tons. Most noticeably, they have more powerful forearms, equipped with longer thumb spikes.

These herbivores need to be strong because this island has large and powerful predators. In particular, Utahraptors stalk the Iguanodon herds on Cornubia. As a group, the raptors are successful carnivores, with different species spread through Laurasia and Gondwana. Most hunt in packs, but this is less common among the larger animals. Unfortunately for the prey here,

Rogue male: even on their own, Iguanodon are capable of protecting themselves against most predators. A male like this one can weigh more than 7 tons and rear up to a height of 16 feet.

THE ARRIVAL OF FLOWER POWER

TODAY FLOWERING PLANTS, or angiosperms, dominate nearly every habitat on Earth. From palms and cactus to beech and oak, from heather moors to wide grasslands, they shape the green landscape we see. Yet, for most of the Mesozoic era, dinosaurs lived in a green and brown world with no flowers at all, and they certainly never saw any grass. However, in the early Cretaceous, even when flowering plants did appear, you would need to have been an observant botanist to spot one. They evolved as small marginal shrubs in a world full of established conifers, ferns, and cycads. The first flowers were not only small, they probably had no scent or color. The mystery is why this rather unassuming new group of plants eventually took off with such vigor that they drove so many others to extinction. The scientific definition of an angiosperm is that it has covered ovules. This means that the female reproductive parts are covered by special tissue layers which protect them from drying out, being eaten

This 140-million-year-old fossil, found by American and Chinese scientists in Nanjing, is the oldest known flower. The blooms are small and likely to be wind-pollinated. Insect-attracting flowers evolved only later.

by insects, or contracting a fungal infection. The male pollen can only fertilize such a plant by landing in the right place and growing a tube into the ovule down which the sperm can pass. The seed that then forms has its own food supply and when dropped is

Modern flowers are very different from the first Mesozoic varieties, however, some species, including magnolia (illustrated below) and drimys (a flowering evergreen), can trace their lineage back to the time of the dinosaurs.

capable of sprouting and forming a new plant. From this innovation blossomed a set of characteristics that transformed the world's vegetation.

For whatever reason, angiosperms were quicker to colonize areas that had, been cleared of other plants. They grew to seed faster and recovered more readily from damage. Then a number of outside factors started to contribute to the flowers' success.

During the Jurassic period, the sauropods developed mass grazing to a new level. Herds moved through an area, churning the ground with their feet and decimating the vegetation. This "dinoturbation" would have left behind ideal environments for flowers to exploit. In the early Cretaceous the climate over most of the Earth's land surface became moister, and in many areas lush vegetation developed. Competition for light became more intense, which also suited flowering plants.

Finally, as the Cretaceous progressed, flowers developed a closer relationship with insects. With their protected ovules, they needed to ensure that the pollen grain reached the right place. Insects already visited flowers to eat the pollen and then carried the excess from one plant to another. Flowers started to produce nectar to attract insects, who became regular visitors. When flowers developed color and scent to make themselves even more attractive, insects such as bees came to specialize in feeding on nectar. This process, called co-evolution, benefited both organisms. With so much working in their favor it is not surprising that flowering plants were so successful.

Utahraptors are large, about 19 feet long, and they hunt in packs.

About a mile from the lake where the old Ornithocheirus is bullying for his supper, a low outcrop of granite backs up against the Huon forest. A herd of Iguanodon are idly plucking saplings from between the bare rocks. It is late afternoon and the long shadows thrown by the rocks hide danger. Right below the Iguanodon, in deep shadow, two Utahraptors make slow progress toward their quarry.

Utahraptors are truly beautiful predators. They are covered in a well-defined black and yellow pattern with a pale cream underbelly. Their sleek, well-muscled bodies are held in perfect balance by a small, highly mobile tail that constantly adjusts and readjusts as the animal slinks forward. Each Utahraptor weighs almost a ton, and if they surprise an Iguanodon, the Iguanodon will be lucky to escape. Their heads hardly move when they walk and their eyes remain locked on the prey ahead. Their forearms are tucked up high, with their long grappling fingers held against their ribs. Each step reveals a flash of the long, black claw on the second toe, distinctive of this group of predators.

These raptors have obviously spent some time working their way around to this position because the rest of their pack is still on the edge of the forest. They are both females, and female Utahraptors do most of the hunting. Somewhere nearby will be a dominant male, but he will rarely hunt. If a kill is made, he will claim his share and save his energy for the challenges that come from other males. The two stalking Utahraptors reach the edge of the outcrop unnoticed. The Iguanodon are slowly moving away from the predators and the distance the raptors will have to sprint once they are in the open is increasing. Utahraptors do not usually pursue their prey for any distance and the Iguanodon could soon outpace them, running on their long back legs. It is time to attack.

The larger female springs silently onto the outcrop and heads for the herd. She has chosen her victim, a sturdy subadult on the edge of the group. She is spotted immediately and the Iguanodon start their screeching bellows of alarm. The rest of the Utahraptor pack appear from the forest, but the herd is

OPPOSITE **Elegant killer: a Utahraptor stops for a drink. He is constantly alert and the midday sun betrays the tools of his trade, his sickle-like toe claw and long, grappling hands. This species is the largest of the raptors, standing almost 7 feet high.**

already striding away toward a large meadow of white Protoanthus. Most of the Utahraptors are out of the chase before it even starts, but the lead female manages to gain on the Iguanodon before he can get into his stride. She leaps. While she travels through the air, her long fingers, tipped with hook-like claws, spread out. Her legs come forward, and as she lands on the Iguanodon's rump, she tries to drive her lethal hind claws into his flank. However, the leap was mistimed. Her feet fail to find their target and, although the Iguanodon stumbles when she lands on him, he remains on his feet. While her claws rake across his back, his bellows turn into an ear-splitting scream. He rears and bucks in a panicked frenzy. The predator loses her grip and tumbles to the ground. She instantly springs up again, but she is in a dangerous position, right in front of the Iguanodon. He rises up and knocks her back down with one forearm, then, swinging the other across, drives a thumb spike deep into her shoulder. The Utahraptor breaks free and scrabbles away, one arm dangling uselessly.

The Iguanodon turns to catch up with the rest of the herd, and continues his deafening alarm screams. The second stalking Utahraptor is too far behind to take advantage of the work started by her pack mate and the predators abandon the chase. The injured female pauses on the forest edge. She is badly wounded but still stands a chance of recovery. The pack will continue to make kills and if there is enough food to go around she will be able to eat even though she may be too weak to hunt. Attacking big prey is always dangerous and most of the older females carry a number of healed wounds.

Utahraptors live in a wide variety of environments and adapt their hunting techniques accordingly. On the wide open plains of northern Appalachia they always hunt in large packs, but among the hill forests to the west they are frequently solitary. In Cornubia they usually live in small packs. If they hunt alone their success rate is as low as 15 percent. As a pair this rate doubles to one in three attacks ending in a kill. After that it does not seem to matter how many there are in the pack since they fail most of the time. Members of a pack also appear to specialize. Some of the smaller animals pursue the prey but are rarely the first to attack. The larger individuals concentrate on ambush and leaping on the prey. If the prey is small enough they may approach from any

angle, but with Iguanodon they never attack from the front. In one other respect Utahraptors are unique. They willingly attack healthy prey, even large males, not just the young or weak like other predators do.

The Utahraptor pack reforms and the members greet one another with what looks like a formal dance. In fact, it is a sophisticated visual "language" that reinforces the dominance hierarchy within the group. The lower orders approach others with their heads down and their ringed tails flitting furiously from side to side. The more dominant animals stand upright and greet others by spreading out their arms and claws and waving them up and down. There is little noise and every member seems to know her place. The dominant male is still nowhere to be seen.

'Utahraptors willingly attack healthy prey, even large males, and do not appear to select the young or weak like other predators do.'

About a mile away, at the far end of the Protoanthus meadow, the fleeing Iguanodon slow down and resume feeding. Meanwhile the Utahraptors have not given up on the hunt. After a flurry of displays, one by one they trot off after the herd. When the lead raptors reach the Protoanthus shrubs, they fan out, sinking down among the flowers to hide. To the west the sun begins to sink below the horizon. Although the Iguanodon herd continue to feed, they bunch closer together.

About two hours after sunset, one of the large female Utahraptors rises up from her crouching position about 60 yards from the herd. She starts to run toward the nearest Iguanodon and issues a series of short barks. She is not trying to catch her prey off guard. About 20 yards away, she stops and continues her loud display. The Iguanodon become nervous. They mill around, stomping their front legs and bellowing at the predator. She holds her ground and soon other Utahraptors appear, again stopping short of the herd and doing their best to intimidate the herbivores. At the moment it is impossible for them to attack any single member of this tight-knit group without risk of being injured by another. Their aim is to keep pushing the herd until it breaks up in the darkness and one of them is isolated.

The night wears on and for a while it appears as if the pack's tactics will fail.

Suddenly, one raptor seizes her chance at the back of the herd and leaps on a female Iguanodon, successfully digging her hind claws into her flank. The giant herbivore bucks and reels, screeching in pain. In doing so she stumbles into another Iguanodon and sends the raptor tumbling off her back.

Although this attack has failed, the panic caused is enough to send several of the younger Iguanodon running off into the darkness. A young male breaks away from the group right past a waiting raptor, which leaps on to his haunches, kicking her claws deep into his side. Like before, the attack produces a loud and furious defense, but within moments a second Utahraptor appears out of the darkness and latches on to the herbivore's other side. The weight and shock of these two large predators tearing, kicking, and biting his back are soon too much for the young Iguanodon. Unable to dislodge them, his back legs crumple, exposing his belly, and the predators are quick to eviscerate him.

More of the Utahraptor pack appear when it becomes clear from the noise that the Iguanodon is dying. While the herbivore gasps his last breath, they settle down to feast with much squabbling and displaying to establish who gets the choice parts.

Morning reveals a gory scene. All the Utahraptors are resting by the corpse, covered in blood. The pack will remain around the dead Iguanodon for a few days, warding off any other predators attracted by the smell. Each one will eat its fill, and by the time they leave, there will be very little left.

Nearby, the waters of the lake are still, reflecting the golden clouds above. On a small island in the center the Ornithocheirus shifts uncomfortably in his sleep. The day warms and huge dark shapes start to pull themselves out of the water. The Ornithocheirus suddenly finds himself sharing his island with numerous big black turtles. He tries waddling away from them, but soon he is surrounded. The day is not yet warm enough for him to soar, therefore he takes off and flaps his way slowly to a turtle-free piece of shore. He lands awkwardly and, after closing his wings, turns to take a drink.

Close behind him is a dense patch of pines. Between their trunks an understory of cycads and ferns twist up through the branches, creating an impenetrable barrier. After the Ornithocheirus lands an unfamiliar chatter starts up deep in the forest. He ignores these sounds until suddenly a tiny, brightly colored creature flies out of the thicket and dive-bombs him. It is followed by a second and a third, and before the old male can take evasive action, he is being

THE ORIGIN OF BIRDS

THERE CAN BE FEW subjects in paleontology that have attracted as much controversy as the origin of birds. In 1861, a beautiful fossil of what looked like a half-bird/half-dinosaur was dug up in Germany. About the size of a magpie, it had the wings and feathers of a bird but the teeth and tail of a reptile. It was called *Archaeopteryx* and was the first of seven similar fossils that have now been found. Eight years later Thomas Huxley suggested that birds had evolved directly from dinosaurs and this is when the arguments started, since some paleontologists supported and some vigorously opposed Huxley's view. The two camps have been labeled the dinosaurians, who maintain that birds are the living survivors of dinosaurs, and avians, who believe in the uniqueness of this exceptional group of animals. A number of remarkable finds in China in the 1990s have provided the most conclusive evidence so far in support of the dinosaurians, who now gleefully call birds "small, feathered, short-tailed dinosaurs."

When Huxley first suggested that birds were descended directly from dinosaurs, it

seemed obvious. He noted no fewer than 35 features that the two groups shared, including their lightweight bones, bipedal stance, three-fingered hand/wing, and hinged ankles. However, even in Huxley's time, some people believed that this was an example of convergence, two different creatures evolving independently to look the same. Besides, dinosaurs were believed to be cold-blooded reptiles, and powered flight (as opposed to gliding) requires the highly energetic metabolism of a warm-blooded creature. Then it was pointed out that dinosaurs' "wishbones," which play an important part in flapping flight, had disappeared in the course of evolution and that birds could not have "reinvented" them. To add further doubt, although *Archaeopteryx* was a pretty good "missing link" between dinosaurs and modern birds, it was too old. The dinosaurs most

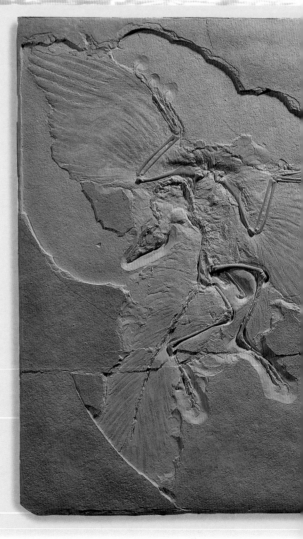

A beautifully preserved *Archaeopteryx* from the Solnhofen limestone in Germany. Since it was first discovered in 1861, this half-dinosaur/half-bird has been seen as the archetypal "missing link" between the two groups.

attacked by a half a dozen of these aggressive little animals. His presence has clearly upset them, and despite the enormous size difference, they are attempting to chase him away.

On the edge of the forest several others of these small creatures sit on branches, calling to each other with high-pitched, rasping whistles. These are not pterosaurs. Their flight is far too fast and erratic. They are dinosaurs that have taken to the air and, for the first time, are challenging the supremacy of the pterosaurs. They are members of a new group of animals, birds, which have their roots back in the Jurassic but have started to blossom in the Cretaceous.

closely related to birds were the dromaeosaurs or raptors that first appeared in the mid-Cretaceous period. *Archaeopteryx* existed millions of years earlier, in the late Jurassic.

For decades scientists actively looked elsewhere for possible ancestors for the birds. Theories that they descended from pterosaurs, crocodiles, mammals, and lizards were all proposed, but the only tenable idea was that they evolved from some still unknown reptile that existed around the time dinosaurs appeared. Then, in the late 1960s, John Ostrom's study of the raptor *Deinonychus* gave fresh hope to the dinosaurians. He revisited and extended Huxley's arguments and systematically analyzed the characteristics shared by dinosaurs and birds, characteristics such as the half-moon wrist bone that allowed both raptors and birds to swivel their "hands" sideways. In flight, birds use this ability to

A young hoatzin clings to a twig. This species is unique among birds because the young still have a claw halfway down the wing. This could be a throwback to an ancestral state, before the creature's "arms" developed into wings.

draw their wings in during the upward stroke and to push them out on the downward stroke, therefore helping to attain more lift. The carnivorous dinosaurs probably used the same technique to tuck their long hands up against their bodies when they were running and then flick them out to catch prey.

During the 1970s, the idea of warm-blooded dinosaurs became widely accepted (see A Hot-blooded Dispute, page 104) and paleontologists also started to find small

dinosaur wishbones among fossils, which further endorsed the dinosaurians' views. However, by the 1990s, the arguments were as alive as ever, with embryological studies contradicting the relationship between birds and dinosaurs.

Behind all these arguments lay feathers, an extraordinarily complex adaptation for flight that is unique to birds. Before their appearance on *Archaeopteryx,* there was little evidence of them and little reason to suppose they existed earlier than this find. What would any animal do with a protofeather? It had long been suggested that feathers could have first appeared as insulation for small, warm-blooded carnivorous dinosaurs, and this view seems to be supported by the Chinese finds, particularly *Sinosauropteryx,* a small dinosaur covered in what look like primitive shaggy feathers. Previous imprints of dinosaur skin showed flat, pavement-like scales. Sadly, it is rare for soft tissue to be fossilized and this area of study is fraught with misinterpretation. However, the evidence for feathered dinosaurs is now as strong as that for furry pterosaurs, and most experts have accepted the latter.

OPPOSITE Home maintenance: an Iberomesornis attends to its nest. This strong, agile little flier lives in dense forests. He is covered in specialized scales called feathers, which are essential for flight and for keeping him warm. They are also brightly colored for display purposes.

Their scales have developed into "feathers," long, flattened structures with a central spine rimmed by thousands of tiny branches that lock together to form a sort of double blade. Feathers are a highly specialized adaptation of the rough, downy scales that cover some other small carnivores, and are the key to bird flight. They are very light, yet when layered together, give the bird a large surface area which can be finely adjusted to create maximum lift. They are also strong, so that if they are hit by branches or twigs, they do not tear, instead they can be groomed back into place. All this allows the little birds to live happily in dense thickets like the one behind the Ornithocheirus. They have even taken to laying their eggs in the trees, keeping them snugly supported by small collections of twigs, moss, and leaves. These aerial nests are safe from attack by other small dinosaurs.

These particular birds are called Iberomesornis and they are small compared to their dinosaur cousins, only about 3 or 4 inches long. They are also beautifully patterned, like tiny jewels against the dull green conifers. Their bodies are blue and they have white heads and red-tipped wings. When they fly, they flash deep purple under their wings. They are attacking the Ornithocheirus because he is a threat to their nests, which sit high in the branches only a few yards away. Their boldness against such a huge enemy must be based on their confidence as fliers. Despite the pterosaur's attempts to snap at them with his fearsome beak, he never really comes close. When more Iberomesornis scuff him, they draw blood with their long, sharp claws. He is forced to flee by creatures less than one hundredth his size.

The Ornithocheirus takes off, but his progress across the lake is slow. It is still early in the morning and there are no thermals. Fortunately, he finds a head wind and manages to rise away from his dazzling little tormentors. The birds continue to attack him, even as he pulls away from the lake. He heads for the southern cliffs to wait for the first of the morning thermals to take him off the island. He is in full breeding colors and should be at his physical peak, ready to compete with other males in a long and arduous mating ritual. However, his age and arthritis are taking their toll, and although there are few outward signs of decline, he is far from ready for the future.

HAIRY DEVILS

EVEN IN THE NINETEENTH century, scientists recognized that pterosaurs must have been very different creatures from dinosaurs. None of the arguments for claiming that dinosaurs were cold-blooded applied if the reptile indulged in the highly energetic activity of flapping flight. The pterosaurs' tiny bird-like bones clearly suggested that they were warm-blooded animals (see The Origin of Birds, page 188). In the 1920s close examination of a beautifully preserved pterosaur skeleton from Solnhofen in Germany revealed a pattern of hollows and stripes on the stone next to the fossil. These were interpreted as being the imprints left by hair follicles and tufts of hair. The idea that anything other than mammals had hair was controversial and, because this sort of soft tissue preservation can be confused with such other phenomena as crystal formation, many doubted the conclusions drawn from the find. It was not until 1970 that a fossil discovery finally convinced most palaeontologists that pterosaurs were covered in fur. Russian scientist A.G. Sharov found a pterosaur in Kazakhstan, which he called *Sordes pilosus,* or "hairy devil," because preserved with the skeleton were thick tufts of hair. It is now accepted that pterosaurs had hair over their bodies but not on their wing membranes, tails, or faces, similar to the pattern found nowadays in bats. The hairs were thick and short, ¼–⅓ inch (5–10 millimeters) long. They would not have been like mammalian hair because, like feathers, they evolved from scales, but they did perform the same function, stopping heat loss. This was proof that pterosaurs must have been warm-blooded. Why else would they have needed insulation?

For decades, scientists argued about whether or not pterosaurs were furry. Then, in 1970, this fossil, called *Sordes pilosus,* was found with what looked like tufts of hair over its body in a pattern similar to that found on bats.

On close inspection the hair appears obvious, but many other factors, such as bacterial activity, might have left similar-looking traces in the fossil find.

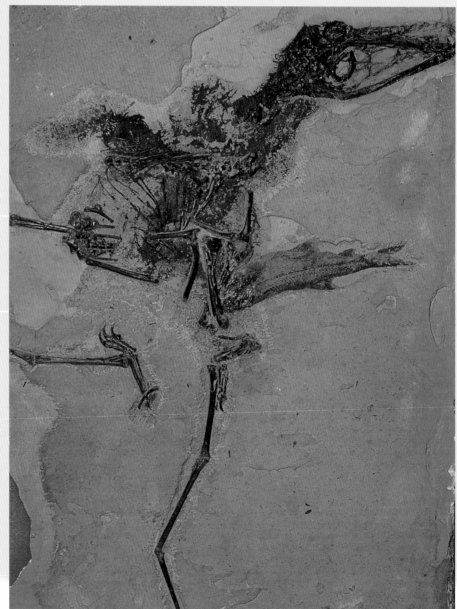

The Battle to Mate

THE BEACHES OF CANTABRIA

On a long, open beach on the north coast of Cantabria stands a lone rock. Jutting out of the sand, it has resisted the ebb and flow of the tide for generations. Once a year it performs a unique task. It lies in the center of the Ornithocheirus' breeding site and acts as a focal point when thousands of these huge pterosaurs sail in from all over the globe. Then the rock is dwarfed, and it becomes a black pebble swamped by a sea of flapping gray wings. This is one of the most spectacular displays in nature. A beach two miles long and a half a mile wide plays host to the largest pterosaurs in the world.

The males arrive first to stake out their territories. Each needs enough space to display his red beak crests and show off the power of his wingbeat. Aggression and competition are intense, and as the beach fills up, vicious fights break out between the rivals. The biggest risk in these contests is that males will use their sharp, fish-catching teeth to tear an opponent's wing. Several days of this establishes a brutal order, where the most powerful males occupy the largest sites toward the center of the beach.

The old male arrives late. There are already a mile and a half of squabbling Ornithocheirus below him, the world's entire male breeding population. He slowly descends toward the beach and aims for the center of the group, hoping to land and carve out a choice display area for himself. When he glides low over the other males, he is met by a forest of clacking red beaks. It will not be an easy task. In flight his delicate wings are fully exposed to his rivals' sharp teeth. He needs to be on the ground with his wings safely packed away if he is to fight his corner successfully. He continues to search in vain for a space to land, slowly losing height all the time. He beats his wings to rise up, but as he does, another male clamps his teeth over the old pterosaur's wing tip. He flaps frantically, tearing his wing membrane in his struggle to free himself. More beaks snap at him and chaos breaks out among the overexcited pterosaurs. The old male lands and manages to close his wings, but he is already badly wounded. Two others continue to attack him, striking at his long wing fingers. He tries to fight back, but he is on the defensive. Soon, bleeding and torn, he is

ABOVE The mating game: when a female finally signals that she is willing to mate, the male is quick to mount her. Afterward, she will leave, but he needs to be ready to try again with other females.

RIGHT Putting on a show: male Ornithocheirus display vigorously in the blistering midday sun. Each pterosaur has to protect its patch not only from its neighbors, but also from new arrivals flying in.

forced to take off. He spreads his wings and jumps, but is brought down again by one of his rivals. He is now fighting for his life. He cannot walk out of the display area without being bitten to death and it is vital that he becomes air-borne. Again and again he jumps, receiving terrible wing wounds as he does, until finally the wind picks up off the sea and he manages to catch a life-saving gust that carries him away.

Exhausted and bleeding, he lands in the shallows far from the other Ornithocheirus. One wing hanging limply in the water, he attempts to preen himself. This was the worst possible start to his breeding season. He will never have the energy to fight his way to a prime site and his wings are too damaged to put on an attractive display. While the evening shadows lengthen he waddles toward a dry sandbank covered in driftwood. He sits alone among the skeletal shapes of dead trees, blinking as a wound on his forehead drips blood into his deep blue eyes. Although he is safe here from the other males, he stands no chance of attracting a female.

Food for the next generation: after the mating displays are over many males lie dead or dying on the beach, mostly through exhaustion. A young Ornithocheirus feeds up before beginning his long journey down the coast.

Sunrise brings a fresh northerly wind, and by late morning the females have begun to arrive. There is bedlam on the display beach. The males warble and clack their beaks while the females circle above. Frequent fights break out, but as the females land, the males turn their attentions to displaying. The females are about the same size as the males, but with smaller crests. After they have landed, they walk slowly through the mass of frantic males. By spreading his wings and waving his red beak, each male tries to encourage a prospective mate to stop. Meanwhile, she is doing her best to push to the center of the display area in her search for a strong partner. When she eventually chooses a suitable one, the female will mate only once and then immediately depart. The males nevertheless stick it out for the duration, mating with as many females as they can subdue. They leave only when the females stop arriving.

The sight of the arriving females rouses the wounded old male and he once again tries to enter the display area. This time he waddles toward the beach, attempting to force his way past the other older pterosaurs and young males on the edge. He makes some headway, since he is considerably larger than the juveniles, but he does not have the stamina to push far. There are already several dead Ornithocheirus floating in the shallows. Infirmity has made this their last season and the stress of the flight here means they did not even have one last chance to mate. The corpses have attracted the attention of a group of scavengers, who surgically dismember the giant gliders, searching for what little meat they have to offer. The old male desperately needs rest and food in order to recover, but he will get neither for at least the next few days. His drive to mate suppresses all other instincts, and while there are females circling above, he will continue to fight, display, and clack his beak.

The weather is perfect. The wind drops and there is hardly a cloud in the sky. The sun beats down and temperatures soar into the high 90s. Although the females come and go, the males continue to cling to their temporary piece of beach.

It is a punishing ordeal for all the pterosaurs. After three days, the beach gradually starts to empty. Some males have died from heat exhaustion, some from their wounds, but the majority have left, having mated as frequently as they could.

On the morning of the fourth day a row of dead pterosaurs stretches along the tide line, their huge, fragile bodies rolling up and down in the shallow waters. A few sit on the sand since their wings are too badly torn to take off, quietly awaiting their fate. The beach teems with all sorts of carnivores gorging on the bounty. Anonymous among the dead is one large male Ornithocheirus, his wings in tatters, his head pecked, and his deep blue eyes clouded over. Despite this ignominious end, the old male pterosaur was a success. In his 40 years he probably sired several thousand offspring and it is likely that some of them were on this beach, competing and succeeding where he finally failed.

'A row of dead pterosaurs stretches along the tide line, their huge, fragile bodies rolling up and down in the shallow waters.'

5

106 MILLION YEARS AGO

Spirits of the Silent Forest

THE EARTH 106 MILLION YEARS AGO. It is the height of the Cretaceous period and the world is warm and humid. Massive volcanic activity on the seabed continues to force the continents apart, pushing up the ocean floor and creating some of the highest sea levels ever recorded. The growing North Atlantic is dividing the huge northern landmass of Laurasia into North America to the west and Asia to the east, while South America has drifted further away from Africa.

Isolated by the movement of the continents, dinosaurs continue to diversify into a myriad of different species. More herbivore designs have evolved, among them the duck-billed dinosaurs, and the carnivore family, the theropods, have produced elegant, ostrich-like omnivores.

Far to the south, the areas that will become Australia and New Zealand remain fused to Antarctica as one giant continent. This is a strange land indeed. Much of it lies within the

A female Leaellynasaura stops by a frozen pond to call for the rest of her clan. In temperatures this low it is very dangerous for individuals to become separated.

SPIRITS OF THE SILENT FOREST

Antarctic Circle, yet there are no frozen wastelands, no ice fields, just a vast expanse of forests and marshes. For half the year this region basks under 24-hour sun. For the other half it endures unremitting darkness and freezing temperatures.

This is perhaps the most extreme habitat that dinosaurs have ever had to tolerate. Some of those who live here are summer visitors, migrating to the far north when winter looms. Others are strange ancient creatures, long extinct elsewhere in the world, but surviving in this environment because no competing species has evolved. A few have adapted to cope with the extreme conditions and remain here all year. Through the long winters they scrape a living under the flicker of the Southern Lights. These are the spirits of this silent forest.

Ferns flourished in the polar regions, but it took flowering plants a long time to adapt to the harsh climate.

LIFE IN A TIME OF WARMTH

AROUND THE MIDDLE of the Cretaceous period, sea levels reached their highest point in the Mesozoic era, 650 feet (200 meters) above today's norms. In these oceans, bony fish and sharks continued to thrive, but the ichthyosaurs went into decline. New, longer-necked creatures known as plesiosaurs appeared and with them the spectacular mosasaurs, long serpentine predators evolved from small terrestrial lizards.

So abundant were the phytoplankton in these waters that their compressed bodies now form thick layers of chalk throughout the modern world in areas that once lay under the sea, such as the White Cliffs of Dover.

On land the climate was still warm and the changes in plants and animals started to follow a pattern. The flowering plants established themselves among the understory while low shrubs colonized river valleys and flood-plains, especially in areas around the Equator. Palms were among the first flowering trees to develop. However, for a long time there were very few woody species, and flowering plants were slow to spread to the higher latitudes, especially in the south. Certain ancient groups of plants, such as the cycads and bennettites, went into decline.

Among the animals the division between north and south became clearer. The sauropods died out in Laurasia to be replaced by herbivorous duck-billed and armored dinosaurs. In the south the sauropods continued to flourish as a group called the titanosaurids, some of which were armored. In fact, there is evidence that some reappeared in the north too.

Birds apparently flourished in both northern and southern hemispheres. Slowly they became more specialized and better fliers. They developed a deeper-keeled breastbone to support larger flight muscles, and some species began to lose their teeth and tails. Oddly, they also quickly evolved flightless forms for running and diving. Throughout their history birds have always been able to lose the ability to fly if it is not required.

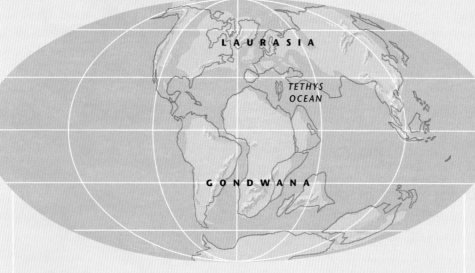

In the mid-Cretaceous the sea levels reached their highest during the time of the dinosaurs. Large parts of Asia, Africa, and the Americas were flooded. At the same time, the Atlantic floor was separating North and South America from Europe and Africa. The northern continents of Laurasia were completely cut off from the southern continents of Gondwana by the Tethys Ocean. India was already moving north toward Asia, but the rift valley between Antarctica and Australia had not yet been flooded. Europe was a series of islands, and North America was split by an inland seaway. Around a quarter of today's dry land was flooded. Diversity among plants and animals increased as they evolved on separate land masses. Warm equatorial currents bathed the polar regions.

Around this time the polar regions went through a period of extraordinary richness. There was no ice at either pole, and species of conifer in the north diversified even while they were declining at the Equator.

To the south there is abundant evidence of the forests that must have covered the South Pole in the coal deposits left in places, such as New Zealand, which are full of fossilized conifers and ferns. However, these forests present experts with a conundrum. Even if the temperatures were mild, how could such rich forests survive two to three months of total darkness? If a plant uses energy by growing and respiring, but is simultaneously unable to create food with sunlight, it will kill itself. As a result, these polar forests must have been extraordinary places dominated by extremes of light and dark. In spring, the sun would rise and gradually establish 24-hour days through the summer. However, it would never climb high in the sky. Instead, it would continually sweep low around the horizon. In autumn the sun would set for the last time for months,

and throughout the winter the darkness would vary from twilight to complete darkness.

Finds in Alaska and Australia show very similar flora thriving in these conditions at both poles. Superficially, they were like the indigenous forests of New Zealand today, dominated by conifers, like the ancient podocarps (such as rimu) and tree ferns. The word podocarp literally means "foot fruit," and the family is distinguished by the swollen stalks that form their "fruit," said to be shaped like feet.

The old polar forests would have been more open than today's, with the taller canopy trees spread out to catch the low summer sun. During the light months the

A giant among insects: the weta evolved about the same time as dinosaurs and has clung on in New Zealand because, until humans arrived, there were no mammals on the islands. Wetas occupy the same niche that mice and rats inhabit elsewhere.

forest would have grown continuously, but in winter the trees must have either dropped their leaves or had some way of becoming dormant. Understory plants, such as ground ferns, probably all died back to their roots. Estimates of average temperatures vary from fairly mild, like present-day New York, to something more extreme, like Anchorage, with an average temperature not much above 32°F (0°C). Winter temperatures and light levels must have been low enough to force the plants into dormancy. Indeed, geologist Andrew Constantine claims evidence of permafrost in the same layers as dinosaur bones in Australia. This would imply that dinosaurs lived in areas where it never got warm enough to thaw out the ground.

Whatever the explanation, the "flowering" of the poles lasted for only part of the Cretaceous. By the end of the Mesozoic, there is evidence that the climate had started to cool slightly and this seems to have had a disastrous effect on the delicate balance of life at the ends of the Earth.

Tree ferns are ancient plants with a history that goes back to the Carboniferous period, more than 100 million years before the age of dinosaurs.

Even though the polar forests had 24-hour light in the summer, the sun never climbed very high in the sky, so the plants had to take maximum advantage of its low-angled rays.

Set in stone: this is the petrified trunk of a 100-million-year-old tree at Curio Bay in New Zealand. At that time the country was part of the Antarctic landmass and was covered in thick forest.

The First Daylight

A dull pre-dawn light spreads across the horizon, illuminating a landscape covered in forest. Rivers trace silvery lines through the dense vegetation, and along their banks icy puddles are melting. It is the beginning of spring at the South Pole. Elsewhere in the world the seasons slip by, sometimes wet, sometimes dry, but with very little to mark their passing. Here at the pole spring transforms life. For the past two months there has been no sun at all and the forest has been in a state of suspended animation. Now the weak glow on the horizon signals the start of a season of continuous growth and, just as the plants take their cue from the light, so do the resident animals.

The forest's long winter silence is broken by a series of guttural screeches. On the trunk of a huge fallen podocarp tree two small brown and green dinosaurs are threatening each other. In the ferns around them, similar creatures chatter and hoot in alarm. The social structure of a clan of Leaellynasaura is being disrupted by the mating season. All winter the clan's strict hierarchy has helped its members survive on the dark forest floor, ensuring that in a time of shortage the fitter individuals get food before the weaker ones without having to fight for it. However, the mating season is a time to challenge the rules, perhaps establish a new order.

This particular clan is made up of 20 dinosaurs, including adult pairs, lone males, and juveniles. Like all Leaellynasaura clans, it is dominated by a single breeding pair, and although all the adults mate and a number of females lay eggs, it is usually only the dominant female who successfully raises young. Of the nearly 200 eggs the females may lay between them, about a quarter will not live long enough to leave the nest, while over half can expect either to be killed by predators in their first few months of life or not to make it through the winter. If 15 young survive, it will be a good year.

During the brief mating season there is often fierce competition among the males as younger members of the clan try to displace the dominant one. This competition usually takes the form of loud calling and posturing. Only

THE POLAR DINOSAURS

HE CREATURES IN this chapter are based on finds made in Australia. At the time of the dinosaurs the land that would become Australia lay a long way south of where it is today, attached to a vast polar continent. This means that fossils dug up recently near Melbourne started life within the Antarctic Circle. Although the area was covered in forest rather than snow and ice, its climate was still extreme by Mesozoic standards. Each one of these characters had to find its own way of exploiting the 24-hour sun in the summer and surviving permanent darkness during the long, cold winters.

EROMANGA SEA

P O L A R   F O R E S T S
•—— Rift Valley

The state of Victoria lay at the end of a large inland sea that split the area that now makes up Australia. To the northeast were highlands and to the south a rift valley.

LEAELLYNASAURA

A small, elegant biped that lived in clans on the forest floor, distinguished by the big eyes and enlarged optic lobes that enabled it to see in the dark. This creature was well suited to being a permanent resident of the polar forests.

EVIDENCE Mainly one skull found in the Otway Range (Dinosaur Cove), south of Melbourne, Australia.

SIZE Adults were about 7 feet (2 meters) long and stood about 20 inches (50 centimeters) tall at the hip. Their heads were about 7 inches (17 centimetrers) long and they could browse up to 4 feet (1.3 meters) off the ground. They weighed about 22 pounds (10 kilograms).

DIET General herbivores, i.e. a diet of ferns, mosses, and club mosses. May have specialized in more highly nutritious parts of plants, such as fruit and new shoots.

TIME Between 112 and 104 million years ago.

MUTTABURRASAURUS

A solid, muscular herbivore, distantly related to *Iguanodon* and distinguished by an enlarged snout that might have been used to produce a distinctive call. Able to migrate in and out of the Antarctic Circle to exploit summer growth.

EVIDENCE One partial skeleton found 500 miles (800 kilometers) north of Melbourne, near Muttaburra in Queensland.

SIZE Could be as much as 30 feet (9 meters) long and about 6.5 feet (2 meter) at the hip. Browsed at anything up to 16 feet (5 meters) and weighed about 3–4 tons.

DIET Big enough to tackle most plants, i.e. cycads, ferns, and conifers.

TIME Around 110 million years ago.

DWARF ALLOSAUR

A smaller descendant of the fearsome Jurassic carnivore *Allosaurus*, but still the largest killer in the area.

EVIDENCE Controversial identification from one ankle bone found in the Otway Range, near Melbourne, Australia.

SIZE About 20 feet (6 meters) long and 5 feet (1.5 meters) at the hip, although it could probably rear to about 7 feet (2.2 meters). Its head was about 2 feet (60 centimeters) long and it weighed more than half a ton.

DIET A general carnivore and scavenger.

TIME Between 104 and 112 million years ago.

KOOLASUCHUS

A relic of a bygone age when amphibians ruled the world. Survived only in the polar forests because the water was too cold for crocodiles that dominated more equataorial regions.

Capable of walking on land, but preferred water. Distinguished by a massively powerful skull.

EVIDENCE Two jaw bones found in the Strzelecki Ranges, south of Melbourne, Australia.

SIZE Almost 16 feet (5 meters) long but only 1 foot (30 centimeters) high. It weighed more than half a ton, a large proportion of that being its 20-inch (50-centimeter)-wide skull.

DIET Fish, crayfish, mollusks; anything aquatic and small enough to fit in its huge mouth.

TIME Between 112 and 140 million years ago.

occasionally do rival Leaellynasaura actually kick or bite. Even a minor wound on animals that rely on speed and agility to escape when danger threatens can be fatal if it slows them down.

One of the Leaellynasaura on the trunk is the dominant male. He is around six years old, measuring almost 10 feet from the tip of his long, stiff tail to his pincer-like beak. Like all of his clan, his predominantly dingy–brown coloring is enlivened by a brilliant pattern of green along his back. However, what sets him apart from the others is his size. His challenger is only about three years old and at least 20 inches shorter. It is not a serious contest. The defeated male soon signifies submission by lying down and lowering his head as close to the broad trunk of the podocarp as possible. The large male could now chase him out of the clan, forcing him to survive in the forest by himself or join another

group. However, he merely turns away, the weakness of the challenge saving the smaller male from serious reprisals.

The tension subsides. The clan returns to feeding and keeps a watchful eye for predators. Many of the larger carnivores are still absent and the clan, having remained in the forest throughout the dark winter, is ideally placed to take advantage of all the new growth the moment it appears. However, they will not enjoy that privilege for long. While the days lengthen and the temperatures rise, larger herbivores migrate down from the north and start to graze through the forest. With them come predators, such as the polar allosaur, the largest and fiercest carnivore in the region. The Leaellynasaura will mate and be ready to nest and lay their eggs within eight weeks. Three weeks after that, a new generation will be running around. It is a fast reproductive cycle, but one that keeps these small and potentially vulnerable creatures a step ahead of their enemies.

Above all, these Leaellynasaura are survivors. They belong to a group of dinosaurs called the hypsilophodonts, small, bipedal herbivores that have been around since at least the middle of the Jurassic period. Fast, with powerful back legs and grasping forearms, they have thrived for millions of years in upland areas across the globe. However, these polar Leaellynasaura have a unique feature which differentiates them from their relatives. Since their chosen habitat confines them to semi- or complete darkness for much of the year, they have developed extraordinary eyesight. Their eyes are huge, and they have two tiny bumps on the back of their skulls to accommodate enlarged optic lobes.

In the dim light of the clearing the clan members browse through ferns, mosses, and liverwort, often stripping trees bare with their sharp claws or digging holes to expose fern rhizomes. Their feeding is quick and precise, and their heads are bent low while they search for nutritious morsels among last year's dead ferns. They have posted a sentinel to warn of any approaching

LEFT A challenging time: during the mating season fighting breaks out within the clan. This is a dangerous time for the little herbivores, but it ensures that only the strongest members reproduce.

danger. Perched high on a tree stump nearby, he stands erect on his back legs, making tiny movements with his rod-like tail to keep him balanced on the tree. His head is alert to the slightest sound or movement, twitching back and forth as he scans the forest. All the mature members of the clan take their turn as the lookout, giving everyone a chance to feed in peace. At the moment all is quiet, so the sentry clicks his beak to produce a chattering noise that will reassure his companions, most of whose heads are buried in the undergrowth.

At this time of year the Leaellynasaura's main concern is rival clans moving into the area and competing for the little food that is available. Although they do not have clearly defined geographical territories and will tolerate the movement of individuals between clans, as groups they are aggressive toward each other. This keeps the population evenly spread through the forest. If an area is

FROZEN IN TIME

FOR MUCH OF the twentieth century it was assumed that dinosaurs did not live near the North and South Poles. Although there were no permanent ice-caps, the poles were dark for half the year and temperatures must have fallen below a level it was thought dinosaurs could tolerate. Dinosaur bones found in Alaska in the 1960s challenged this belief since they were similar to animal remains found in the American Midwest, it was suggested that these dinosaurs might have migrated north in herds to exploit summer grazing. However, recent finds in Australia have offered another explanation. Some dinosaurs might have specialized in life at the poles.

Many millions of years ago, as Australia slowly drifted away from Antarctica, a small area of flood-plain was buried beneath the Earth's surface as the rift valley between the continents sank. Then, in the last 30 million years, the same area was pushed up again as the hard sandstone of the Otway and Strzelecki Ranges just south of Melbourne. On the coast, the sea exposed the 120-million-year-old flood-plains and the bones of animals

Dinosaur Cove is just south of Melbourne and not easily accessible. The paleontologists exploring it had to rely on support from both volunteers and commercial groups to reach the fossils in the cliffs.

particularly rich in food, the clans do not forage widely, therefore there are fewer confrontations and population density is high. Numbers within a clan may become too large to be practical and the group will split. In poor food areas the opposite is true. If lack of food causes a clan's numbers to fall drastically, it may no longer be able to hold its own against other groups, therefore it is likely to disband or become absorbed into another clan.

An hour after the first light if dawn appears on the horizon, its weak glow disappears. The first day of spring is over. Fleeting though it was, it has changed life in the depths of the polar forest irrevocably. Now both plants and animals will begin to break out of their dormant states and prepare for the 24-hour sun that is to come.

The days are getting longer quickly and there are no more morning frosts.

that had fallen there. A group of paleontologists, led by Thomas and Pat Rich, started to explore this coast in 1980. It was not an easy task. In the area that is now called Dinosaur Cove they had to use mining equipment to dig tunnels into the cliff. However, their reward was to find a distinctive community of dinosaurs which they believe had adapted to thrive in the unique dark and light regimes of the polar forest. Dominant among these animals was a group called the hypsilophodontids, small, bipedal herbivores thought to have inhabited upland areas elsewhere in the world. Several species were found, but one was of particular interest. Called *Leaellynasaura* (after the Riches' daughter), a well-preserved skull revealed not only large eye sockets, but also bumps on the back of the head that could have accommodated enlarged optic lobes. Thomas Rich has suggested that this was a specific adaptation for seeing and remaining active during the long winter darkness.

This view is controversial because it means that the *Leaellynasaura* would have had to cope with

A jewel in the rock: this is the top of a skull of the dinosaur *Leaellynasaura*. Its most striking features are the large eye sockets and the tiny bump on the back of the skull which could accommodate an enlarged optic lobe. Rich believes that *Leaellynasaura* had very good night vision, helping it survive in the long polar winter.

sub-zero temperatures and would therefore have needed some way of generating body heat (see A Hot-blooded Dispute, page 104). Not only that, but also one of the strongest arguments suggested to explain the extinction of dinosaurs is that either volcanic activity or a meteor impact filled the atmosphere with so much waste that the sun was blocked out and the world was plunged into a temporary ice age. If a group of dinosaurs had already adapted to such conditions, why didn't they survive? Unfortunately, there are so few dinosaur remains in Australia that even if they had held on there longer than elsewhere in the world, we would be lucky to find any evidence.

The Forest Awakens

The warmth of the sun now produces heavy mists that hang just below the level of the tallest trees. Beneath the tree ferns an opulent carpet of ground ferns is growing and the clan of Leaellynasaura is taking full advantage of it. They are feeding near an old river gully that has filled with water, forming a dark, still pond. Suddenly their sentry's reassuring clicking turns into a sharp hoot of alarm. Just above the edge of the pond is a low, dark cave and the sentry has spotted movement within it. The spring temperatures have woken its winter resident.

A giant Koolasuchus raises herself from the dead leaves at the back of the cave and pushes her massive head out to test the air. The entire clan focuses their attention on this huge amphibian. Her black lidless eyes, perched on top of her head, give her a perfect all-around view of the forest. She opens her mouth to reveal fearsome rows of teeth, designed for slashing and cutting up the fish that form the major part of her diet.

She slips out of her cave and drags herself along the bank, clutching at podocarp roots for leverage. As her body emerges, it is seen to be small and strangely at variance with her formidable jaws and heavy, spade-shaped skull. Away from the water, the Koolasuchus is a bewildered landlubber, out of place alongside the lithe, fast-moving dinosaurs nearby. Most of the vast amphibians that ruled the Earth long ago have since died out. Crocodiles have taken over their niches throughout the rest of the world, but at the South Pole, where her reptilian rivals would not survive the winter, the Koolasuchus clings on.

Although the moist cave is an ideal spot for hibernation because there is no danger of flooding, the small pond in front cannot supply anything like enough food for a creature the size of a Koolasuchus. She will spend the summer in the lush green waters of the river, ambushing shoals of fish with her huge gape. To vary her diet, the river will also provide her with a rich bounty of turtles, crayfish, and clams. However, the river is a 100 yards away and the Koolasuchus faces a potentially hazardous trek from her winter refuge to her summer home.

GIANT SURVIVOR FROM THE PAST

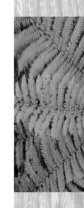

MAGINE A SALAMANDER that weighs half a ton, with teeth up to 4 inches (10 centimeters) long and you have *Koolasuchus*, one of the fiercest amphibians ever to hunt the world's rivers. It had a large, flat, spade-shaped head with powerful jaws, and its eyes, placed on top of its head, gave it clear all-around vision. A *Koolasuchus* skull also had a pattern of grooves across the surface. This was filled with nerve tissue and allowed the animal to sense vibration in the water, warning it of the approach of other creatures. Although it had a strong swimming tail, *Koolasuchus* probably hunted by lying motionless at the bottom of the river until its prey came close enough for it to spring open its huge mouth and suck them to their doom.

Evidence that *Koolasuchus* hunted in the polar forests comes from two 32-inch (80-centimeter) jaws dug up in Victoria, Australia. The most remarkable aspect of these jaws is that they are there at all. *Koolasuchus* belonged to a family of creatures called labyrinthodont amphibians, a group so old that they were already in decline when dinosaurs first appeared on Earth. It had always been thought that they died out 50 million years earlier than this find suggests, toward the end of the Jurassic period, and were replaced in similar niches throughout the world by crocodiles. However, it now seems that they hung on for some time in the extreme south. Palaeontologist Thomas Rich believes this is evidence of a "relict" fauna thriving at the South Pole. In other words, because the polar forests were an extreme environment in which many creatures found it difficult to live, animals that did manage to adapt to it had some measure of protection from those displaced to less severe habitats.

The carnivorous allosaurs were also thought to have become extinct by the time of the Australian finds, but the discoveries there included a small ankle bone. Some scientists believe this could have belonged to a pygmy species of allosaur that might have outlasted its cousins by adapting to the cold south.

Last refuge: all over the world crocodiles rule the waterways, but in the polar rivers ancient amphibians, such as this *Koolasuchus*, were still the top predators.

The *Koolasuchus* had a pattern of grooves running across its head and around its eyes. These were sensory pits for detecting vibrations in water and allowing him to hunt in muddy rivers.

She moves clumsily. Her belly drags through the leaf litter and the width of her skull makes it difficult for her to push through the tangle of last year's dead ferns. A larger predator would make short work of her, but fortunately the only creatures around to hear her crashing through the undergrowth are the Leaellynasaura, and they are already beginning to lose interest. The sentry keeps his huge eyes fixed on the giant amphibian, but he has resumed his reassuring chattering. Although the Koolasuchus would soon demolish the carcass of a Leaellynasaura that lay wounded or dying at the water's edge, she has neither the speed nor the agility to hunt on land. Even if she were to blunder into a clearing full of Leaellynasaura, she would have little chance of catching one.

After an exhausting journey the Koolasuchus reaches the banks of the wide green river. She stumbles over the pebbly beach, through a scrappy stand of horsetails and slips into the lazy flow. The water is full of small invertebrates, such as water fleas, ostracodes, and the algae, to which it owes its color. It is too opaque for Koolasuchus to see far, but now that she is back in her own domain she does not need her eyes. The pale lines that crisscross her head reveal a sophisticated sensory system for picking up vibrations in the water. While she sits motionless at the bottom of the river, her tiny brain constructs a "motion map" of her surroundings. When anything that might be potential food disturbs the patterns on this map, she is ready to leap out of the darkness.

A Moment to Breed

OCTOBER–LATE SPRING

Now the sun will not set until next March. Instead it merely dips toward the horizon every 24 hours, in token acknowledgement of the existence of night. The structure of the forest has evolved to take advantage of this low, angled light. The tallest trees, the mighty podocarps and araucarias, are spread out, forming an open upper canopy. This allows enough light through to form a denser mid-canopy of tree ferns and cycads. Below this, a very lush forest floor is covered in plants adapted to poor light. Having lain dormant all winter, these plants are now making up for lost time. Bright young fronds start to unravel from the crowns of tree ferns and new leaves fill the podocarp canopy.

Among the branches primitive birds such as Nanantius swoop from tree to tree, the iridescent blue on their backs flashing in the sunlight. Nanantius do not sing, but individuals chatter as they court, display, and challenge one another in the warm spring air. The sound mixes with the hum of spring-hatched insects. The vibrant din of life has replaced the winter silence. Somewhere in the distance the bellow of a large predator adds to the noise. For the Leaellynasaura this is not a welcome sound.

The females of the clan will soon be ready to lay their eggs. Similar to the mating, there is a sense of urgency. The young have to reach a certain size before the next winter, otherwise they will succumb to the cold. Like most dinosaurs, Leaellynasaura are ground nesters, and this is a very vulnerable time for them. They have found a slight rise in the ground under a mature tree fern. An old araucaria stump provides a good look-out point, and there is already a young male standing to attention on it, eyes scanning the forest, beak clicking reassuringly. In fact, the clan and its ancestors have used this spot several times before, but each year the search for a suitable nesting site starts again.

The female Leaellynasaura are frantically gathering leaf litter into piles. Their slim brown arms delicately shape the mounds into perfect incubators so that, when they lay their eggs, the warmth of the decomposing leaves will buffer them against variations in temperature. The dominant female builds her nest at the highest point and the others surround her. Younger females build most of the outer piles. Their nests are not situated securely and not as expertly attended. Therefore their eggs will be more vulnerable to predators and to shifts in temperature than those of the dominant female. Few of their young are likely to survive. This may seem harsh, but it is nature's way of giving some of the young the best chance of survival. The dominant pair are passing on the strongest genes and their offspring will be closely related to most of the clan. From the moment they hatch, all the clan will help to look after them. As a result, the survival rate among this dominant litter is high.

'The young have to reach a certain size before the next winter, otherwise they will succumb to the cold.'

Once the eggs are laid, the nests need constant attention. The temperature has to be monitored and the leaves changed regularly. The males and females of each pair will take turns doing this while their partners feed. However, the clan is tied to the area, which makes them vulnerable. Leaellynasaura are capable of fleeing through thick forest at incredible speed. At the sound of an alarm call they can vanish into the undergrowth instantly, running and jumping through the thickest vegetation. However, they will not willingly abandon their nest site, so their first line of defense during the incubation period is to avoid discovery altogether.

A small group of Leaellynasaura have separated from the nesting area and come down to feed on the edge of the forest near the river. At the point where a small tributary spills into the main river, the rocks are covered in a thick layer of moss, and between them new ferns and liverworts have burst into life. This is

Testing the temperature: a dominant female Leaellynasaura uses her beak to check that the nest mound is the right temperature for her eggs.

an unusually open area for the security-conscious dinosaurs, but the lure of rich new food is irresistible.

A hundred yards down the river they have been spotted. Poised behind some low podocarp scrub is an adult male allosaur. It was his call that echoed through the forest earlier. He is not a winter resident, but now that the temperatures are rising, the forests are becoming more attractive to those who spent the harsh winter elsewhere. Like the Koolasuchus, he is the last of his lineage, holed up in his polar stronghold but threatened with extinction. The allosaurids were the dominant predators of the Jurassic, but now in the Cretaceous they have been superseded, often by smaller pack hunters. This male is only about 16 feet long, a dwarf compared to his ancient ancestors, but still easily large enough to dispatch a Leaellynasaura.

Slowly he works his way through the deep scrub along the bank, his round yellow eyes constantly checking the distance between himself and his prey. His head carries a powerful jaw and his expression is sculpted into an angry frown by ridges of horny studs. The sentry cannot hear him because of the rush of the river and has not spotted the green- and yellow-striped line of his back against the scrub. The other Leaellynasaura continue to feed, occasionally looking around and sniffing the air, but equally oblivious. The allosaur picks his way carefully, but the scrub is dense and he frequently has to stop to check his position in relation to the clan.

When he reaches the last line of vegetation before the river, not 20 yards from the clan, he stops to assess his chances. He is almost three times as big as his intended prey and, in a straight race on flat ground, could run them down. However, here by the river the ground is neither flat nor straight, and the Leaellynasaura's agility and acceleration will count for everything. The only thing the allosaur has on his side is the element of surprise, and in an instant he loses it. It is hard to tell whether the sentry has seen the predator's tail move, smelled his distinctive odor, or just heard his stomach rumble, but he lets out a harsh, shrill hoot. The clan explodes in different directions. The allosaur leaps from the scrub, claws out and mouth open.

One clan member has accidentally fled toward the predator and the allosaur immediately closes in on him. While he does, the little herbivore jumps and swings his stiff tail rapidly to one side, a feat that enables him to twist and change direction in mid-air. The allosaur's mouth snaps at nothing and as he turns to try and grasp the Leaellynasaura, he loses his footing on the mossy rocks. He thrashes his arms twice and regains his balance. Only the slight angry twitch of his tail reveals any disappointment. His expressionless face scans the bank, but the clan has evaporated.

His attention is drawn by a series of deep rumbling calls further down the river. He raises his head and sniffs the air, picking up the familiar smell of his most frequent prey, Muttaburrasaurus. At the same moment a 3-ton cow

Silent hunter: a male polar allosaur waits in ambush under a tree fern. Since his eyes are on the side of his head, he has excellent all-around vision and can remain motionless while scanning for prey.

appears around a bend in the river. She is followed by another and then another until a small herd of 30 Muttaburrasaurus are advancing through the shallows. They have migrated 500 miles south from their wintering ground along the edge of the Eromanga Sea. While they moved along the coast, they formed huge migratory herds numbering many thousands. However, now they have reached the southernmost point of their journey, and they have broken into smaller groups, moving up river valleys in search of rich summer grazing.

The dwarf allosaur has tracked them for most of the journey. He is not large enough to take on a fully grown adult, and the herd structure protects many of the juveniles, but the rigors of migration take a heavy toll on the smaller animals and an allosaur is always ready to attack the weak or the sick. Because of this, the herd is dominated by older, larger individuals, some of

Back again: after a migration of almost 500 miles, the first Muttaburrasaurus arrive in the polar forest, their summer grazing grounds.

whom have been making the annual journey for decades.

Muttaburrasaurus are distantly related to Iguanodon, with their heavy back legs and smaller forearms, but they still generally walk on all fours. A big male can measure as much as 26 feet from nose to tail, making the herd a formidable wall of moving muscle. Their bodies are pale green with mottled black backs and white stomachs, but their most distinctive feature is an enlarged "Roman" nose with bright orange stripes on either side. The skin on the side of the nose is loose and when a Muttaburrasaurus wants to call, he inflates his

MONSTROUS SOUNDS

CONTROVERSY SURROUNDS THE dinosaur *Muttaburrasaurus*. It is known from only one partial skeleton, and although it is thought to be related to the *Iguanodon*, some scientists dispute this.

One thing that is clear from the fossil, discovered near Muttaburra in Australia in 1981, is that the animal had a very large

Fossil evidence shows that *Muttaburrasaurus* had a large "Roman" nose, and it is possible that skin stretched over this allowed it to produce a complex range of calls.

nose. Complex and enlarged nasal cavities are a feature of the duck-billed dinosaurs, or hadrosaurs, that flourished later in the Cretaceous and are also related to the iguanodontids. Since the beginning of the twentieth century, paleontologists have puzzled over the purpose behind this bewildering array of headgear. In some the nasal bone forms a high crest, in others a flattened helmet, and in one, *Parasaurolophus*, the nose has grown a long, backward-facing tube, like a snorkel. It was originally suggested that this decoration might help the duck-bill dinosaur to breathe while it fed on underwater plants, but then scientists realized that it was a "blind-ended" tube, meaning it is, bent over in an inverted U-shape and sealed at the top, and therefore could not act as a snorkel. It is unlikely that the tubes conferred any improved sense of smell, and even if they did, this would not explain the variety of shapes. However, they might have been highly colored and used for species or sexual identification.

More recently, after close examination of

Parasaurolophus' nasal crest, a new hypothesis has been suggested. Paleontologist David Weishampel has analyzed the air passages within the tube and concluded that the structure was designed to create sound. A powerful snort would produce a low, resonant hoot, and different-sized animals, whether babies or adult males or females, would create different tones. Weishampel even demonstrated his point by building a replica and blowing into it to produce a noise rather like that of a didgeridoo. Later he advanced the work by using a computer to calculate the resonance of the chambers and the air flow produced by *Parasaurolophus'* lungs. The computer created an eerie set of calls varying from long, low hoots to blaring squawks of alarm.

Such detailed work has not been done on the other hadrosaurs, but it would be reasonable to guess that they were all capable of making unique calls and that sound was very important to them. The one thing that has not fossilized is the soft tissue that surrounded these facial instruments, and therefore we can only guess at any sounds that might have been created.

orange sacs and expels air through his mouth, using his nasal cavity to provide resonance. The result is a distinctive low honk that carries through the dense forest and helps individual members of a herd to keep in touch with each other. By closing his mouth and driving air quickly through his nostril, a Muttaburrasaurus can also produce a penetrating high-pitched alarm call.

Calls from the first herd are answered by another group across the river. These Muttaburrasaurus have found a large fern-covered flood plain just upstream from the Leaellynasaura clan. The giant herbivores have settled there to nest and several large females have started to excavate holes in which to lay their eggs. These will be spaced one animal's length apart so that there is room for the parents to come and go without disturbing others. Each hole is 3 feet deep with a wall around it about 20 inches high. Having scraped out the earth, the female lines the nest with vegetation, lays her eggs in it, then covers them over with more leaves. Unlike the "compost heaps" used by the Leaellynasaura, the vegetation is there primarily to keep the eggs cool and out of the glare of the sun's rays.

'A distinctive low honk carries well through the dense forest and helps individual members of a herd to keep in touch with each other.'

The herd's activity has attracted the attention of the dwarf allosaur. He stands motionless on the forest edge, looking for signs of weakness. He is unlikely to find any because the long journey south has weeded out most of the old and sick. Also, on the journey up river, all the Muttaburrasaurus have fed well. In time, however, the young will hatch, the mothers will be weakened by the effort of providing for them, and the allosaur will have his meal.

In the meantime, he tests out the herd by advancing on a lone female. However, the moment his striped body appears, the herd begin to hoot alarm and make fake charges at the allosaur, hoping to scare him off. He quickly retreats, but the herd does not relax until the predator is out of sight.

With the arrival of the Muttaburrasaurus, the transformation of the forest is complete. From the dark silence of a few months ago, it has turned into a thriving habitat with many forms of life taking advantage of the endless sunlight.

The New Generation

High above the podocarps, lines of pterosaurs migrate south, their effortless flight maintained by the warm moist air rising from the forest. When they reach higher ground, they follow each other into a soaring spiral, climbing high into the sky before peeling off and gliding for many miles across the dark green landscape. Beneath the tree ferns, the Leaellynasaura clan has laid their eggs. The parents, under the watchful eye of a sentry, are tending their leaf incubators. The little dinosaurs have to work hard to keep the temperature in the nests steady at about 88°F, because the air temperature can exceed this on some days. Under the cool of the tree fern they constantly test the temperature

BRINGING UP BABY

ALTHOUGH DINOSAUR EGGS were first discovered in France in 1859 and whole nests were dug up in Mongolia in 1923, it is only recently that they have been truly appreciated as sources of information. Ingenious work on tiny egg fragments and delicate fossil nests have now produced a wealth of scientific evidence.

It is almost certain that all non-avian dinosaurs reproduced by laying eggs in nests on the ground. These nests varied from simple straight rows to carefully constructed circular depressions with rims around the outer edge. Eggs varied in size and shape, but were never much larger than a soccer ball. Their shells were hard, but contained numerous pore canals to let gases diffuse in and out, enabling the developing dinosaur to breathe. They also frequently had lumps and bumps on the surface to prevent

them from packing together too tightly. These precise adaptations, which ensured that each egg had access to sufficient oxygen, would seem to confirm that the eggs were laid and then buried under either vegetation or soil.

In 1922, on an expedition through Mongolia, paleontologist Roy Chapman Andrews discovered fossilized dinosaur nests with their eggs still arranged in neat circles. For decades these were viewed merely as interesting curios, but now paleontologists have realized how much information they can give us about the way dinosaurs behaved.

A few fossil clutches show that some dinosaur mothers took great care in arranging their eggs. In a circular clutch of 24 Troodon eggs found in Montana, the top of each elongated egg points toward the center. At another site in Montana there is evidence that some dinosaurs laid their eggs in hatcheries, with each nest one body length apart.

Clutch sizes varied enormously, but generally dinosaurs were what is called "r strategists," which means they tended to have many offspring but invested little energy in protecting them. (Mammals, on the other hand, are "k strategists." They have fewer young, but devote more time to raising them.) This has enormous implications when scientists try to work out the fate of the hatchlings.

Some finds suggest very caring mothers. A unique fossil from Mongolia shows a bipedal Oviraptor in what appears to be a brood of the nest with their beaks. Too hot and they have to pull leaves off the top, too cold and they start packing the eggs with more layers.

Temperature is not the only threat to the clan's eggs. Scampering through the leaf litter of this polar forest are several species of mammal. Few are bigger than one inch long, but some are large enough to see a dinosaur egg as a perfect meal. For millions of years mammals have been only a small part in the ever-changing drama of life on Earth, yet their numbers and species has never decreased. In fact, they have now started to increase. This is particularly true in the polar region where their warm-bloodedness and ability to hibernate have allowed them to prosper in a climate that is difficult for reptiles. Their

Usually it is impossible to match egg remains to a particular dinosaur, but just occasionally the whole embryo is fossilized inside, as with this baby *Mussaurus*. *Mussaurus* were prosauropods (see Chapter 1), and some scientists believe they looked after their hatchlings.

position over a clutch of eggs, although it is hard to prove exactly what the creature was doing there. Exquisite work by Jack Horner in Montana showed that baby *Maiasaura* were very dependent on their parents. When they hatched, their bones were still soft, and Horner found their eggshells crushed up in the nest, suggesting that, once hatched, the babies stayed there. There was also evidence of vegetation that might have been brought there by an adult.

Other fossils imply that mothers took less care of their offspring, or abandoned them altogether. Some fossil clutches have been left with the shells relatively undamaged, suggesting that the young were advanced enough to have left the nest soon after they hatched, before they crushed the empty eggs. Footprints frequently show juveniles in groups with no adults, and adult groups with no individuals under a certain size. It is very unlikely that a 60-ton sauropod, with her head on the end of a 40-foot (12-meter) neck, would have made a good mother to a brood

of several hatchlings no more than a meter (3 feet) long.

Mothering must have varied from species to species, but in most dinosaur populations there were probably many more juveniles than adults, leading independent lives by exploiting slightly different niches. Whatever they ate, bone analysis shows that baby dinosaurs grew very fast. Some hatchling sauropods put on 5–7 pounds (2–3 kilograms) a day, which is about the same growth rate as a baby blue whale fed on mother's milk. Strangely, the quality of plant food provided by conifers and ferns is very low, so it is hard to see how they obtained such a rich diet.

A valley full of the remains of a sauropod hatchery has recently been found in Argentina. Thousands of shell fragments and tiny bones litter the ground, which was probably once a river flood plain. These fossils must have survived only because they were buried in mud when the river flooded. However, there is no evidence of carefully constructed nests at the site.

Always hungry: young Leaellynasaura remain in their mound nest for up to two weeks while their bones harden and they learn to move around like the adults. During this time they are fed regurgitated vegetation by their mother and other members of the clan.

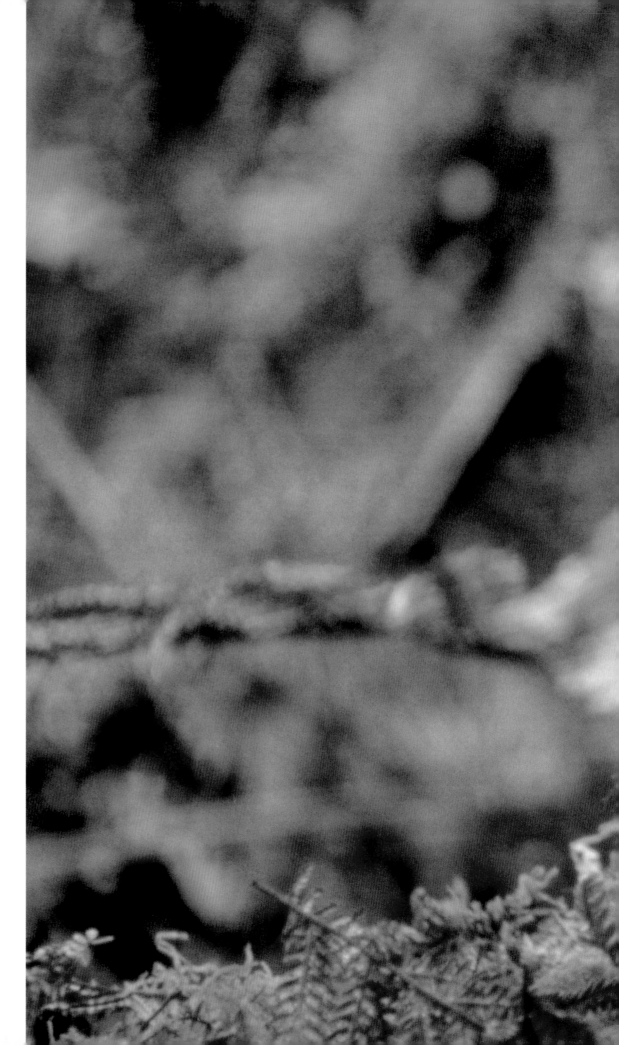

success causes problems for the clan because not only do some mammals eat eggs, but also others have turned away from their traditional diet of insects and started eating seeds and young shoots. This is direct competition, and it is with particular venom that the Leaellynasaura stamp and scratch at the leaf litter whenever they see a furry face.

One mother Leaellynasaura spots a black-haired Steropodon near an outer nest. He is one of the larger mammals, with well-developed teeth, capable of making a meal out of her eggs. Her response is a low call of alarm. She darts toward the Steropodon, who stands his ground and sits back on his hind legs, curling his lip to bare his teeth. The dinosaur is wary, and she knows the mammal can deliver a nasty bite. She turns and, using her hands, flicks leaf litter and soil at him through her back legs. Another clan member joins her. The mammal is quickly overwhelmed and retreats into the forest, but he knows where the nest site is and may be back.

During the next few weeks, mammals attack the nests repeatedly. As usual, it is the outer nests that suffer the greatest damage. However, the Leaellynasaura take turns patrolling their egg mounds and, 20 days after the eggs were laid, the ground suddenly starts to sing. From beneath their huge piles of leaves and fern fronds the young are about to hatch. They call continuously from inside their eggs as they try to break out. Carefully the parents remove the leaves to reveal their tight clusters of eggs. One by one, cracks appear in the eggs and widen as the young use their legs and backs to pry open the shells.

The moist hatchlings are no more than one foot long. Compared to the adults, their tails are short, their forelimbs long and their eyes large. Most noticeably they have bristle-like spines running around their necks and down their backs. These are important because they trap a layer of air next to the skin. Should temperatures become unseasonably cold, these long scales could help save the youngsters' lives. While the baby Leaellynasaura grow and become more active, the scales disappear. To start with, the young will stay in or

'One by one, cracks appear in the eggs and widen as the young use their legs and backs to pry open the shells.'

OPPOSITE **Tidying up: her brood having hatched, the female Leaellynasaura disposes of all the shells. There are always some eggs that fail to hatch. The mother will eat these so that she can reabsorb their nutrients.**

225

near the nest. They are not fast or agile enough to keep up with the feeding clan, although they are capable of scrabbling clear of the nest on all fours should they be discovered by a predator.

In the dominant nest, two out of the 12 eggs have not hatched. This is not uncommon, even for an experienced parent, and once it becomes obvious that no young are going to emerge, the mother consumes the eggs to conserve their nutrients and prevent the smell from attracting mammals.

The nesting area is now an odd mixture of activity and silence. For long periods the nests are quiet. The tiny brown and green nestlings sit asleep or motionless as insects buzz and hum around them, occasionally twitching while the odd mite finds a new host. A nursemaid sentry is always left on watch. The rest of the clan are out feeding as usual. The older members will not digest all their food, and some will be stored in their crops to be regurgitated back at the nest site to feed the young. When the adults return to the nesting area, they chatter and click to the sentry. The nests burst into life as the young hoot and call for attention. The dominant female regurgitates a wad of greenery and places it on the edge of her nest, where the young squabble over who should have the largest share.

Lost and found: when a hatchling wanders away from its nest, it is vulnerable. However, its short, piercing alarm call quickly attracts an attending adult.

A single lone call stops the adults feeding. One nestling has wandered from the mound and is lost. While the youngsters grow, this will happen more frequently. Two female clan members bound into the undergrowth in search of the lost nestling. He has not gone far, but is busy scrabbling in the wrong direction. One of the adults scoops him up in her forearms and carries him back to his nest. This constant care by the rest of the clan ensures that, as long as the nest site is not discovered, most of the young survive this nest-bound period.

Storm Clouds Gather

Huge rain clouds start to gather from the west. The polar forest prepares for one of its regular seasonal downpours. The rain arrives in the orange light of the summer night, turning the sky a dirty brown. There is little wind and the cool water falls in big, heavy droplets. The Muttaburrasaurus mothers stand over their nest mounds, shielding their hatchlings from the worst of the downpour, water bouncing off their speckled green backs. The noise of the rain drowns out the forest chatter and the surface of the wide river shimmers with raindrops in the dull light. Under the fern canopy, the Leaellynasaura clan is protected from the direct rain, but soon the water starts to run down the fronds and drip onto the nest site. The young, now fully mobile, are huddled in a small crèche around an adult.

The rain continues through the night and much of the following day. The river starts to swell and one by one the sandbanks disappear. On their flood-plain nursery the Muttaburrasaurus show little concern, but if the rain continues for much longer, their mounds could be in trouble. The Leaellynasaura are more mobile, but the forest floor, soaking up the moisture like a huge sponge, is becoming sodden, and small ponds begin to appear.

Then, as if in response to an invisible signal, the rain stops and within minutes the clouds break to let through the midday sun. Although the sun never reaches the same height as it does at the Equator, it is still strong enough to send temperatures rocketing. Within an hour the forest is steaming. A thin mist fills the understory and picks out every shaft of sunlight. Many of the animals sit and enjoy a steam bath amid the leaf litter and dense fern thickets. Unfortunately, with the clearer weather, the insects return, among them dense clouds of biting flies. The female flies need to drink plenty of dinosaur blood if their bodies are to manufacture enough protein to produce eggs. When they rise from the river margins, the flies identify potential hosts from the carbon dioxide they breathe out.

Over most of their bodies, dinosaurs are immune to insect bites. The flies' mouthparts cannot penetrate the mosaic of scales typical of dinosaur skin.

However, even the giants of the Mesozoic era have some soft spots. When the Muttaburrasaurus relax on the steaming flood plain, biting flies gather around their eyes, noses, and ears. Rows of insects line the soft tissue of their orange nose sacs, and their tranquil steam bath becomes increasingly uncomfortable. Several adults toss their heads in irritation and shift around, trying to avoid the swarms. Within minutes, a number of 3-ton dinosaurs are being driven from their resting places by insects only a millimeter long.

The newly hatched Muttaburrasaurus, sitting in their nest hollows, cannot move away easily and soon the same swarms plague them. The flies carry a blood-borne disease that can cause anaemia in the Muttaburrasaurus, although this is rarely a primary cause of death. More often than not it merely slows them down and a predator's teeth finishes them off.

SUCKING DINOSAUR BLOOD

I N THE BOOK *Jurassic Park*, the dinosaurs are created from the genetic material left in a mosquito after it has drunk blood from a dinosaur and then become stuck in tree sap, which over millions of years became solid amber. Like the best science fiction, half of this story is true. Amber *has* shown that dinosaurs must have been plagued by tiny blood-sucking flies.

Entomologists can tell a lot about an insect from its mouthparts, and fossilized biting midges found in Canada still bear witness to the huge prey whose blood they must once have drunk. Modern midges often feed exclusively on specific host animals, which may be birds, mammals, reptiles, or even other insects. Special sensory hairs on the midges' mouthparts help them find their prey by detecting the gaseous plume of carbon dioxide given off by the animals as they breathe. Midges that regularly suck the blood of small hosts, such as birds and other insects, have lots of these sensory hairs. Those that feed on larger prey tend to have fewer. The biting midge fossils have very few of these hairs and, at the time these fossils were alive, the only prey large enough to explain this were dinosaurs.

Since skin impressions from dinosaurs mostly show that they had close-fitting scales, the midges must have concentrated on soft skin areas, such as eyelids, nostrils, and ears. Some scientists claim that the few heat-sensor hairs on the antennae of the Canadian fossils support the idea that dinosaurs were warm-blooded. However, living species of midge that feed on fish (which are cold-blooded) frequently have heat sensors, and some midges that feed on mammals (which are warm-blooded) do not, so this evidence is not conclusive.

Amber preserves insects beautifully, even when they are millions of years old. Cretaceous amber has revealed that dinosaurs must have been tormented by biting flies.

An allosaur comes down to drink by the river. He has obviously just made a kill. His green snout and jaw are splashed with dark blood. He, too, is tormented by flies, shaking his head and clawing with his forearms to disperse the mat of insects around his eyes. He dips his head in the water and drags it from side to side, providing temporary relief.

The Leaellynasaura are more used to the flies, and their sleep is disturbed not by insects but by juveniles from their own clan, playing in the steam. While the youngsters jump and skip among the adults, they learn crucial moves that could one day save their lives. Their bodies are fast assuming the proportions of an adult and their tails are stiffening. Many have lost the long scales with which they were born. They are also trying out new foods, such as club mosses, liverwort, young ferns, and podocarp seedlings they find on the forest floor.

Plagued by insects: an adult Muttaburrasaurus is surrounded by a swarm of biting flies. Most of his skin is too thick for them to penetrate, but they cluster in his ears and around his eyes.

After a couple of hours of sunlight the steam clears and a wind picks up, dispersing the tormenting clouds of flies. The clan moves nearer the river to graze. As usual, the adults settle down to frantic scratching and nibbling among the vegetation. The sentry perches on a collapsed cycad looking out for any enemies who might be lurking nearby. Occasionally, some of the clan drink from the river's edge. It is probably the noise of their lapping and splashing that attracts the attention of a Koolasuchus lying at the bottom of the river. Although the amphibian would be lucky to catch a fully grown Leaellynasaura, a juvenile is a different matter.

Close call: a young Leaellynasaura leaves the clan to drink in the river, unaware of the danger from predators such as Koolasuchus. Fortunately, he is fast enough to leap clear of the giant amphibian's ambush and he returns to the protection of an adult.

While she moves into the shallows, the Koolasuchus not only senses their vibrations but also, with her all-around vision, she sees the clan on the bank. Despite her size, her head and body are almost flat, allowing her to move through a mere two feet of water and remain invisible from the bank. At this point the bank drops steeply down to the river's edge. When one young Leaellynasaura drinks, he does not realize he is only one jaw length away from the huge amphibian.

The Koolasuchus lunges and the clan scatters, but it is too late for the youngster to turn and run. Instead he leaps upward, a move he has practiced in play. When the Koolasuchus snaps her mouth shut, he lands on top of her head, tumbles off to one side, and stumbles back up the bank. Out of the water the Koolasuchus cannot move her head fast enough for a second snap and instead stops where she is, watching the retreating dinosaur. Meanwhile, the rest of the clan returns. The juvenile hoots with distress, but the adults recognize that the threat is not serious and start to taunt the Koolasuchus. The frustrated amphibian retreats into the water, but not before she has been pelted with mud and pebbles by the clan.

The Last Flourish

FEBRUARY–LATE SUMMER

The days are still warm and long, but there are a few signs that the year is progressing toward autumn. The female podocarps are developing their distinctive red "fruit" and many ferns are heavy with spores. Among the dinosaurs, the young are gaining weight and keeping pace with the adult groups. On the edge of the flood plain a dwarf allosaur has brought down an old male Muttaburrasaurus. The rest of the herd continue grazing nearby, apparently unconcerned. It is difficult to judge why the predator has been successful this time. The old bull could have been wounded or ill, but it is a big kill for the allosaur and he will not be able to eat it all himself.

Out of the fern thicket, another allosaur approaches, drawn by the smell of a fresh kill. He is smaller and advances with head lowered. This could be a submissive pose, but it also puts him in a good position to retreat should the larger allosaur react badly to his approach. In fact, a bad reaction is almost guaranteed. Allosaurs are lone hunters and do not willingly give up kills. The larger predator stops feeding and freezes in an aggressive pose, letting out a low hiss. The interloper continues to advance, presenting the first with a dilemma. There is far more meat here than he can eat and more carnivores are bound to arrive soon. Does he waste time and energy fighting off the new-comer, or does he eat his fill and leave? He obviously decides on the less aggressive option and returns to the carcass, contenting himself with an occasional hiss or snap in the direction of the other allosaur. While the two predators feed, smaller dinosaurs and even a few mammals arrive and hover in the fern thicket, waiting for leftovers. The carcass will last a few days, but eventually everything will be eaten.

Deep in the forest a cacophony of hooting breaks out. The clan is feeling threatened, not by a predator or a pack of mammals, but by other Leaellynasaura. The sentry has spotted a rival group grazing nearby and the entire clan responds aggressively. Adults of both sexes advance through the ferns, bobbing and hooting threateningly. The intruders hoot back and chatter, but do not retreat. The assault party moves nearer, still bobbing and jumping. When they are close enough, they flick litter in the direction of the other clan. However, the newcomers are only probing the first clan's strength, hoping to find them weakened by illness or injury. When the home team put up a good show, the confrontation evaporates. The interlopers quickly bound back to their own part of the forest.

Later in the day the Muttaburrasaurus herd moves along the edges of the forest in search of podocarp and cycad fruit among the branches. Raised up on their hind limbs, their beaks can reach to a height of 16 feet or more. Although their forelimbs are primarily designed for walking, with small hooves at the end of their digits, they can be used to great effect to drag down

The kill: a dwarf allosaur has brought down an old Muttaburrasaurus. After he has eaten his fill, the remains of the 4-ton carcass will feed many other predators.

ABOVE Every year the podocarps fruit, providing a late bounty for the herbivores in the forest. The distinctive red berries are in fact swollen stems with the seeds at the end.

branches during feeding. The juveniles now browse with the main herd and, like the adults, will eat anything that does not move. Their huge digestive tracts are capable of extracting nutrients from the most unlikely plant material, even the sharp, resin-covered, poisonous leaves of the cycads.

The clan is attracted to the sound of the Muttaburrasaurus. They know they are not threatened by the giant herbivores. If anything, they are safer among the herd, hidden from predators by their vast bulk. Also, the Muttaburrasaurus

LEFT **Dinosaurs in the mist: in the low light of late summer three Muttaburrasaurus feed on young podocarps. Around their feet a clan of Leaellynasaura pick up the podocarp fruits (above) that the large dinosaurs drop.**

are messy eaters, spilling podocarp fruit on the ground as they clutch and bite at the trees. The Leaellynasaura scamper among the feeding herd, plucking the leftovers from around their feet. Despite the benefits of scrounging a free meal, however, there is risk attached to this activity. With 3-ton giants stamping and stumbling around them, the clan members have to be prepared to move quickly while they feed or they are in danger of being squashed by their huge benefactors.

Winter's First Bite

Shortly after another heavy downpour, the sun finally slips beneath the walls of the rift valley toward the west. In the dim gray light the forest shivers. There will be no steam baths for the animals for many months to come. From now on the nights will rapidly become longer. Soon complete darkness will blanket the clan's home. There is a chill in the air and the character of the forest seems to be changing. Pterosaurs are already filing back from the darkening south and many bird species are following.

At the first sign of sunset, the Muttaburrasaurus herd becomes agitated and start a twilight call. Their loud, low bellows echo across the forest and are

answered by other distant herds. After a summer dispersed among the rich polar feeding grounds, thousands of Muttaburrasaurus will come together, drawn by the urge to migrate north once more, chasing the dwindling sun.

Ironically, given that its population is rapidly diminishing, this is probably the noisiest time of year in the forest. A clan of Leaellynasaura, feeding on the forest edge, is forced into the open by a group of Muttaburrasaurus. Immediately, one Leaellynasaura darts for a high vantage point to act as sentry, but the herd is causing a lot of disturbance, and the noise of its calling deprives him of the use of one of his senses. This is unfortunate, since slowly creeping toward them through the podocarp scrub is an allosaur. Still worse, the movement of the herd is pushing the Leaellynasaura toward her.

When they come closer, the allosaur slowly flexes her claws and shifts from leg to leg. Oblivious to the danger, the sentry tumbles off his perch again and the clan breaks up, intending to run through the herd to the safety of the forest. Right at this moment the predator strikes. She is on open ground, the Leaellynasaura have no warning and their attention is on the herd. A supreme killer like the allosaur does not need any more help than this. Her jaw closes on a male subadult before he even sees her and, with one flick of her neck, she breaks his back.

The allosaur stands over the body of her victim with a strip of Leaellynasaura skin hanging from her teeth. The effort of her attack hardly registers in her breathing. She bends down and nudges the carcass. Then, placing her foot firmly on the rib cage, she locks her jaw around the Leallynasaura's hip and tears off a leg. Lifting her head she throws the leg to the back of her throat to swallow it whole.

Not far away, in the sanctuary of the forest, the clan is soon restored to calm. While they regroup, a sentry takes up his post on a nearby podocarp trunk.

LEFT When the days start to shorten, a small family group of Muttaburrasaurus begins the long trek north, leaving behind a forest that will soon be in 24-hour darkness.

Ambush in the forest: the allosaur is a very effective ambush predator. Even though the Leaellynasaura are faster, if he can get close enough, they stand no chance. One bite of his jaws can break their backs.

Darkness Descends

APRIL—WINTER ARRIVES

Cold comfort: a female Leaellynasaura breaks the ice on a pond with her beak. Even in winter, temperatures this low are rare in the forest and they put the little herbivores under enormous stress.

Every day twilight comes earlier. A wintry silence settles across the plain. Even at its height, the weak gray sunlight barely penetrates to the gloom of the forest floor. The Leaellynasaura are still busy. Although most of the ferns have turned woody and brown, there is plenty of rotting fruit and fungus. The clan is also adept at digging for roots and rhizomes.

During this damp period, the Koolasuchus rises to the edge of the river and waits. Probably driven by the fading light, she is leaving the river to return to her dark cave in the forest. Just as it was in the spring, this is a hazardous expedition, taking her out of her element. However, the larger summer residents have long since left. She pulls her black glossy body out of the water, struggles up the bank, and trundles into the forest. The clan is nowhere near and she reaches the pond within an hour, unmolested. Then she works her way along its muddy banks to find her cave. The entrance has become overgrown during the summer, but she recognizes the smell and pushes her way through the ferns. Once inside, she settles among the moist litter and prepares for hibernation.

The sky begins to clear just as the sun sets for one final time behind the western horizon, turning the evening clouds red. Most of the clan stop feeding. The clear skies mean that, for the first time this year, the temperature drops toward freezing. The Leaellynasaura huddle in groups, sharing each other's body warmth. It is dark and still among the dormant trees. High above, the sky is alive with curtains of greens and purples that whip and roll across the polar night. They are the Southern Lights, visible again for the first time in months.

The weeks pass and cold has gripped the forest. There have been warm periods during the long polar night, but now frost covers the leaves in even the deepest parts of the forest. The mammals, so common in the summer, are nowhere to be seen since they have retreated into their burrows.

Outside, the clan of Leaellynasaura remains active in the darkness, their keen eyes picking out what food the forest has to offer. They do not possess the mammals' ability to hibernate, but as the temperature continues to drop, they start to behave strangely. They gather into a huddle, wrapping their long legs and necks around each other. Then slowly they all stop moving. The low temperatures have forced them into a state of torpor. Like hibernation, torpor saves precious energy, but it is a short-term response and may happen several times in the course of the winter. When temperatures rise again, the Leaellynasaura quickly revive and break into activity.

Turning Full Circle
THE RETURN OF SPRING

Sunrise, and a watery blue light spills across a silent landscape. Spring is returning to the polar forest. Beneath the open canopy and the spreading tree ferns, a dark brown pond fringed with ice gently steams in the cold morning air. The sunlight reveals the frozen body of a small green and brown dinosaur on its banks. It is the dominant female Leaellynasaura. Her perfectly preserved body suggests that she died of exposure during a severe cold snap.

In the center of the pond, the brown water parts to reveal a huge flattened head with vacant black eyes. The head waits motionless, watching the bank for movement, then slips toward the dead Leaellynasaura. The water surface hardly registers the smooth movement. The Koolasuchus has woken early this year and is in need of food. She rises out of the pond and clamps ahold of the lifeless body. Slowly she drags her prize into the water.

Nearby the rest of the clan are scraping the last morsels of winter food from the forest floor before the new growth of spring. Another Leaellynasaura has replaced the dominant female in the hierarchy and the males are beginning to fight. The year has come full circle and it is the mating season again.

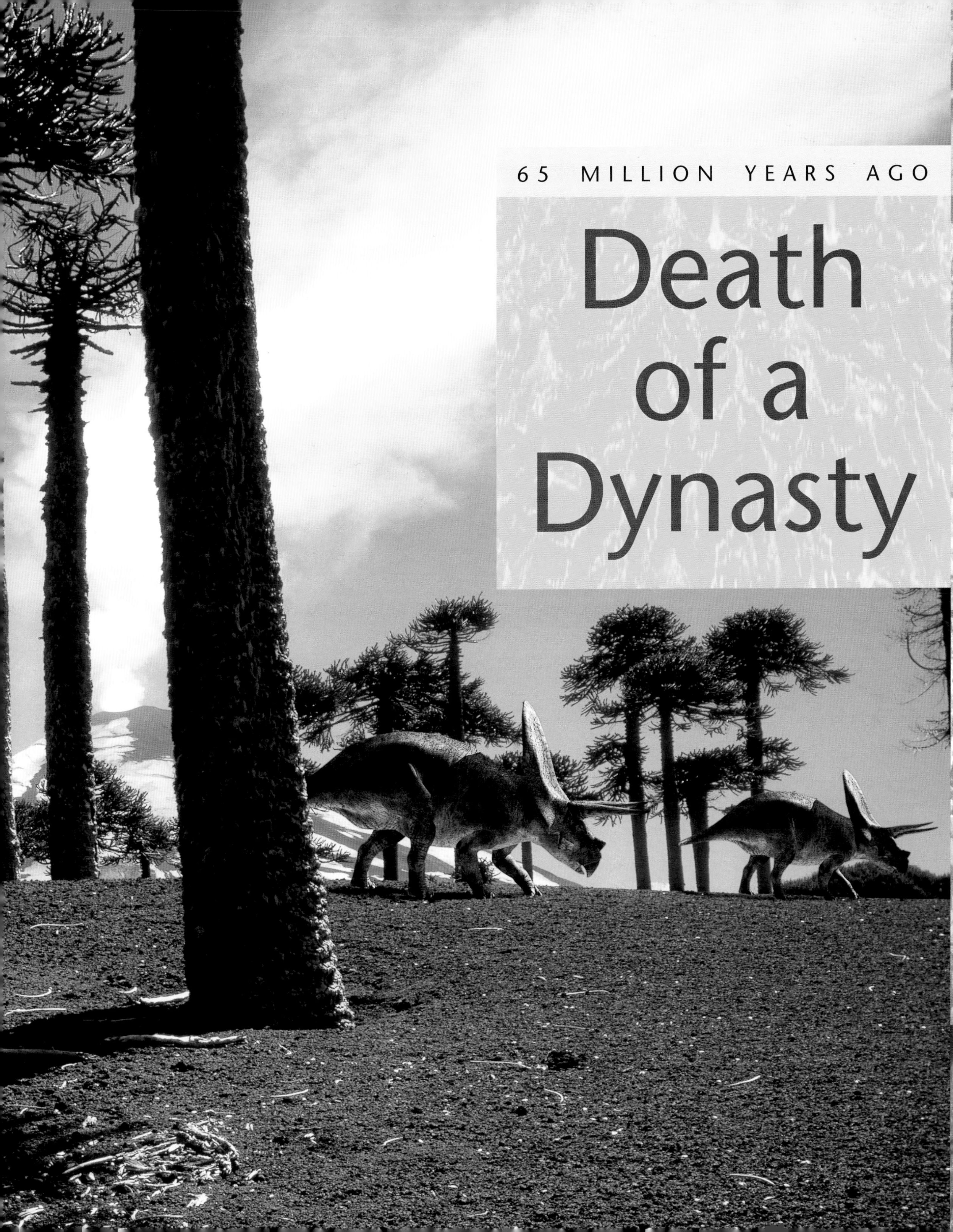

65 MILLION YEARS AGO

Death of a Dynasty

6

THE EARTH 65 MILLION YEARS AGO. The Earth's Mesozoic era is drawing to a close and most of the huge old landmasses are now divided up into smaller continents. For 180 million years the world has been warm, with no ice-caps and little change between the seasons. However, this long period of apparent stability has been deceptive. The same epoch has witnessed massive changes among all its living creatures, including the evolution of most of the modern groups of animals.

The landscape has transformed from a dry world dominated by conifer forests to a moist green place full of flowering plants. This has favored the small mammals and birds, two groups that have steadily increased in number and variety, as have the ubiquitous insects. However, there have also been losers. Gone are the ichthyosaurs and pliosaurs in the oceans, with the ammonites in sharp decline. Only one or two giant

Scene of desolation: with the volcano still smouldering in the background, a family of Torosaurus cross an ash field in search of food. The only plants to survive the recent eruption are mature araucaria trees, whose branches are too high for the dinosaurs to reach.

species of pterosaurs remain, and the explosion of flowers has driven many species of fern and cycad to extinction. Through all of this, dinosaurs have remained hugely successful and show no signs of decline. Vast herds of new herbivores have evolved to graze on the soft flowering vegetation, and different predators have appeared to eat them. None of these is more fearsome than Tyrannosaurus, the king of the dinosaurs.

However, there are major environmental changes on the way, and events are conspiring to subject life on Earth to its biggest test since the massive Permian extinction. Subtle alterations in the world's atmosphere and a catastrophe plummeting down from outer space is about to bring this last age of the giant reptiles to an abrupt end.

Glorious blooms: at the end of the Mesozoic, flowering plants have become hugely successful. For much of the Cretaceous they have grown no larger than shrubs, but now there are several varieties of flowering trees forming dense forests.

DINOSAURS FOR EVER

EVEN BEFORE ANY disaster struck, the end of the Cretaceous was a time of change. Globally, temperatures started to fall. This did not lead to the formation of icecaps, but life at the poles was hit hard and the lush polar forests, which had been rich enough to leave behind coal deposits, died out, to be replaced by more open habitats. At the same time, sea levels were falling and this led to the loss of the epicontinental seas. Toward the end of this period, pterosaurs went into decline. The only forms that survived were the huge, toothless species that specialized in fishing. Birds continued to thrive and diversify. Among the new species were flightless marine forms, similar to modern

Snakes appeared toward the end of the age of dinosaurs and are, therefore, a relatively recent group of reptiles. One theory behind their lack of legs suggests they originally lost them adapting to aquatic life.

divers. However, it was not competition with birds that finished off the pterosaurs. Instead, as temperatures across the world dropped and the sea currents around continents

altered, the weather became more unpredictable, making it more difficult for these vast creatures. The loss of warm, shallow seas also robbed them of their favorite hunting grounds. From then on, the group was doomed.

In the water, other reptiles were in decline. Ichthyosaurs had already died out and plesiosaurs and the sea lizards, mosasaurs, were also going. Other marine creatures were suffering. Reef-forming clams, squid-like belemnites, and even the ever-present ammonites were disappearing.

On land, flowers became the dominant type of plant, representing 50–80 percent of all species. This success was mostly at the

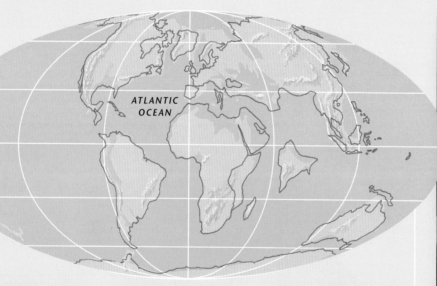

ATLANTIC OCEAN

Sixty-five million years ago the world's continents had started to take on a modern configuration. The Atlantic Ocean had almost completely separated the New World from the Old World. The giant southern continent of Gondwana broke up as Australia moved north and

Antarctica settled over the South Pole. India continued north on a collision course with Asia. The inland seaway that had split the North American landmass for so many millions of years retreated. Sea levels rose and fell, with land bridges occasionally connecting Asia

to Europe, Africa to Europe, and South and North America to each other. Despite this there was a tendency for continents to develop their own endemic range of plants and animals. Places such as Australia and Madagascar remain unique to the present day.

expense of cycads and ferns. Insect-specific flowers had evolved, as had the first social bees and ants. However, most flowers still relied on wind or general insect feeding for pollination. A few flowering plants had developed into trees, and in the south the southern beech did well. Around the Equator palms grew in large numbers. In most places conifers continued to dominate the upper-story, pines and redwoods to the north and podocarps and Araucaria to the south. In the colder temperatures pines did particularly well at high latitudes and altitudes, which they still do today.

Animal populations varied enormously from one continent to another, but there was

no shortage of dinosaurs. In western North America the herbivores included armored ankylosaurs, ostrich-like ornithomimids, and dome-headed pachycephalosaurs, but the duck–billed hadrosaurs were by far the most successful. During the late Cretaceous, numbers of horned dinosaurs increased to make them the second largest group of grazers. They were hunted by small carnivores, such as raptors, and considerably larger ones, such as *Tyrannosaurus*. Another curious predator was *Troodon*. With its grasping hands and large eyes, it was potentially a specialist night hunter and its most likely prey were mammals, whose numbers were rising rapidly. One species to emerge as this time was the marsupial *Didelphodon*, related to the modern-day opossum.

Many of these American creatures also occurred in Asia because the two continents were periodically joined by a land bridge at the Bering Straits. However, dry central Asia appears to have had a unique mixture of small bipedal dinosaurs and birds. During this time, Europe was a collection of large islands, and in the mid-Cretaceous also shared many dinosaurs with America. However, as the Atlantic opened up, it became isolated, developing its own raptors, duck-bills, and armored dinosaurs. Some islands showed signs of this isolation by protecting animals that were extinct elsewhere and developing dwarf species. Fossil finds of southern Gondwana predators and herbivores in Spain and France also suggest that land bridges with Africa might have opened.

For the last few million years of the Mesozoic the duck-bills or hadrosaurs were by far the most successful group of dinosaurs. There are many superb fossils of these animals.

The southern continents of South America, Africa, Madagascar, Australia, India, and Antarctica were all separate, but shared a common difference from the north. The titanosaurids, or southern sauropods, were the dominant herbivores and the predators belonged to a group known as the abelisaurs. *Tyrannosaurus* never seemed to have ventured south, even though there is evidence of a North/South American land bridge. Perhaps this is because some abelisaurs grew as large and fearsome as *Tyrannosaurus*. Unfortunately, the fossil record for this period on these southern continents remains poor, so it is difficult to construct a complete global picture. However, there was no sign that dinosaurs were about to disappear off the face of the planet.

Palms were among the earliest flowering plants to grow as trees. With their spreading crown of leaves and tough stems, they look like cycads, but the similarity is superficial.

The evolution and success of many insects seems to parallel the increasing complexity of flowers. Late Cretaceous fossils show fused petals and funnel-shaped flowers, which would have depended on insects pollinating them.

Moths belong to one of the most common groups of today's insects, called Lepidoptera. Over time, most have become specially adapted to feed on flowers.

A Fading Paradise

It is the wet season on the eastern coast of Laramidia and a dense fog has blown in from the Pierre Seaway. It is typical of this time of year. These warm, moist mists can sometimes lie over the low plains for several days, trapped in the still air between the mountains and the shallow sea. The forests here are unique, with trees covered in plants that absorb moisture from the air. The trunks of the giant araucaria are swathed with light green lichen covering and softening their craggy bark. Dense layers of moss also hang from the branches of the southern beech, and even the low shrubs, such as magnolia and bay, drip with long clumps of moss. In marshy areas the layers of green dressing are even thicker, making the huge swamp cypress that grow there almost unrecognizable. From higher ground, the whole area looks as if it is covered in a thick, green blanket, which is why it is called the Blanket Forest.

However, this beautiful forest is under threat. Only a few hundred miles to the north, where the plains open out, the blanket is completely absent. Each year the seaway is slowly retreating further south, and with it go the fogs. The range of the Blanket Forest has shrunk to a few thousand square miles, a small percentage of what it once was. Its prospects of survival as a habitat are made even more bleak by its mountainous neighbors. Dominating the uplands is a series of snow-capped volcanoes, which are dotted every few miles down the length of the range. They are young and active, and in several places long black tongues of old lava reach into the forest. Many of the volcanoes have constant plumes of smoke and ash drifting from their peaks, and the sulfur frequently mixes with the fogs, making them more acidic. Some of the more delicate plants have already disappeared, and the exposed trees are losing their coverings altogether. Although the region supports a wide variety of animals that have adapted to life under the blanket, many are now endangered.

At the forest's edge on some raised ground, a pair of female Ankylosaurus tear at the moss and lichen. Although not endangered, these extraordinary creatures are rare. They are visitors here, attracted to the forest by the amount of greenery within their reach. They are not choosy feeders and use their long

A FINAL FLING

EVIDENCE FOR ALL the animals in this chapter comes from the Hell Creek Formation in the western United States (see page 277), or from associated fossil beds. All of them seem to have flourished right up until the sudden disappearance of the dinosaur. Many of them represent the largest or most decorative of their group. In the past this has been used as evidence that the dinosaurs became too big and lumbering to survive and that is why they died out. However, this is to forget the giant sauropods and the fact that dinosaurs reinvented themselves several times during their long history. There is no obvious reason why these should have been the last of the dinosaurs. Instead, being so large and well-preserved, it is not surprising that the Hell Creek dinosaurs are some of the most famous.

The Pierre Seaway is all that is left of the old Western Interior Seaway that once separated Laramidia from Appalachia, and it is slowly retreating south. Volcanic mountains run down the spine of Laramidia, with the Blanket Forest on its eastern flanks.

TYRANNOSAURUS

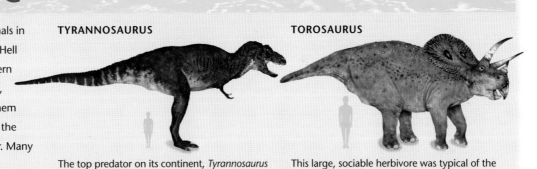

The top predator on its continent, *Tyrannosaurus* had longer teeth and a larger head than any other terrestrial carnivore, yet it also had a short body and short arms.
EVIDENCE Over 20 individuals have been found, most of them in recent years. Only three complete skulls are known, but remains have been discovered all the way from Alberta to New Mexico.
SIZE About 45 feet (14 meters) long and could have weighed up to 5 tons. Its mouth had a gape of over 3 feet (1 meter) and could probably remove as much as 150 pounds (70 kgs) of meat in one bite.
DIET A top predator, exclusively carnivorous.
TIME 67–65 million years ago.

ANKYLOSAURUS

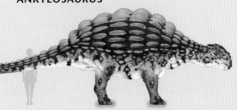

The biggest of all the armored dinosaurs, *Ankylosaurus'* body had become one fused box. Its skull was so heavily reinforced that there was little room for a brain inside, but its wide hips contained a huge gut for digesting any plant material thrown in there.
EVIDENCE Three fairly complete specimens from Alberta, Wyoming, and the Hell Creek Formation in Montana.
SIZE About 33 feet (10 meters) long and about 10 feet (3 meters) at the hip. For its size, it was very heavy, around 7 tons.
DIET Herbivore, feeding on low vegetation.
TIME 70–65 million years ago.

TOROSAURUS

This large, sociable herbivore was typical of the horned dinosaurs, with a powerful beak for grazing and three horns on its face. Its unique characteristic was the largest of all display crests.
EVIDENCE Seven partial skulls and several pieces of skeleton from Alberta to New Mexico.
SIZE Almost 25 feet (8 meters) in length, with a skull (including crest) of over 6 feet 6 inches (2 meters). Weighed around 7 tons.
DIET Very strong beaks allowed it to tackle the toughest of vegetation, even small branches.
TIME 67–65 million years ago.

ANATOTITAN

Anatotitan was closely related to *Edmontosaurus*, some of the largest hadrosaurs, or duck-billed dinosaurs, ever to have lived.
EVIDENCE Three species of *Edmontosaurus* have been identified in Hell Creek and nearby formations, based on about 16 skulls and associated skeletal elements. Three skulls and partial skeletons of a creature identified as *Anatotitan* have also been found at Hell Creek, but it has recently been suggested that this might have been a large *Edmontosaurus*, and that *Anatotitan* did not exist after all.
SIZE *Edmontosaurus* was about 40 feet (12 meters) long, stood about 11 feet (3.5 meters) at the hip and weighed about 4 tons. *Anatotitan* was about 43 feet (13 meters) and 5 tons.
DIET General herbivores.
TIME 67–65 million years ago.

APPALACHIA

LARAMIDIA

PIERRE SEAWAY

tongues and sharp beaks to crop anything up to a couple of yards off the ground, whether it is leaf, lichen, or twig. However, they only graze at the edge of the forest because their huge bulk prevents them from entering into the denser areas.

Looking at the Ankylosaurus in the thick fog, with moisture running off their shiny black backs, there is no doubt that these are armored dinosaurs. Since the days of their distant relative Polacanthus, this group of animals has developed a heavier defensive covering. Instead of having light, strong skele-

tons like many dinosaurs, their bones have gone into overdrive, fusing verte-brae, ribs and bony plates to create an impenetrable armor. At around 32 feet long and weighing over seven tons, Ankylosaurus is the largest of them all. Their backs are heavily plated and covered in low spines, and their heads have fused into dense, reinforced boxes. Even their eyelids are armored. Their tails are stiffened and at the end of each sits a large, bony club. While the females crop the lichen, this lethal weapon bobs quietly from side to side. However, if needed, it could smash the leg of the largest predator.

These formidable defensive weapons protect the solitary lifestyle of the Ankylosaurus. Despite being slow, they have no need for herd security and they also do not appear to have the intelligence for sophisticated social behavior. The enormous thickening of their skulls has left only a small space for the brain. Most of their senses are poor, except for a keen nose. Occasionally, in the Blanket Forest, females can be drawn together by the smell of good grazing, but the males are aggressive loners and never tolerate the presence of other Ankylosaurus unless there is a chance of mating.

Having stripped the lichen from the base of a large arau-caria, the females turn and head downhill to another patch of thick blanket moss. When they leave, they cross a small, open area where volcanic rock shows through the light fern scrub. The clearing is surrounded by gigantic trees which disappear into the fog above. In the center, a huge pile of moss and lichen has been dumped as if it had fallen from the branches overhead. When they pass this heap, the Ankylosaurus stop and sniff the air while their tails flick nervously back and forth. Something in the scent from the pile worries them. One bellows and hurries out of the clearing, quickly followed by her companion.

The pile of vegetation is a Tyrannosaurus nest and it stinks of this ruthless predator. Normally, a female

LEFT **Built to survive: a 7-ton Ankylosaurus sniffs out some fresh new growth of southern beech. His heavily armored back, massive club tail, and reinforced skull make him almost impervious to attack, even from the mighty Tyrannosaurus.**

Tyrannosaurus protects her nest closely, but this clearing is unnaturally silent. There is a hint of another smell coming from the nest, the odor of decay.

The noise of the Ankylosaurus disturbs a small, hairy Didelphodon that has been burrowing at the edge of the pile. He sits up to sniff the air. His whiskers twitch while his eyes strain to follow the retreating bulk of the Ankylosaurus disappearing into the mist. Didelphodon is one of the largest mammals in this forest, weighing several pounds. His black and gray coat is soaked by the moist air and the damp pile of moss he has been excavating. Once he is sure that the dinosaurs have left, he cleans himself, meticulously working over his belly fur to make sure he has not picked up any mites. The same smell that repulsed the Ankylosaurus has attracted this little opportunist. A Tyrannosaurus egg is a huge meal for a Didelphodon. He starts to wash his face just as a large shadow passes over him.

'Every mother Tyrannosaurus will defend her nest to the death, and she is larger and more powerful than a male.'

The Didelphodon is fast, but he has no time to use his quick reactions. He has failed to spot a male Tyrannosaurus silently stalking him a few yards away. A short lunge is all the giant carnivore needs in order to grab the mammal, impaling him on his long teeth and then flipping back his head to swallow him whole. Tyrannosaurus are the largest predators on the continent, in fact, one of the largest predators ever. This young male is 40 feet long and weighs nearly 5 tons. However, he is not a caring parent protecting the nest. He has been attracted for the same reason as the Didelphodon. He smelled the pile of moss and is hungry. To the male a clutch of a dozen or so large eggs is not only food, but also an opportunity to eliminate potential competitors even before they hatch. He knows he has to be careful. Every mother Tyrannosaurus will defend her nest to the death, and she is larger and more powerful than the male.

This wariness of the mother is the reason he stalked the nest so cautiously and that the Didelphodon did not hear him. In fact, he has probably been watching the site for some time. Females often hide themselves nearby and appear only if there is a threat. However, since the Ankylosaurus were not chal-

lenged, the male Tyrannosaurus felt bold enough to move in. Standing over the nest, he checks the scent signals. A mother Tyrannosaurus continually attends to her eggs, turning the nest pile and ensuring a constant temperature for incubation, but this nest is too cold. Now that the male is close to it, he can smell the decay. He claws at the pile with his back legs, then reaches down with his tiny forearms to pull the eggs out.

Soon the clutch of long, cream–colored eggs is revealed and, still checking regularly in case the female should return, he picks them up one by one and swallows them. Having such long teeth, he breaks several eggs in the process and small, immature Tyrannosaurus embryos slither out. He eats them as well. Looking at the fragments of eggshell, it is clear why the female abandoned the nest. Many of the eggs were broken long before the male arrived, their rotting

High-risk meal: a Didelphodon feeds on a Tyrannosaurus embryo. A mother Tyrannosaurus usually protect her nests, even from small mammals. However, if the eggs fail, the giant predator will abandon them, leaving a feast for smaller creatures, such as Didelphodon.

contents being the source of the smell. With such large eggs the exact thickness of the shell is vital. The mother creates the eggshell just before she lays and it would appear in this case that something upset the process. The shells are uneven, suffocating the embryos under too many layers of calcium in some places and cracking through weakness in others.

The most likely explanation for this goes back to the high volcanic activity in the area. The acid rain that is affecting the Blanket Forest is also dissolving the nutrients in the environment, which are needed to help the Tyrannosaurus lay down eggshell inside her body. Not only that, but the lava flows to the north has upset the annual migration of one of the Tyrannosaurus' most common prey, the duck-billed dinosaur Edmontosaurus. Every year these herbivores follow the rains from north to south and back in a 600-mile round trip. The lava flows have broken and delayed this migration, and in many places this far south the Edmontosaurus have failed to appear. The Tyrannosaurus rely on this source of food, and the absence of the herds probably worried the mother at a crucial time before laying. Still, she did lay and protect the nest before her nose told her that the clutch was doomed.

While the male finishes off the last of the eggs, a long, sonorous bellow echoes through the Blanket Forest. It is the mournful mating call of a female Tyrannosaurus. In this area, each female establishes a home range of hundreds of square miles, therefore this is probably the same individual who abandoned the nest. Without eggs or young to care for, females quickly become fertile again, but finding a mate can take some time. Population density in Tyrannosaurus depends on the availability of food, but even in rich feeding grounds, such as the northern plains with their vast herds of duck-billed and horned dinosaurs, the females still maintain exclusive home ranges of around 30 square miles. The males, however, range over thousands of square miles. They are solitary and rarer than the females. Each male's range encompasses those of several females and overlaps with those of other males. His entire adult life is spent fighting other males and searching for receptive females. On this occasion, both are lucky because she will not have to call for days, and he will be the first male to respond.

Away from the herd: an Anatotitan stops to drink at the edge of the forest. Anatotitan is one of the larger species of hadrosaurs, or duck-billed dinosaurs. They usually live in herds and are the most successful group of dinosaurs in Laurasia.

With such large, aggressive predators, it is never that simple. The male cocks his head in response to the mating call. The sound is confused by the thick vegetation and the moisture in the air, but the female is clearly close. Each bellow sets off a cascade of smaller calls through the forest as its echoes disturb birds and smaller dinosaurs. The male knows he cannot simply approach the female and mate since that would only lead to more injuries. Instead, Tyrannosaurus indulge in a ritual called "courtship feeding." A male makes a kill and then uses the carcass to attract the female. While she feeds, he attempts to mate. The larger the kill, the longer the female stays around and,

since the male has to mate several times to ensure successful fertilization, he will often look for a dangerously large kill. Many die this way, either by being speared by the horns of a fully grown Triceratops or crushed by an Anatotitan. However, since the sole aim of a male Tyrannosaurus is to mate, he is prepared to risk his life in courtship feeding. This male barks in response to the mating call and defecates on the abandoned nest. Although this will not attract the female, it will alert her to his presence and may stop her wandering out of his reach.

Very early morning is the best time to see this part of the Laramidia coast, before the fog rolls in. Beyond the marshy coast of the Pierre Seaway there is a thin strip of flood plain dotted with numerous clear blue lakes. The vegetation is scrub, with patchy groups of trees, and the low light picks out herds of duck-bills feeding at the water's edge. Beyond this plain rises the pale green Blanket Forest, layer upon layer stacking up against the foothills of the distant volcanoes.

'Normally Tyrannosaurus is an ambush predator, using surprise to help him overcome his prey.'

The male Tyrannosaurus stalks out into the open. He lowers his tail and stretches up as high as his legs will allow, surveying the scene. His black and speckled gray coloring blends well with the dawn light, but today camouflage is not his primary concern. Normally he is an ambush predator, using surprise to help him overcome his prey, but the female's calls have subtly changed his hunting technique. He now makes himself obvious and directly approaches a group of duck-billed Anatotitan grazing nearby. A fully grown Anatotitan is marginally larger and more bulky than a Tyrannosaurus, and this animal's tight herd structure makes it a difficult target. The herbivores hoot in alarm and begin to move away. The Tyrannosaurus continues to approach, pushing the Anatotitan into more hurried reactions. Some rock back on to their hind legs and trot toward a nearby lake. Several large males turn to confront the predator. The Tyrannosaurus skirts around them but continues to work his way nearer. He is hoping that by pushing the group, he will force a sick or old individual to betray itself. The male duck-bills check his advance. He turns and tries moving the other way.

When the fog thickens it is clear that the Tyrannosaurus is not going to achieve his kill without a direct attack on a healthy male Anatotitan, and he is reluctant to try this.

A series of bellows from the far side of the lake provides the Tyrannosaurus with another option. Slowly through the fog, a herd of Torosaurus appear. These giant horned herbivores weigh up to 8 tons and dominate the coastal plains. Torosaurus have the most magnificent crests of all the animals in this group, a 6-foot-long frill set over a three-horned face. This gives them the largest skull of any dinosaur, in fact, of any land creature. This decoration can

protect the animal, but is primarily there to impress mates and intimidate rivals. Both sexes have frills, but in the breeding season, the bulls enhance their displays by flushing the crests with blood and creating two vibrant eyespots.

The Tyrannosaurus first notices these colorful frills when he approaches the herd. This group is mating and which means the bulls will be fighting. In any fight there will be a loser, and the loser will be exhausted and possibly injured, prime targets for a predator. He watches while the Torosaurus go through their mating rituals. There are no permanent hierarchies within the herd. The bulls challenge for temporary dominance around receptive cows. This involves the male standing next to and "tending" a female. If a rival approachs, he immediately dips his head to display the full range of colors on his crest. Sometimes this is enough, but frequently the aggressor will mimic the other's display movements. Then the two males will go through a complicated set of moves involving dipping the head and waggling the crest, all to communicate their strength. These crest displays are important and enough to settle most challenges. The winner continues to tend the cow, standing in her way if she tries to move off, and eventually they copulate. If the cow is not happy with her mate, she will try to break free, running through the herd to shake off her attendant male.

LEFT Danger signal: a female Torosaurus flushes color patterns into her crest and stamps the ground to see off a threat to the youngster grazing next to her. Her spectacular horns are enough to deter even the most determined predators.

Beside the lake, two evenly matched males have been displaying since sunrise. One is an experienced male, probably over 50 years old. There is a long tear in the center of his crest from a previous fight and the top of his back is heavily scarred from predator attacks. His rival is much younger, but almost as large. His crest has two fine, dark eyespots and his hide is smooth and less scarred. Gradually, their head-dipping and waggling comes to a halt which is a bad sign. The older male bellows loudly. Then, suddenly, the young challenger lurches forward and they engage horns. The older bull stumbles back from the

A BUNCH OF SHOW OFFS

THE FIRST HORNED dinosaur to be discovered was *Triceratops* in 1889. It had three facial horns and a sizeable crest made of solid bone extending out of the back of its head. It was suggested that this would have made a formidable defense against predators and the idea stuck. However, several other horned species have been found since and *Triceratops* remains the only one with a solid crest. The rest had large holes in the middle of their frills, which in life would have been covered by stretched skin full of blood vessels. This does not make them ideal defensive structures. Then it was proposed that the crests provided an anchoring point for huge jaw muscles, enabling the animals to slice through the hardest of plant material with their beaks. However, animals such as *Torosaurus* have crests 6 feet 6 inches (2 meters) long, and there is no point in having

muscles stretched out that far since it would not provide significant extra strength.

In recent years, the crests, like so many other frills and plates in dinosaurs, have come to be seen primarily as sexual displays. In the mass graves of horned dinosaurs it was discovered that immature individuals had under-developed crests, making crest growth an adult characteristic. It is more difficult to prove that there was a difference between the sexes because we have no reliable way of sexing the finds. However, since the head display may also have identified a species, it is possible that both sexes had these structures.

Studies of the horns, which come in all shapes and sizes, show that some were ideal for locking together in a fight, as deer antlers do today. Although its defense must have been a major feature of an animal's development, especially with the large

Vision was probably very important to dinosaurs. The bizarre crests of the duck-billed dinosaurs, such as this *Parasaurolophus*, could have supported visual displays, as well as being used for making distinctive calls.

single-horned species, sex and species recognition were probably more important in shaping these bizarre structures.

The same argument has been applied to the eyebrow and nose crests on carnivores, the nose shapes of duck-bills, and even some of the spines of armored dinosaurs, all with good reason. Sex is an important driving force in evolution and is the primary cause of many extreme growths in modern mammals and birds. Also, the closest living relatives to dinosaur, birds, and crocodiles, both have color vision, and the majority of mammals see in black and white. It is not unreasonable to assume that dinosaurs had good color vision. Visual displays could, therefore, have formed an important part of their lives. It is possible that the odd bony lumps and bumps we now see in many fossil skeletons represent all that is left of a wild collection of brightly colored displays that filled the Mesozoic world.

The crest of the *Triceratops* is unusual among horned dinosaurs because it is solid. Usually, crests have two holes in the middle, which would suggest that defense was not their primary role.

force of the attack. The two long forehead horns and the shorter nose horns lock together tightly. The two animals pause again, eye to eye, their heads lowered in combat. Torosaurus are large, heavy dinosaurs and their forelimb posture is slightly squat, making them slow but extremely stable. For each bull, it is like trying to shift a boulder the same size. With their heads firmly locked, they shift their weight to try to gain an advantage, and when they do, the strain on their necks is enormous.

While the mist thickens the bulls continue to try and subdue each other. Their horns rasp and grind as the headlock slips and tightens. Each one grunts and snorts with the exertion of moving his opponent even the tiniest amount. After an hour, neither animal appears to have gained anything, but both are close to exhaustion. Suddenly the older bull disengages and retreats. The younger male pursues him for a few hundred yards, bucking his head and trumpeting his victory. Eventually he lets him go. Some distance from the herd the old Torosaurus stops and it becomes apparent why he has retreated. One of his horns is hanging down and he is bleeding profusely over one eye.

Distracted by the pain of his broken horn, he fails to spot the approaching Tyrannosaurus until it is too late. The predator runs out of the mist and sinks his long, puncturing teeth into the old bull's flank. Anchoring himself with his right foot, he uses his short powerful neck to tear off a 65-pound slab of flesh. The Tyrannosaurus is a large predator, but he is still lightly built compared to the Torosaurus. The last thing he wants to do is grapple with this massive prey. Having opened up a huge wound with that single bite, he backs off to wait for another opportunity.

Despite his injury, the Torosaurus swings around and faces his attacker. This is what makes these herbivores so difficult for lone predators to attack. In spite of their size, they can turn rapidly and present the predator with three long horns and a wide expanse of crest. This is a stalemate and Torosaurus have been known to continue grazing while keeping a hungry Tyrannosaurus at bay. However, for this old bull the situation is different. Confused and exhausted, he has a gaping wound in his side and one useless horn. He bellows in anger and pain and looks around for the rest of the herd. Unfortunately, they are

OVERLEAF **Moving in for the kill: a male Tyrannosaurus circles an injured Torosaurus. Although the giant herbivore has adopted a defensive posture, this will be his last stand. The predator's initial ambush inflicted deep gashes and mortally wounded him.**

some distance away and can provide no protection for him. He tries to charge his tormentor, but stumbles to a halt in agony. The Tyrannosaurus stalks one way and then the other.

Eventually, the bull makes a fatal error. He panics and turns, trying to run back to the herd. The predator swiftly catches up with him and again sinks his teeth into his side. This time he shatters part of the hip bone. The Torosaurus stumbles and the Tyrannosaurus bites again. The Torosaurus gets up and faces his attacker. He no longer has the energy to turn and run, so he simply stands unsteadily as shock and blood loss slowly overcome him. The Tyrannosaurus holds back, his mouth already dripping with the blood of several pounds of Torosaurus meat. Realizing that his prey cannot go anywhere, he calls to the female in the Blanket Forest with a series of short, deep barks.

After half an hour, the old bull is still on his feet, and right before he loses consciousness, he finally sees the reason behind his death. A massive female Tyrannosaurus appears out of the mist. Scars disfigure one side of her face and she walks with the slightest limp. Her eyes are fixed on him and are deep red, a sign of age. The pitch of the male's call rises and he is careful not to place himself between his potential mate and the prey. She walks forward slowly, occasionally glancing at the male, but heads for the now prostrate Torosaurus. She sniffs the dying animal, necklaces of saliva hanging from her mouth. She feeds, driving her long teeth into the flesh and ripping off large chunks of skin, meat, and even bone. This habit means that she often breaks her teeth. She does not care since she swallows the bulky mouthfuls whole. While she eats, the male advances toward her, lowering his head and making reassuring coughing sounds. He then sits up, puffing out the red wattle under his chin, an attempt to impress her. When she spots him coming close, she turns and opens her mouth wide, displaying her huge dripping jaw. He recognizes this as a warning. She is not ready to accept him.

After she has filled her stomach, the female crouches down and rests her head on the ground. The male hovers but she shows no inter-

BIG MOUTH

BY COMPARISON WITH the rich variety of feeding methods evolved by dinosaur herbivores, the carnivores were remarkably conservative. The theropod dinosaurs were the carnivorous dynasty of the Mesozoic, and all the predators for 160 million years came from this group. They have been nicknamed land sharks because they probably fed as sharks do, running up to prey, biting a large piece out, and then retiring to see what damage they had caused. From *Coelophysis* to *Tyrannosaurus* they relied on recurved teeth that ensured that the moment they bit their victims, the meat was pulled free. These dinosaurs never developed any chewing mechanism and always swallowed whole. One fossil shows the perils of this. A large carnivore has clearly perished in the process of swallowing, with two long bones stuck in its gullet. There were some refinements over the years. Raptors used their grappling hands

Tyrannosaurus had the largest head of any dinosaur predator, which could explain its small arms. To remain balanced on two legs, and yet develop such massive jaws, the weight of its arms was reduced.

and long toe claws to inflict wounds before biting the prey. However, Tyrannosaurus was just a large biting machine. Its exceptionally long teeth were its killing weapons, and its arms were irrelevant.

Given that *Tyrannosaurus* was so large and might have been warm-blooded, it would have needed a great deal of meat to keep it going. Palaeontologist James Farlow made an inspired calculation of *Tyrannosaurus'* needs based on a scene from the film *Jurassic Park*, in which the predator ate a lawyer. Assuming a *Tyrannosaurus* weighs 4.5 tons and a lawyers weighs 150 pounds, he estimated it would take 292 legal advisers a year to keep the predator fed. Fortunately, that is the equivalent of only three or four *Triceratops*, and they were much more freely available in the Cretaceous.

est, so the day draws on, with the female sleeping most of the time. Evening lifts the mist and bathes the gory scene with a red hue. The Torosaurus herd have moved on and the presence of two Tyrannosaurus has caused the duck-bills to abandon the lake. With the last flare of sunlight, the female wakes and this time shows more interest in the male. She raises her tail and he approaches quickly from behind. When he attempts to mount her, he uses his tiny forelimbs to steady himself by hooking into the thick hide on her back. The coupling is brief, but it is the first of many. In between, the female sleeps and feeds, but the male never drops his guard. By staying close, he not only increases his chances of fertilizing her by mating repeatedly, but also he can keep other males away.

At first light on the third day there is a tropical downpour. The rain soaks the rapidly decaying Torosaurus corpse, carrying tiny beetle larvae away in stinking rivulets. The female is losing interest in mating and the male is edgy. Just before midday the rain stops and through the clammy, moist air comes the noise of the Torosaurus herd returning. On encountering the Tyrannosaurus pair, they start to harass them. Eventually, the predators have to abandon the carcass. While they slink away, the fragile bond that allowed mating snaps. With no warning the female turns on the male. He is quick to respond, but she still manages to sink a bite into the back of his head. He stumbles away, then turns and flees. She chases him, bellowing and snapping at his tail, but the pursuit will not last long. Despite his wound, the male has done well. It is likely that the female will bear his offspring and he has not mortally damaged himself by fighting other males for the privilege.

That night one of the volcanoes 300 miles north becomes more active. It begins with a series of small eruptions as far away as the Blanket Forest. By morning a thin column of smoke can be seen on the northern horizon. In geological terms this mountain range is young and is still being built. It has been created by Laramidia being pushed west by an ever-widening Atlantic Ocean. While the mountains grow the ecology and climate of the whole area is changing. Lowlands become uplands, rainfall patterns shift and rivers change course. All this happens slowly enough for animals and plants to adapt, but some do it better than others.

A Foretaste of Violence

The northern volcano has finally blown its top. A huge explosion throws millions of tons of hot ash and rubble out to the east, and an area about 125 miles long and 60 miles wide is devastated. Forests, prairies, and lakes are all buried under an ash layer that is 65 feet deep in some places. Hundreds of thousands of animals are caught in this cataclysm, but among the worst affected are the herds of Edmontosaurus. Somewhere in the region of 70 percent of the world's Edmontosaurus population is buried by the eruption, and those remaining are split into isolated groups. Once these duck-bills moved in their thousands down the coastal plains of the Pierre Seaway. Now the largest group to survive the explosion numbers no more than 40. For a herd-living creature such as Edmontosaurus, this is potentially catastrophic. They need high numbers to reproduce successfully and now there is a strong likelihood that the species will become extinct before it can recover. In turn, this would put pressure on other animals that rely on them, not least the big predators, such as Tyrannosaurus. In some areas Edmontosaurus make up more than a half of the diet of the local Tyrannosaurus.

Three hundred miles to the south the eruption's effects are less devastating, but they are still considerable. The following night, a northerly wind brings a cloud of fine dust into the area. When it settles everything gets a covering of ash. By moonlight the landscape looks washed out, as if there had been an extreme frost. The plants desperately need some rain to wash off the dust, otherwise they will start to suffocate. For one nesting colony of duck-billed Anatotitan, the dust is a deadly night-time visitor.

Anatotitan are closely related to Edmontosaurus but larger, about 45 feet long and about 5 tons. They also do not travel in large herds. This group has built a series of nest mounds beside the lake and their ducklets have hatched simultaneously. Even at night, the adults move between the mounds attending their young, bringing them new-growth vegetation to eat and sheltering them from the elements. Unfortunately, there was little they could do to stop the dust cloud as it swept in from the north. Each group of hatchlings sits at the

OPPOSITE **Habitat killer: the northern volcano blows its top, throwing a huge column of ash into the atmosphere. Once the power of the eruption begins to dwindle, the mass of dust crashes down, spreading out in a deadly fan and burying everything in its path.**

267

bottom of a large nest bowl. When the dust begins to fall, it concentrates at the bottom of these bowls, and the young are too small to climb out. The night air fills with the concerned hoots of adult Anatotitan and the panicky calls of suffocating ducklets. Unable to understand what is going on, some adults respond to the calls by dumping more dust-laden food in the nest. The cease-less activity of the huge parents also stirs up the dust, clearing it from between the nests, but settling it into the nest bowls.

By morning there are few ducklet calls to be heard. The adult Anatotitan stand around confused and covered in dust. In one or two nests the young,

Poisoned earth: in such a volcanic area there are many hot springs exuding toxic gases. These frequently suffocate hapless herbivores, and the Tyrannosaurus are not averse to scavenging the carcasses.

although covered in ash, have managed to climb clear of the suffocating layers by scrabbling up the vegetation brought by the adults. However, they are in a minority. Most lie dead at the bottom of the nest bowls. As long as there are a few ducklets left, the adult Anatotitan will not abandon their nests, but midday brings more problems. Heavy rain begins to fall, enough to start washing the plants clean, but it turns the dust in the nests into a clinging paste. The last surviving ducklets die in the quicksand at the bottom of their nest bowls. The adult Anatotitan continue to attend the nests, occasionally fishing out their mud-covered young, but the task is hopeless. This year's brood is doomed and within a few days the Anatotitan group will move on.

For some animals, the volcanic ash is a bonus. The small carnivorous mammals, including Didelphodon, are relatively unaffected by the fall of ash because they live in burrows. When the Anatotitan begin to lose interest in their nests, the mammals seize the opportunity and move in, digging into the drying silt in search of ducklets. By the time the herd leave, the nests are a mass of furry mammals fighting over tiny dinosaur corpses.

After the rain the Blanket Forest looks much like it did before, except that many of the rivers and lakes are clogged with silt. On a small mound the old female Tyrannosaurus is building a new nest. Before starting to nest she has been on a three-month hunting spree, killing and devouring as many animals as she could eat. However, once she lays her eggs, she will starve herself until they hatch, usually about two months. With so many small predators threatening the nest, not to mention other Tyrannosaurus, she cannot afford to leave her eggs unprotected for a moment. For several days she has been selecting mouthfuls of moss and litter to build the large composting mound and is now ready to lay. Tyrannosaurus eggs are big and elongated, and for a successful hatch have to be carefully positioned upright in the nest. To do this the mother will use her tiny but strong forearms to place each egg gently, blunt end down, in a spiral pattern. As the chicks hatch, each will push through the top of its egg and emerge from the shell almost without disturbing the rest of the clutch. It is a long time since this mother dinosaur has seen her eggs reach this stage. When she stops and sniffs the moist air, the omens do not look good.

A Time of Decay

Rising on the warm midday thermals, a huge male Quetzalcoatlus pterosaur floats over an area of volcanic desolation. Thirty-six feet from wing-tip to wing-tip, he is a master of the air currents, hardly ever having to flap his wings. His pristine white body is in strange contrast to the dark volcanic ash beneath.

The Quetzalcoatlus is a rare sight. Once pterosaurs of all shapes and sizes were a common part of most ecosystems. Now the whole group is extinct except for a few lonely giants. It is difficult to blame any one factor for their demise. Certainly bird numbers and species have boomed through the Cretaceous, and the birds have proven more adept than the flying dinosaurs at living amidst dense vegetation. The smaller pterosaurs disappeared first, but in more recent times a drastic fall in sea levels has hit the huge gliding pterosaurs very badly. Most of these species specialized in fishing in warm, shallow seas.

'Deinosuchus grows to over 40 feet in length and, at over 2 tons, will happily challenge a Tyrannosaurus if it ventures near the water.'

Quetzalcoatlus is a good example. To feed he flies low over the water, lowering his long, stiff neck and scooping fish out of the water with his toothless bill. The vast areas of flooded land called epicontinental seas were ideal for this type of feeding. They were highly productive, invariably calm, and the pterosaurs could harvest freely from vast shoals of fish. However, when sea levels fell, the first things to disappear were the epicontinental seas. Rivers became longer as the water retreated into the deeper seaways. In this area the Pierre Seaway is on the retreat and soon, for the first time in millions of years, Laramidia and Appalachia will become one continuous landmass. With this slow but steady loss of habitat, the future for Quetzalcoatlus looks grim.

This particular male must have been displaced by the eruption. He was lucky to survive. The huge pterosaurs are delicate gliders and any caught in the dust cloud would have found it impossible to keep aloft. He circles higher and higher on the volcanic foothills and heads south, away from the ash-covered landscape. He can see green on the horizon and can smell water in the air.

Distances mean little to him since he can cross continents without much effort. The northerly winds speed his flight, and within three or four hours he has covered well over 60 miles. For most of the afternoon he has been flying parallel to the seaway and eventually he starts to spiral down toward a large, freshwater lake just inland. A long, sandy shore on its western edge provides the ideal landing and take-off strip. He glides slowly until he stalls a yard above the sand and touches down on his back legs, stowing his delicate wing membranes and flipping his wing fingers across his back. Then, leaning heavily on his hands, he waddles down to the water's edge for a drink. He is vulnerable and nervous on the ground and spends more time looking around than drinking.

Dinosaur killer: since the early Mesozoic, crocodiles have been successful freshwater predators. Some, such as this Deinosuchus, have grown to enormous sizes and frequently pluck dinosaurs from the riverbanks while they are drinking.

He has good reason to be wary. The area consists mostly of flooded marshes, and although he can spot no large dinosaur predators, that is because they have been chased out of the habitat by giant crocodiles. One species of crocodile, Deinosuchus, grows to more than 40 feet in length and, at over 2 tons, will happily challenge a Tyrannosaurus if it ventures near the water. Deinosuchus will hunt in either fresh or marine water and has developed the technique of ambushing land creatures at the water's edge into an art. The lake at which the Quetzalcoatlus is drinking has several large Deinosuchus in it, but he cannot see them because a tiny aquatic fern covers most of the water, hiding the killers in its depths. However, as the pterosaur dips his bill, the crocodiles sense the vibration. About 20 yards away a huge armored head quietly breaks the surface. Translucent eyelids wipe the fern leaves from the Deinosuchus' orange eyes as he watches his prey. Then he slips back under the water and, with one flex of his tail, glides toward his victim. The Quetzalcoatlus does not see this but he seems nervous and turns to take off.

At that moment the water in front of him erupts. The Deinosuchus lunges forward, the pterosaur stumbles back, and the crocodile manages to grab his right wing claws. He throws open his remaining wing to intimidate his attacker and stabs at his head with his bill, but these defenses are hopeless. The crocodile's armor plating means that he can hardly feel the pterosaur's attack and, despite his size, the Quetzalcoatlus weighs less than 220 pounds. The Deinosuchus' jaws snap his right wing like a twig. His delicate bones are no match for the predator's crushing bite. The crocodile then pulls his flapping victim into the water. While he does, another crocodile rises out, grabs the pterosaur's neck and breaks it with a twist of his body. The Quetzalcoatlus' fight is over in seconds. When he is dragged under, the tiny ferns float back

MESSAGES LEFT IN THE BONE

AS WELL AS recording the shape of an animal, a fossil skeleton can contain clues to the health of its owner. Only about one per-cent of diseases leave their mark on the bones, but these include arthritis, which has been found in two *Iguanodon* ankles, and severe infections, such as the abscess found in a duck-bill jaw. Gout has been found in the arms and toe of a *Tyrannosaurus* and, given that in humans it is associated with eating too much red meat, it is not too surprising.

It used to be thought that dinosaurs suffered a lot from osteoarthritis because their back vertebrae often appeared fused. This has since been revealed as a condition known as diffuse idiopathic skeletal hyperstosis or DISH. This occurs when the ligaments running next to the vertebrae become calcified and gradually lock the backbone into a rigid shape, but it is not

The fused vertebrae of a sauropod. This could be due to illness, but might also be a natural process to help the animal support the huge weight of another during mating.

associated with any disease. In fact, it looks as if it might have been an adaptation to help dinosaurs support their weight over their back legs. Duck-billed hadrosaurs, horned dinosaurs, sauropods, and *Iguanodon* all show this condition in their back vertebrae, which could have helped them hold their tails high. *Stegosaurus* needed a highly flexible tail for defense, so did not suffer from DISH. Horned dinosaurs, such as *Triceratops*,

show fusion of their neck vertebrae, but this could have been to help them support such a large head.

In addition to the clues resulting from disease, severe injuries can leave healed fractures in the bone. One *Tyrannosaurus* find shows a wound so severe that the animal has twisted its neck backward and up. Certain injuries seem more common in certain species, giving clues to their owner's way of life. Fractured ribs have been found in the remains of sauropods, possibly caused by leaning against other objects. Carnivores frequently have healed fractures in their limbs, betraying the perils of tackling larger, heavier prey. Duck-bills often have crushed vertebral spines, which could be the result of trampling, but it has also been suggested that these skeletons belonged to females who suffered back problems from the weight of males leaning on them during mating.

DEATH OF A DYNASTY

into position as if to draw a veil over the dismemberment that is taking place beneath the surface.

The night is cool and the next morning brings the first fog for some weeks to the Blanket Forest. While its moist fingers creep among the trees, they touch a sleeping Tyrannosaurus. Slowly the droplets build up on her back and trickle down her flanks. Pools gather around her nostrils and a large butterfly lands to drink. Butterflies are yet another extraordinary design produced by the hugely successful insects. Throughout the time of dinosaurs, more insect species have appeared to take advantage of every habitat available. The butterflies, with their long tongues and delicate wings, are the latest and have evolved to feed specifically on flowers. This one succeeds in tickling the Tyrannosaurus, which wakes with a sneeze, propelling the butterfly into the bushes. The predator flexes her neck and lifts her scarred head. She looks sick and haggard. Her red eyes are sunken and cloudy, and she has not eaten for seven weeks. About 25 yards in front of her, and still bathed in morning light diffused by the fog, is her nest, a pile of moss and litter. She rises to her feet and stalks over to it, limping slightly. She has gout in one of her legs and it has become more painful as her health has deteriorated. Two Didelphodon have been exploring the nest in the night, but they scatter as she approaches. She does not chase them. Instead she steps around the nest, checking it and smelling for signs of damage. All must be well because she returns to her hiding place.

What she has not noticed, curled up in the compost, is an extraordinary-looking, long, thin reptile. It is a snake, part of a group of highly specialized lizards which have been evolving throughout the Cretaceous to move without using legs. Snakes can slip through the undergrowth at high speed, propelled by waves of muscle contractions passing down their bodies, and are designed to hunt warm-blooded creatures. While mammals have become more common, snakes have developed a unique ability to spot their "heat signatures" in the dark. On either side of the snake's head, between her eyes and her nostrils, are her "pit organs," capable of sensing tiny changes in temperature. When she moves around in the undergrowth at night, the warmth of the mammals' bodies betrays them.

Beginning of the End

The sun rises on a desolate scene. All the open forests and marshes along a huge swathe of the south-western edge of the Pierre Seaway are dead. The once-lush plains stink of rotting vegetation and the humid air is thick with insects. All shade has gone and the trees are now leafless and left standing as naked snags. This is yet another devastating side effect of the eruption several months ago. The thousands of tons of dust that were deposited in the area were gradually washed down out of the forests by the streams and rivers. However, when the dust reached the slow-flowing estuaries, it was all dumped, killing the delicate

freshwater ecosystems, flooding drier habitats and suffocating the roots of trees. It will take years for this area to recover. In addition, the huge volcano looming behind the Blanket Forest is showing signs of restlessness. It is only a matter of time before it follows the example of its northern cousin.

Underneath a group of palms with brown, limp leaves a group of duck-billed Anatotitan snuffle among the litter for some fresh growth. Their stomachs are shrunken and they call frequently to each other in low hoots. The duck-bills have an efficient method of grazing. Their wide "bills" can crop the lowest shoots, and then hundreds of teeth can grind down even the toughest plants. However, they do not do well on rotting food. There is virtually nothing

Futile display: two Anatotitan scrap against a backdrop of desolation. A once-rich lake has been strangled by a lava flow and is now no more than a stagnant pool where Deinosuchus wait to ambush thirsty dinosaurs.

for them to eat, and if they are to survive, they must move on. Unfortunately, Anatotitan are territorial and they will not migrate away. The group wanders through the palms to the shores of a stagnant lake to crop a small patch of horsetails that has struggled up through the silt.

The crocodiles have done well in the silted marshes. They have been able to move from one muddy pool to another, hunting the weakened herbivores. Several Anatotitan from this group, even one fully grown adult, have been dragged to their deaths by giant crocodiles. The duck-bills watch the muddy water warily as they feed on the horsetails. Normally they would move much further from crocodile-infested water, but that is impossible now. A large splash in the stagnant lake sends the group wading in panic through the mud. The opaque waters settle again and, driven by hunger, the Anatotitan slowly return to the horsetails. Preoccupied by the threat from the water, they completely miss another predator stalking through the dead trees toward them.

The large female Tyrannosaurus stops a short distance from the Anatotitan herd and scans the group for weaklings. The duck-bills are in poor health and she feels bold enough to make a direct attack. Some yards behind her, hiding in the bushes, is a group of three young Tyrannosaurus chicks. She has at last managed to hatch a successful brood. They are only a few days old and still have the mottled backs and the baleful yellow eyes of youngsters. Their heads and limbs are all proportionally larger than the adults and they are already fast runners. Their mother ignores them while she steadily stalks her prey. However, the long months of starvation have taken their toll on her. Her limp has become more pronounced since the gout has become worse and she looks painfully thin. She moves closer and then breaks into a lop-sided trot. Too late, the nearest Anatotitan sees her, hoots an ear-splitting alarm call, and turns to wade away. The Tyrannosaurus has approached on slightly firmer ground and jumps on the fleeing duck-bill as she reaches the deeper mud. A bone-shuddering bite on the haunches leaves the prey stunned and bleeding. The duck-bill wallows in

THE EXCEPTIONAL HELL CREEK

THE HELL CREEK Formation is a deposit dating from the very end of the Cretaceous period and lies on the borders of Montana, Wyoming, and the Dakotas. Since its discovery at the end of the nineteenth century, it has proved a rich source of dinosaur fossils, including large numbers of *Triceratops*. Between 1902 and 1908, paleontologist Barnum Brown excavated two *Tyrannosaurus*, which were exhibited in the Carnegie and American museums, bringing him instant fame.

Recently, however, Hell Creek has proved useful for a different reason. It is the only dinosaur-bearing fossil bed that crosses what is known as the K-T Boundary, the period between the very end of the Mesozoic and the beginning of the current Cenozoic eras. In many places the formation is more than 330 feet (100 meters) thick and the top few yards lie in the modern Cenozoic era. Sampling of the boundary layers has revealed iridium and crystals of shocked quartz,

Paleontologists expose a hip bone from the Hell Creek Formation, confirming *Tyrannosaurus* as one of the last great dinosaurs. These rocks also include evidence of the extinction that wiped out these creatures.

showing that a meteor impact affected this area. Many scientists have surveyed the type and number of dinosaurs and plants running up to the impact to see if any other type of extinction mechanism was at work.

Unfortunately, the geological resolution, the smallest period of time distinguishable in the rocks, is as much as half a million years, which makes it difficult to pinpoint the moment when any particular species flourished or specific event occurred.

Plant findings show a healthy land that was decimated by the meteor. In the immediate aftermath of the impact there is a "fern spike," when it appears that ferns covered the wounded Earth. The dinosaur remains show no diminution in numbers before the impact, but there is a lack of diversity, with one or two species such as *Triceratops* and *Edmontosaurus* being very common, a possible indication that something was seriously wrong. Pieces of dinosaurs have been found above the boundary, but these are believed to have been eroded out of the ground and redeposited in more modern soils. Otherwise the message of Hell Creek is clear: the huge reptiles that were common before the boundary completely disappeared after it.

the mud, wildly thrashing its back legs. Two more shuddering bites leave the prey crippled and drowning in its own blood. The rest of the group offer no resistance and flee. Once the Tyrannosaurus is sure her prey is dead, she drags it out of the mud. The three Tyrannosaurus chicks break cover and run toward their mother. They have seen the kill and immediately run over and start tearing at its intestines.

While the young feed, the muddy waters nearby move. The Anatotitan's blood has flowed into the lake and other hungry predators are arriving to join in the feast. Several large Deinosuchus rise up out of the water and slip on to the bank. One by one they edge forward, opening their mouths wide as a challenge. The chicks, both curious and afraid, back away from the kill. The

A born carnivore: a young
Tyrannosaurus plucks at a
piece of Anatotitan liver that
his mother has dropped.
Hatching from such a large
egg, a juvenile Tyrannosaurus
is soon a formidable predator
in its own right.

mother Tyrannosaurus roars and stamps a foot, more as a warning to her young than as a threat to the crocodiles. In the end, she hardly resists the Deinosuchus at all. There are far too many for her to fight off and some of the larger adults are almost as big as she is. She turns and abandons her kill, with her youngsters following after her reluctantly.

Several days pass and the temperatures become uncharacteristically cool. At night the western sky glows red as huge lava fields build in the mountains. With the duck-bill population so badly hit, the Tyrannosaurus is finding it difficult to catch enough food to support her young. Eventually, she loses another hatchling. The two larger siblings turn on the third weaker one while he sleeps and eat him. The mother's behavior becomes more erratic as the lack of food takes its toll.

It is mid-afternoon and the Tyrannosaurus settles down to sleep on the warm rocks. Her young continue to make pleading noises, but they maintain a cautious distance. Lost in a deep sleep the normally alert predator fails to notice the arrival of a mother Ankylosaurus in the low shrub nearby. Following behind her are a pair of youngsters or scutelings. Although they do not have the spikes and club of their parents, they are still heavily armored. Their backs are already covered in plates and small knobs of bone. This, and the presence of their mother, makes them very difficult prey.

Nevertheless, the hungry young Tyrannosaurus immediately turn their attention to the scutelings and start a clumsy attempt at stalking them. While the adult Ankylosaurus feeds, the little Tyrannosaurus manage to hop within a few yards of their prey. They have no idea of how dangerous Ankylosaurus can be, so they get ready to pounce. It is then that the mother smells them and starts her rumbling alarm call. The scutelings immediately trundle toward her while she swings her tail in threat. The call wakes the sleeping Tyrannosaurus, who scrabbles to her feet. She is only 30 yards from the armored herbivore. The mother Ankylosaurus sees the predator and panics. She charges with her head tucked down. The Tyrannosaurus manages to leap to one side, but the moment the charging Ankylosaurus loses sight of her target she pivots around and swings her giant tail club in defence.

In almost any normal situation, the Tyrannosaurus would have withdrawn from this dangerous confrontation, but the moment the Ankylosaurus' club smashes into her gouty knee she is doomed. The explosive pain freezes one side of her body and, shrieking in alarm and confusion, she collapses on to the Ankylosaurus. Reading this as an attack the herbivore steps up her activity. She tips the predator to the ground and starts to pound her with her club. Giving blow after blow she beats the resistance out of the Tyrannosaurus whose bones are built for speed and power, not this kind of onslaught. For a few seconds she struggles, but then the club lands a fearsome blow on her skull and her fiery red eyes fade into unconsciousness.

While this furious confrontation is taking place, the young Tyrannosaurus have been trying their luck with the scutelings. They have little idea what to do with two armored boxes and abandon their attack. For several minutes the adult Ankylosaurus stands near the dead Tyrannosaurus, bellowing. Then she must sense that the predator is dead because she turns and calls for her scutelings. They appear and the family move away, leaving an eerie silence and the smell of blood.

Morning finds the Tyrannosaurus crumpled on the lava field, her head in a pool of blood. Her two chicks approach tentatively. At first they seem timid. They call to her, but she does not move. They have learned to give her a wide berth, so they hang back, but their calls become more impatient. Soon the smell of death and their hunger have a predictable effect. One hatchling moves forward and drinks from the pool of blood. The other tugs at the flesh. Their mother will continue to provide them with food until other predators chase them away.

Death from the Skies

IMPACT DAY ON EARTH

Just as the chicks are tearing at their mother's flesh, a light appears on the horizon to the south. It grows swiftly in intensity and the Tyrannosaurus look up in curiosity, their mottled faces lit by the new light. Their eyes flicker and then they return to their mother's carcass. Unknown to them, a comet six miles wide and traveling at 18 miles per second has just hit a shallow sea 2000 miles away to the south. The distant glow they see represents an explosion of about 100 million megatons, enough to open a hole 125 miles wide and ten miles deep in the planet's crust. Life on Earth will never be the same again.

THE END WAS NIGH

ALMOST AS INFAMOUS as dinosaurs themselves is the fact that they all died out in a very short space of time. To understand this event we have to put it in context. Extinction is an integral part of evolution. All creatures eventually die out and this does not imply "failure." Over 90 percent of the organisms that have ever lived are extinct. Evolution is a dynamic process and there is a constant turnover of species.

However, extinction does not occur at an even rate. There appear to be quiet periods in the history of life, punctuated by "mass" extinctions. In the past 550 million years there have been five major extinctions, when over 50 percent of animal species died. The most significant of all wiped out 95 percent of life (see page 28) at the end of the Permian era, before the dinosaurs evolved. The most recent one occurred 65 million years ago and has attracted more attention than all the others because it finished off the dinosaurs.

There have been over 80 theories suggested to explain the demise of the dinosaurs. These include plague, constipation, mammals eating their eggs, racial senility, a nearby explosion of a supernova, and being hunted down by aliens. However, any theory has to explain a very odd pattern of extinction. Herbivorous and carnivorous dinosaurs were badly affected, as were lizards, sharks, marsupials, and a range of marine organisms. However, other mammals, crocodiles, turtles, frogs, salamanders, and numerous other marine organisms survived relatively unscathed.

As this large hole in Arizona shows, meteors are enormously destructive. At the end of the Mesozoic an object at least 6 miles (10 kilometres) wide crashed into the Gulf of Mexico, probably driving the dinosaurs to extinction.

For a few minutes the young Tyrannosaurus continue to eat unbothered. The glow decreases, but a dark plume is growing in the sky from the south. Suddenly, the ground begins to shake. The Tyrannosaurus look up quickly, then crouch down in fear. The shaking continues and throws them off balance. Sweeping across the flood-plains and marshes, a hurricane-like shock wave slams into the Blanket Forest. Massive araucaria are snapped like twigs. The young Tyrannosaurus are ripped from their mother and thrown into a maelstrom of flying rocks, wood, and vegetation. For a moment the wind drops, but then it returns, tearing at the land in the opposite direction. The forest is devastated, but the worst is yet to come. While the huge dark plume grows larger

Geologically active areas pour gases into the atmosphere, and, at the end of the Mesozoic, as India collided with Asia, there was an enormous amount of volcanic activity. Some speculate that this is what killed the dinosaurs.

One problem facing current analysis of the extinction is that the data is biased toward the western United States. The best and most detailed quantitative work has been done in places such as the Hell Creek Formation (see page 277), which was a lush coastal plain in the Cretaceous. This area must have been subject to different stresses from those that occurred in places such as the desert of inland China, but comparative data does not exist.

Research has revealed that there were at least three forces at work at the end of the Cretaceous, which would have made life pretty miserable for most organisms. A large crater in the Gulf of Mexico and a layer of the rare element iridium all around the world suggest that an asteroid or comet six miles wide hit Earth at this time. It could have caused severe acid rain, global wildfires, and, since a layer of debris spread around the planet and blocked out the sun, a prolonged "impact winter." For hundreds of thousands of years on either side of this event the movement of India up against the Asian continental plate produced massive, sustained volcanic activity. Now known as the Deccan Traps, this activity generated enough flood basalt to cover an area the size of Alaska and Texas together with lava almost ½ mile deep. This could have caused global cooling, and among the poisons ejected into the atmosphere would have been selenium, which is particularly toxic for developing embryos in eggs. Finally, there was a big drop in sea levels and a 25–percent increase in land surface. This was at the expense of the epicontinental seas and might have caused the fragmentation of animal populations.

No single doomsday theory fits all the evidence, but since we know that all these events were taking place at the same time, it is possible that they all played a role in the mass destruction. In fact, taken altogether, it is a wonder that anything at all survived.

and larger, temperatures begin to rise. Burning hot rocks slam into the ground and spontaneous fires start up among the piles of debris. The temperatures continue to climb and the animals that survived the shock wave now start to burn alive. A larger earthquake, measuring about ten on the Richter scale, rocks the mountainside and the giant plume of debris from the explosion blocks out the sun. While the unnatural darkness descends, tiny balls of molten rock rain down from the sky, bringing death in their wake. Across the entire landscape, anything that can burn ignites.

Finally, the noise of the impact hits the beleaguered Blanket Forest, a deafening split in the atmosphere as if the Earth itself were screaming. However, there are no ears left to hear it. Twisted and crushed between two huge flaming araucaria lies the mother Tyrannosaurus, her neck thrown back and her

Last stand: a female Tyrannosaurus joins the evening chorus against the backdrop of a smouldering volcano. Late Cretaceous sunsets are nearly always this red because of the material thrown into the atmosphere by volcanic activity.

mouth gaping open. The molten rain gradually strips the flesh from her face, exposing her dagger-like teeth. Her long struggle to reproduce has come to nothing. Life in Laramidia is over.

The debris from the comet explosion spreads out like a deadly fan across the Mesozoic Earth, signaling the end of an era. By cutting out the sun, this deadly blanket throws the world into an unnatural winter, and animals and plants die in the billions. Eventually, the skies clear, but a second nightmare follows as greenhouse gases overheat the atmosphere.

It takes the ailing Earth millions of years to recover, but at last forests return and ferns spread once again. The most notable absentees from this fresh green world are the giant dinosaurs. From all their myriad forms, only the birds survive as testimony to the agility and beauty of this mighty dynasty.

Bibliography

Archibald, David J., *Dinosaur Extinction and the End of an Era: what the fossils say*, Columbia University Press (1996)

Bakker, Robert, *Dinosaur Heresies*, Penguin Books (1988)

Behrensmeyer, A. K., Damuth, J. D., DiMichele, W. A., Potts, R., Suess, H. D. and Wing, S. L., *Terrestrial Ecosystems Through Time: evolutionary paleoecology of terrestrial plants and animals*, University of Chicago Press (1992)

Benton, Michael, *The Penguin Historical Atlas of the Dinosaurs*, Penguin Books (1996)

Carpenter, Kenneth, Hirsch, Karl F. and Horner, John R., *Dinosaur Eggs and Babies*, Cambridge University Press (1994)

Colbert, Edwin H., *The Little Dinosaurs of Ghost Ranch*, Columbia University Press (1995)

Crowley, Thomas J. and North, Gerald R., *Paleoclimatology*, Oxford University Press (1991)

Currie, Philip J. and Padian, Kevin, *Encyclopedia of Dinosaurs*, Academic Press (1997)

Dodson, Peter, *The Horned Dinosaurs: a natural history*, Princeton University Press (1996)

Farlow, James Orville and Brett-Surman, M. K., *The Complete Dinosaur*, Indiana University Press (1997)

Fastovsky, David E. and Weishampel, David B., *The Evolution and Extinction of the Dinosaurs*, Cambridge University Press (1996)

Funnell, Brian M., Smith, Alan G. and Smith, David G., *Atlas of Mesozoic and Cenozoic Coastlines*, Cambridge University Press (1994)

Gould, Stephen J. (ed.), *The Book of Life*, Ebury Hutchinson (1993)

Kemp, T. S., *Mammal-like Reptiles and the Origin of Mammals*, Academic Press Inc. (1982)

Long, Robert A. and Houk, Rose, *Dawn of the Dinosaurs: the Triassic in petrified forest*, Petrified Forest Museum Association (1988)

Macdonald, David W., *The Encyclopaedia of Mammals*, Unwin Hyman (1984)

Norell, Mark A., Gaffney, Eugene S. and Dingus, Lowell, *Discovering Dinosaurs*, Little Brown and Company (1995)

Norman, David, *The Illustrated Encyclopedia of Dinosaurs*, Salamander Books (1985)

Norman, David, *Prehistoric Life*, Boxtree Ltd. (1994)

Spalding, David, *Dinosaur Hunters: 150 years of extraordinary discoveries*, Key Porter Books (1993)

Weishampel, David B., Dodson, Peter and Osmolska, Halszka, *The Dinosauria*, University of California Press (1992)

Wellnhofer, Peter, *The Illustrated Encyclopedia of Pterosaurs*, Salamander Books (1991)

Acknowledgements

This book would not have been possible without the skills and creative talent of a number of people. All the computer-graphic animals created in these pictures are the result of work by the animation team at Framestore, led by Mike Milne, an incredibly gifted 3D animator who, from the beginning, shared my dream of making these animals as real as possible. In particular, I would like to thank Alec Knox, who posed the creatures, and Daren Horley, whose designs and exquisite artwork made the dinosaurs' skins look so real.

All the photographic backgrounds were taken by still-photographers on location while we were shooting the TV series. These were Michael Pitts for the underwater material, Carrie Grant for the Californian redwoods, and Ian Macdonald, a very talented and patient photographer, for the rest. Combining these beautiful animals with their backgrounds took the specialist skills of Rob Farrar at Alchemy, to whom I am indebted for sacrificing so much of his personal time to complete the stills under such short deadlines. Several of the stills are not computer graphic but animatronic models shot on location and for these I am grateful to Jez Harris and his team of expert model makers.

The information in the book is available only because of the hard work of countless scientists in the field, and I would like to thank all those in the palaeontological community who helped and advised me. In particular I relied on the enthusiasm and expertise of Jo Wright (University of Colorado) and David Martill (University of Portsmouth). Further advice came from Kent Stevens (University of Oregon), Tom Holtz (University of Maryland), Mike Benton (University of Bristol), David Unwin (Museum für Naturkunde, Berlin) and David Norman (Sedgwick Museum, Cambridge). However, the book is the result of my interpretation of their information and any mistakes are my own.

Finally, I would like to thank Clare, my wife, and my four little ones for their patience and support during the three years this project took.

Tim Haines

Index

Numbers in *italic* refer to illustrations. Numbers in
bold refer to information in the boxes. Subheadings
have been placed in chronological rather than
alphabetical order where appropriate.

Picture credits

BBC Worldwide would like to thank the following for providing photographs and for permission to reproduce copyright material. While every effort has been made to trace and acknowledge copyright holders, we would like to apologize if there are any errors or omissions.

Page 19 page border, repeated on pp. 61, 111, 153, 199, 243: 1 (top) NHPA © Alberto Nardi, 4 Oxford Scientific © G.A. Maclean, 5 Oxford Scientific © Nick Groves/Hedgehog House, 6 (bottom) Robert Harding; 22 Dr. D. M. Martill; 23 (above) Planet Earth © Wayne Harris, (center) Oxford Scientific Films © J.A.L. Cooke, (below) Oxford Scientific Films © Mike Linley; 28 Planet Earth © J.R. Nacivet; 34 Dr. Roger Smith, South African Museum of Natural History, Cape Town; 38 Natural History Museum, London; 46–7 Ardea London © François Gohier; 47 American Museum of Natural History, New York; 53 Natural History Museum, London; 63 Planet Earth © Hans Christian Heap; 64 (above) Bruce Coleman Collection © Gerald S Cubitt; 65 (below) Natural History Museum, London, (right) NHPA © Stephen Dalton; 76 Natural History Museum, London; 80 (above) Museum of the Rockies, Montana, USA © Bruce Selyem, (below) Oxford Scientific Films © Stan Osolinski; 86 (above) Planet Earth/Denver Museum of Natural History, Colorado, USA © Mark Schumann; 86 (below) Ardea London © François Gohier; 94 Ardea London © François Gohier; 94–5 Ardea London /Humboldt Museum, Berlin © P. Morris; 95 & 101 Ardea London © François Gohier; 104 Bruce Coleman Collection © Wayne Lankinen; 108 Ardea London (left) © P. Morris, (right) © François Gohier; 113 Planet Earth © Nancy Sefton; 115 (top right) NHPA © Lutra, (lower left) Planet Earth © Ashley J Boyd, (lower right) NHPA © David Henclin; 120 (above right) Still Pictures © Secret Sea Visions, (center) Planet Earth © Steve Nicholls, (below) Dr Helmut Mayr, Bayerische Staatssammlung für Paläontologie und Historische Geologie, München; 127 Natural History Museum, London; 131 (left) Frontispiece from Thomas Hawkins' *Great Sea Dragons*, 1840, ill. in *Ichthyosaurs: a history of fossil 'sea-dragons'* by S.R. Howe, T. Sharpe and H.S Torrens, National Museum of Wales, 1981, p.23, (right) Planet Earth © Phil Chapman; 134 Institut und Museum für Geologie und Paläontologie der Universität Tübingen; 155 Ardea London © D. Dixon; 156 Dr. D.M. Martill; 156–7 NHPA © Albert Nardi; 157 (center) Oxford Scientific Films © M. A. Chappell, (right) Planet Earth © Jeannie Mackinnon; 164 (below) Natural History Museum, London; 172 (lower right) L'Institut Royal des Sciences Naturelles de Belgique, Brussels (Département de Paléontologie); 174 (above center) Natural History Museum, London, (above right) L'Institut Royal des Sciences Naturelles de Belgique, Brussels (Département de Paléontologie), (below left) Natural History Museum, London, (below center) Ardea London; 178 Professor Alexandr P. Rasnitsyn, Paleontological Institute, Moscow; 182 (top center) D.L. Dilcher and G. Sun, (below left) Planet Earth © Peter Gasson; 188–9 Natural History Museum, London; 189 Aquila © J.J. Brooks; 192 Dr. D.M. Unwin, Institut für Paleontologie, Museum für Naturkunde, Berlin; 203 (lower left) Natural History Museum, London, (center) Oxford Scientific Films © Grant Dixon/Hedgehog House, (top right) Oxford Scientific Films © John Weeber/Hedgehog House; 208 & 209, Professor Pat Vickers-Rich, Monash University, Melbourne & Thomas H. Rich, Museum of Victoria, Melbourne, Australia; 220 Planet Earth © Ken Lucas; 221 Planet Earth © Jorbe Provenza; 228 Prof. Dr. Ryszard Szadzjewski; 245 Oxford Scientific Films © Jack Dermid; 246 (above) Oxford Scientific Films © Michael Fogden; 246–7 NHPA © Stephen Dalton; 247 NHPA (center) © Julie Meech, (above) © Kevin Schafer, (below right) Planet Earth © Martin Rügner; 260 Natural History Museum, London; 265 Ardea London © François Gohier; 266 Still Pictures © D. Decobecq; 272 Professor Bruce M. Rothschild, The Arthritis Center of Northeast Ohio; 277 Ardea London © François Gohier; 280 Ardea London © François Gohier; 280–1 Science Photo Library.

All the other photographs © BBC Worldwide 1999. Digital images created by Framestore; stills composited by Alchemy Creative Services.